DISCARD

W9-BSD-763

THE CHOICE

Also by Zbigniew Brzezinski:

*The Grand Chessboard: American Primacy and its
Geostrategic Imperatives*

*Out of Control: Global Turmoil on the Eve of the
Twenty-First Century*

*The Grand Failure: The Birth and Death of Communism
in the Twentieth Century*

THE CHOICE:

GLOBAL DOMINATION OR GLOBAL LEADERSHIP

ZBIGNIEW BRZEZINSKI

BOOKS

A Member of the Perseus Books Group
New York

Books published by Basic Books are available at special discounts for bulk purchases
in the United States by corporations, institutions, and other organizations. For more
information, please contact the Special Markets Department at the Perseus Books
Group, 11 Cambridge Center, Cambridge MA 02142, or call (617) 252-5298, (800)
255-1514 or e-mail special.markets@perseusbooks.com.

Designed by Scribe

A CIP catalog record for this book is available from the Library of Congress.
ISBN 0-465-00800-3
04 05 06 / 10 9 8 7 6 5 4 3 2 1

CONTENTS

PREFACE

My central argument about America's role in the world is simple: America's power, asserting in a dominant fashion the nation's sovereignty, is today the ultimate guarantor of global stability, yet American society stimulates global social trends that dilute traditional national sovereignty. American power and American social dynamics, working together, could promote the gradual emergence of a global community of shared interest. Misused and in collision, they could push the world into chaos while leaving America beleaguered.

At the outset of the twenty-first century, America's power is unprecedented in its global military reach, in the centrality of America's economic vitality for the well-being of the world economy, in the innovative impact of America's technological dynamism, and in the worldwide appeal of the multifaceted and often crass American mass culture. All of these give America matchless global political clout. For better or worse, America is the global pacesetter, and there is no rival in sight.

Europe might be competitive economically, but it will be a long time before Europe acquires the degree of unity that would enable it to compete politically. Japan, once seen as the next superstate, is out of the race, while China, despite its economic progress, is likely to remain relatively poor for at least two generations and in the meantime may encounter severe political difficulties. Russia is no longer in the running. In brief, America does not have, and will not soon face, a global peer.

There is thus no realistic alternative to the prevailing American hegemony and the role of U.S. power as the indispensable component of global security. At the same time, American democracy—and the example of American success—disseminates economic, cultural, and technological changes that promote growing global interconnections over and above national frontiers. These changes can undermine the very stability that American power seeks to ensure, and can even breed anti-American hostility.

America, therefore, confronts a unique paradox: it is the first and only truly global superpower, and yet Americans are increasingly pre-occupied with threats from a variety of much weaker hostile sources. The fact that America possesses peerless global political clout makes it the focus of envy, resentment, and, for some, intense hatred. These antagonisms can also be exploited, indeed abetted, by America's more traditional rivals even if they themselves are too cautious to risk a direct collision with America. The risks to America's security are real.

Does it follow, then, that America is entitled to more security than other nation-states? Its leaders, as the managers of the nation's power and as the representatives of a democratic society, must seek a carefully calibrated balance between two roles. Exclusive dependence on multilateral cooperation could become a prescription for strategic lethargy in a world in which threats to national and eventually even to global security are evidently on the rise and potentially menace all of mankind. Yet primary reliance on the unilateral exercise of sovereign power, especially if accompanied by a self-serving definition of the emerging threats, could bring self-isolation, growing national paranoia, and increasing vulnerability to a globally spreading anti-American virus.

An anxious America, obsessed with its own security, could find itself isolated in a hostile world. If its quest for solitary security were to get out of hand, it could transform the land of the free into a garrison state imbued with a siege mentality. At the same time, however, the end of the Cold War has coincided with a massive diffusion of the technical knowledge and capability needed to make weapons of mass destruction, not only among states but potentially even among political groups with terrorist motivations.

The American public bravely faced the horrendous reality of "two scorpions in the bottle"—the United States and the Soviet Union deterring each other with potentially devastating nuclear arsenals—but it is more troubled by percolating violence, periodic acts of terrorism, and the diffusion of weapons of mass destruction. Americans sense that in this politically unclear, sometimes morally ambiguous, and often mystifying setting of political unpredictability, there lurks a danger to America precisely because America is the world's predominant power.

Unlike previous hegemonic powers, America operates in a world of intensifying immediacy and intimacy. Past imperial powers such as Great Britain during the nineteenth century, China at various stages in its several thousand years of history, or Rome during half a millennium, just to name a few, were relatively impervious to external threats. The world they dominated was compartmentalized and non-interactive. Distance and time provided breathing space and enhanced homeland security. In contrast, America may be uniquely powerful in its global scope, but its homeland is also uniquely insecure. Having to live with such insecurity is likely to be a chronic condition.

Hence, the key question is whether America can conduct a wise, responsible, and effective foreign policy—one that avoids the pitfalls of a beleaguered mindset but still comports with America's historically novel status as the world's paramount power. The quest for a wise foreign policy must begin with the realization that "globalization" in its essence means global interdependence. Such interdependence does not ensure equality of status or even equality of security for all nations. But it means no nation has total immunity from the consequences of the technological revolution that has so vastly increased the human capability to inflict violence and yet tightened the bonds that increasingly tie humanity together.

Ultimately, the central policy question confronting America is "Hegemony for the sake of what?" At stake is whether the nation will strive to shape a new global system based on shared interests, or use its sovereign global power primarily to entrench its own security.

In the pages that follow, I have focused on what I consider to be the main issues to which a strategically comprehensive response is needed:

- What are the main threats to America?

- Given its hegemonic status, is America entitled to more security than other nations?

- How should America cope with potentially lethal threats that increasingly emanate not from powerful rivals but from weak foes?

- Can America constructively manage its long-term relationship with the Islamic world, many of whose 1.2 billion people increasingly view America as implacably hostile?

- Can America act decisively to resolve the Israeli-Palestinian conflict, given the overlapping but legitimate claims of two peoples to the same land?

- What is needed to create political stability in the volatile new "Global Balkans" located within the southern rim of central Eurasia?

- Can America forge a genuine partnership with Europe, given Europe's slow progress to political unity but increasing economic might?

- Can Russia, no longer a rival to America, be drawn into an American-led Atlantic framework?

- What should be the American role in the Far East, given Japan's continued but reluctant dependence on the United States—as well as its quietly growing military might—and also given the rise of Chinese power?

- How likely is it that globalization might breed a coherent counter-doctrine or a counter-alliance against America?
- Are demography and migration becoming the new threats to global stability?
- Is America's culture compatible with an essentially imperial responsibility?
- How should America respond to the emerging inequality in human affairs, which the current scientific revolution may precipitate and which globalization may accentuate?
- Is American democracy compatible with a hegemonic role, however carefully that hegemony may be camouflaged? How will the security imperatives of that special role affect traditional civil rights?

This book is thus partially predictive and partially prescriptive. Its point of departure is that the recent revolution in advanced technologies, especially in communications, promotes the progressive emergence of a global community of increasingly shared interest with America at its center. But the potential self-isolation of the only superpower could plunge the world into escalating anarchy, made all the more ominous by the dissemination of weaponry of mass destruction. With America—given the contradictory roles it plays in the world—fated to be the catalyst either for a global community or for global chaos, Americans have the unique historical responsibility to determine which of the two will come to pass. Our choice is between dominating the world and leading it.

June 30, 2003

PART I:

AMERICAN HEGEMONY AND GLOBAL SECURITY

America's unique standing in the global hierarchy is now widely acknowledged. Foreigners' initial surprise and even anger at explicit assertions of America's hegemonic role have given way to more resigned—if still resentful—efforts to harness, contain, deflect, or ridicule that hegemony.[1] Even the Russians, who for nostalgic reasons have been the most reluctant to recognize the scale of America's power and influence, have accepted that for some time to come the United States will remain the decisive player in world affairs.[2] When America was struck by terrorism on September 11, 2001, the British, guided by Prime Minister Tony Blair, gained a major voice in Washington by promptly embracing America's declaration of war against global terrorism. Much of the world followed suit, including countries that earlier had themselves felt the pain of terrorist attacks with only limited American commiseration. Worldwide declarations that "We are all Americans" were not only expressions of genuine empathy; they were also expedient affirmations of political loyalty.

The contemporary world may not like American preeminence—may distrust it, resent it, even at times conspire against it. But as a practical matter, it cannot oppose it directly. The last decade has seen occasional attempts at such opposition, but to no avail. The Chinese and the Russians flirted with a strategic partnership to promote global "multipolarity," a term easily decoded as "anti-hegemony." Not much came of that, given Russia's relative weakness vis-à-vis China, as well as China's pragmatic recognition that right now, most of all, it needs foreign capital and technology. Neither of these would be forthcoming if China's relations with the United States were antagonistic. In the last year of the twentieth century, the Europeans, and especially the French, grandly announced that Europe would shortly acquire "an autonomous global security capability." The war in Afghanistan quickly revealed this commitment to be reminiscent of the once famous Soviet assertion that the historical victory of Communism "is on the horizon," an imaginary line that recedes as one walks toward it.

History is a record of change, a reminder that nothing endures indefinitely. It can also remind us, however, that some things endure for a long time, and when they disappear, the status quo ante does not reappear. So it will be with the current American global preponderance. It, too, will fade at some point, probably later than some wish and earlier than many Americans take for granted. The key question is: What will replace it? An abrupt termination of American hegemony would without doubt precipitate global chaos, in which international anarchy would be punctuated by eruptions of truly massive destructiveness. An unguided progressive decline would have a similar effect, spread out over a longer time. But a gradual and controlled devolution of power could lead to an increasingly formalized global community of shared interest, with supranational arrangements increasingly assuming some of the special security roles of traditional nation-states.

In any case, the eventual end of American hegemony will not involve a restoration of multipolarity among the familiar major powers that dominated world affairs for the last two centuries. Nor will it yield to another dominant hegemon that would displace the United States by assuming a similar political, military, economic, technological, and sociocultural worldwide preeminence. The familiar powers of the last century are too fatigued or too weak to assume the role the United States now plays. It is noteworthy that since 1880, in a comparative ranking of world powers (cumulatively based on their economic strength, military budgets and assets, populations, etc.), the top five slots at sequential twenty-year intervals have been shared by just seven states: the United States, the United Kingdom, Germany, France, Russia, Japan, and China. Only the United States, however, unambiguously earned inclusion among the top five in every one of the twenty-year intervals, and the gap in the year 2000 between the top-ranked United States and the rest was vastly wider than ever before.[3]

The former major European powers—Great Britain, Germany, and France—are too weak to step into the breach. In the next two decades, it is quite unlikely that the European Union will become sufficiently united politically to muster the popular will to compete with the United States in the politico-military arena. Russia is no longer an imperial power, and its central challenge is to recover socioeconomically lest it lose its far eastern territories to China. Japan's population is aging and its economy has slowed; the conventional wisdom of the 1980s that Japan is destined to be the next "superstate" now has the ring of historical irony. China, even if it succeeds in maintaining high rates of economic growth and retains its internal political stability (both are far from certain), will at best be a regional power still constrained by an impoverished population, antiquated infrastructure, and limited appeal worldwide. The same is true of India, which additionally faces uncertainties regarding its long-term national unity.

Even a coalition among the above—a most unlikely prospect, given their historical conflicts and clashing territorial claims—would lack the cohesion, muscle, and energy needed to both push America off its pedestal and sustain global stability. Some leading states, in any case, would side with America if push came to shove. Indeed, any evident American decline might precipitate efforts to reinforce America's

leadership. Most important, the shared resentment of American hegemony would not dampen the clashes of interest among states. The
more intense collisions—in the event of America's decline—could
spark a wildfire of regional violence, rendered all the more dangerous
by the dissemination of weapons of mass destruction.

The bottom line is twofold: For the next two decades, the steady-
ing effect of American power will be indispensable to global stability,
while the principal challenge to American power can come only from
within—either from the repudiation of power by the American democracy itself, or from America's global misuse of its own power. American
society, even though rather parochial in its intellectual and cultural interests, steadily sustained a protracted worldwide engagement against the
threat of totalitarian communism, and it is currently mobilized against
international terrorism. As long as that commitment endures, America's
role as the global stabilizer will also endure. Should that commitment
fade—either because terrorism has faded, or because Americans tire or
lose their sense of common purpose—America's global role could rapidly terminate.

That role could also be undermined and delegitimated by the
misuse of U.S. power. Conduct that is perceived worldwide as arbitrary
could prompt America's progressive isolation, undercutting not
America's power to defend itself as such, but rather its ability to use
that power to enlist others in a common effort to shape a more secure
international environment.

On the whole, the public understands that the new security
threat to America dramatized by 9/11 will be a lasting one. The country's wealth and economic dynamism make a defense budget of 3–4
percent of GDP relatively tolerable; this burden is considerably lower
than it was during the Cold War, not to mention World War II. In the
meantime, globalization contributes to such interweaving of American
society with the rest of the world that American national security is
becoming increasingly blended with issues of global well-being.

The task of statesmanship is to translate this underlying public consensus on security into a long-term strategy that will mobilize,

not alienate, global support. This cannot be accomplished by a recourse to jingoism or by panic mongering. It requires the fusion of traditional American idealism with sober pragmatism regarding the new realities of global security. Both point to the same conclusion: For America, increased global security is an essential component of national security.

NOTES

1 In 1997 when I published *The Grand Chessboard: American Primacy and Its Geostrategic Imperatives*, the former German chancellor Helmut Schmidt (in a signed review) was outraged by my acknowledgment of the historically novel fact of American global hegemony. Subsequently, the French foreign minister at the time, Hubert Vedrine, ironically labeled it as "hyperpower."

2 Recent Russian analyses of global trends explicitly concede the continuation of American primacy for at least two decades or so, with no other power even near. See *"Mir na Rubezhe Tisiacheletii"* (collective publication of the Institute of World Economy and International Affairs), Moscow 2001. President Putin's decision to identify himself strongly with America after 9/11 was clearly derived from the realization that open hostility toward America could only worsen Russia's own security dilemmas.

3 Arguably, the international pecking order in 1900 included, sequentially, the United Kingdom, Germany, France, Russia, and the United States, all relatively closely bunched; in 1960 the lead had shifted to the United States and Russia (the USSR), with Japan, China, and the United Kingdom much further back; in 2000 the United States is alone at the top, followed far behind by China, Germany, Japan, and Russia.

1

THE DILEMMAS OF
NATIONAL INSECURITY

For most of America's history as a sovereign nation, its citizens have considered security the norm and occasional insecurity an aberration. From now on, it will be the reverse. In the era of globalization, insecurity will be the enduring reality and the quest for national security a continuing preoccupation. Consequently, deciding how much vulnerability is tolerable will be a perplexing policy issue for the United States as the world's current hegemon, as well as a cultural dilemma for American society.

THE END OF SOVEREIGN SECURITY

America came into its own during an era in which national sovereignty and national security were nearly synonymous. They defined international affairs. The international order of the last several centuries has been based on the premise of nation-state sovereignty, with each state the ultimate and absolute arbiter within its territory of its own requirements for national security. Though that sovereignty was legally defined as absolute, obvious asymmetries in national power not only necessitated major compromises, especially on the part of the weaker states, but also involved significant violations of some states' sovereignty by stronger ones. Nonetheless, when the first global organization of cooperative states was established in reaction

7

to World War I—the League of Nations—the abstract notion of absolute sovereignty resulted in the endowment of equal voting rights to all member states. Symptomatically, the United States, acutely sensitive about its sovereign status and aware of its geographically advantageous security situation, chose not to be part of that body.

By the time the United Nations was set up in 1945, it was clear to the major states that the realities of global power had to be accommodated if the organization was to play any meaningful security role. Still, the principle of equality of sovereign states could not be discarded altogether. The resulting compromise provided for voting equality in the UN General Assembly for all member states, and for a veto right in the UN Security Council for the five leading powers that emerged as victors from World War II. This formula was a tacit recognition that national sovereignty was increasingly an illusion for all but a few very powerful states.

For America, the linkage between state sovereignty and national security was traditionally even more symbiotic than for most other states. It was reflected in the sense of manifest destiny preached by the country's revolutionary elite, which sought to insulate America from Europe's remote interstate conflicts while representing America as the standard bearer of an altogether novel, universally valid conception of how a state should be organized. The linkage was reinforced by the awareness that geography made America a sanctuary. With two huge oceans providing extraordinary security buffers and with much weaker neighbors to the north and south, Americans considered their nation's sovereignty to be both a natural right as well as a natural consequence of peerless national security. Even when America was drawn into two world wars, it was the Americans who crossed the oceans to combat others in distant lands. Americans went to war, but war did not come to America.[1]

After the end of World War II, with the onset of the largely unexpected Cold War with a hostile ideological and strategic foe, most Americans initially felt protected by the U.S. monopoly of the atomic bomb. The Strategic Air Command (SAC), with its unilateral capability (at least into the mid-1950s) to devastate the Soviet Union, became the nation's security blanket, much as the two-ocean Navy had been earlier. SAC both symbolized and perpetuated the notion that security is inherent in America's special position, even though insecurity had become the norm in the twentieth century for almost all other nation-states. To be sure, American troops in Germany and Japan were protecting others while also protecting America—but they were also keeping danger geographically distant from America.

It was not until the late 1950s, and perhaps not even until the Cuban Missile Crisis, that America was jarred into recognition that modern technology had made invulnerability a thing of the past. The 1960s saw a surge in national anxiety over the "missile gap" (with Soviet leaders deliberately claiming a greater capability for, and greater numbers of, their missiles than they actually had), demonstrated by growing fears that nuclear deterrence was inherently unstable, by a preoccupation among strategists over the possibility of a disarming Soviet nuclear strike as well as over the growing risks of an accidental nuclear discharge, and eventually even by an effort to develop new forms of technologically advanced space-based defensive systems such as anti-ballistic missiles. The intense national debate on these issues eventually led to a consensus that a relationship of stable deterrence with the Soviet Union was attainable only through mutual restraint. That paved the way in the 1970s for the ABM Treaty and then the SALT treaties, and in the 1980s for the START treaties.

These treaties were, in effect, a recognition that America's security was no longer entirely in American hands but depended in part on accommodation with a potentially lethal antagonist. That the antagonist was similarly vulnerable and that its conduct seemed to be guided by a similar recognition of its own vulnerability provided a degree of reassurance, making the acceptance of shared vulnerability psychologically easier for the American public. To be sure, the arrangement did not eliminate the risk of mutual destruction, but its apparent rationality and predictability tended to soothe national anxieties. As a result, the Reagan administration's attempt, in the early 1980s, to regain America's invulnerability through the proposed Strategic Defense

Initiative (SDI)—space-based defenses against a Soviet ballistic missile attack on the United States—failed to mobilize overwhelming public support.

This unexpected public moderation was doubtless partly due to the expanding American-Soviet détente, which further reduced fears of a nuclear collision, but it was also prompted by the public's sense that the Soviet bloc and even the Soviet Union itself were facing a massive internal crisis. The threat was perceived as fading. Indeed, following the collapse of the Soviet Union in 1991, Soviet missiles ceased to be the subject of arms reduction agreements but instead became the object of American dismantling teams, with U.S. funds and techniques enhancing the security of the storage depots for the formerly awe-inspiring Soviet nuclear warheads. The Soviet nuclear arsenal's transformation into a beneficiary of U.S. protection testified to the degree to which the Soviet threat had waned.

The disappearance of the Soviet challenge, coinciding as it did with the overwhelming display of technologically novel U.S. military capabilities in the Gulf War, quite naturally led to renewed public confidence in America's unique power. The U.S.-led and technology-driven revolution in military affairs (RMA) spawned not only new weapons and tactics, which dictated one-sided outcomes of the two short wars in 1991 and 2003 against the Soviet-armed Iraq, but also a new sense of American global military superiority. For a brief while, America again felt almost invulnerable.

That new mood coincided with widespread recognition that the fall of the Soviet Union signaled a more drastic shift in the global distribution of political power. While the wars against Iraq in 1991 and in Kosovo in 1999 dramatized America's widening lead in the application of technology to military purposes and its ability to strike at other nations with relative impunity, American preponderance increasingly was perceived abroad as not only military. It was at least as evident in the "soft" dimensions of power, in scientific innovation, technological adaptation, economic dynamism, and more intangibly in sociocultural experimentation. By the 1990s, many foreign commentators recognized America—sometimes with intense resentment—not only as the global hegemon but also as humanity's unique (and often disturbing) social laboratory. The rapid dissemination of the new Internet connectivity was but one manifestation of the massive global impact of America as the world's social pioneer.

In the process, America's role on the world scene has become more "dialectical" than ever: the American state, relying on its dominant power, acts as the bastion of traditional international stability, while American society, through a massive and varied worldwide impact facilitated by globalization, transcends national territorial control and disrupts the traditional social order.

On the one hand, the combination of the two reinforces America's established inclination to see itself as the model for everyone else, with American preponderance even increasing the country's sense of its moral vocation. The U.S. Congress's tendency to mandate the certification of other states' behavior by the U.S. State Department is symptomatic of the current American attitude, which is increasingly cavalier toward others' sovereignty while remaining protectively sensitive about America's.

On the other hand, the combination of American power and globalization is changing the nature of U.S. national security. Modern technology is eliminating the effect of geographic distance, while multiplying the variety of means, the destructive radius, and the number of actors capable of projecting violence. At the same time, the reaction against globalization focuses resentment on the United States as the most obvious target. Thus globalization universalizes vulnerability even as it concentrates hostility on America.

Technology is the great equalizer of societal vulnerability. The revolutionary compression of distance by modern communications and the quantum leap in the destructive radius of deliberately inflicted lethality have punctured the nation-state's traditional protective umbrella. Moreover, weaponry is now becoming post-national in both possession and reach. Even non-state actors such as underground terrorist organizations are gradually improving their access to more destructive weaponry. It is only a question of time before, somewhere, a truly technologically advanced act of terrorism takes place. In addition, the same "equalizing" process is providing poorer states such as North Korea with the means to inflict damage to a degree once restricted to a few rich and powerful states.

At some point, this trend could have apocalyptic consequences. For the first time in history, it is possible to contemplate a non-biblical "end of the world" scenario—not an act of God but a deliberate unleashing of a manmade, global, cataclysmic chain reaction. The Armageddon described in the last book of the New Testament, Revelation 16, could pass for a nuclear and bacteriological global suicide.[2] While the probability of such an event may remain remote for some decades, the inevitable reality is that science will continue to enhance the human capacity for acts of self-destruction that organized society may not always be able to prevent or contain.

Short of such an apocalyptic outcome, the list of violent scenarios that could ensue as a consequence of international tensions or as byproducts of Manichean passions is bound to expand. Such scenarios, ranging from the more traditional to the more novel, include:

1. a central and massively destructive strategic war, at this stage still feasible though unlikely, between the United States and Russia and perhaps in twenty or so years between the United States and China, as well as between China and Russia;

2. significant regional wars fought with highly lethal weaponry, for example between India and Pakistan or between Israel and Iran;

3. fragmenting ethnic wars, particularly within multiethnic states such as Indonesia or India;

4. various forms of "national liberation" movements of the downtrodden against existing or perceived racial domination, for example by the Indian peasantry in Latin America, the Chechens in Russia, or the Palestinians against Israel;

5. lash-out attacks by otherwise weak countries that have succeeded in building weapons of mass destruction and in finding ways for their delivery either against neighbors or anonymously against the United States;

6. increasingly lethal terrorist attacks by underground groups against particularly hated targets, repeating what occurred in the United States on 9/11, but eventually escalating to the use of weapons of mass destruction;

7. paralyzing cyber-attacks, undertaken anonymously by states, terrorist organizations, or even individual anarchists, against the operational infrastructure of the advanced societies in order to plunge them into chaos.

It is common knowledge that the tools for such violence are becoming more diversified and accessible. They range from highly complex weapons systems—particularly the various types of nuclear weapons designed for specific military missions, available to only a few states—to less efficient but still deadly nuclear explosives designed to kill large numbers of urban dwellers; and from nuclear explosives to chemical weapons (lethally less efficient) and bacteriological agents (less precisely targetable but highly dynamic). The poorer the state or more isolated the group that seeks to use these weapons, the more likely it is to resort to the less controllable and discriminating means of mass destruction.

Global security dilemmas in the early decades of the twenty-first century are thus qualitatively different from those of the twentieth. The traditional link between national sovereignty and national security has been severed. To be sure, traditional strategic concerns remain central to America's security, given that potentially hostile major states—such as Russia and China—could still inflict massive damage on the American homeland if the international structure were to break down. Moreover, the major states will continue to refine and develop new weaponry, and maintaining a technological advantage over them will continue to be a major preoccupation of U.S. national security policy.[3]

Nevertheless, major wars between more developed states have already become a rarity. The two world wars, originating in the most advanced region of the world at the time—Europe—were "total" in the sense that they were fought with the most advanced means available, in order to kill both combatants and non-combatants indiscriminately. But each side still anticipated its own survival while pursuing the destruction of its opponent. Although total in their goal, these wars nonetheless were not suicidal.

With Hiroshima and Nagasaki giving "total" an altogether new meaning, and with the dissemination of atomic weapons among the major Cold War rivals as well as others, the notion of victory in a total war has become an oxymoron. This fact was acknowledged and institutionalized through the adoption by the United States and the Soviet Union of the strategy of mutual deterrence. Given that the nations that can best afford the most destructive weaponry are most often the ones that have the most to lose from using it, one can still envisage a total war between India and Pakistan, but no longer between France and Germany. It is only a slight exaggeration to say that total wars are becoming reckless acts that only poorer states can afford.

Wars among more developed states (however unlikely), and by developed states against less developed ones (more likely), will henceforth be fought with increasingly precise weaponry and will be designed not to totally destroy the opponent's society (and thereby court counter-devastation), but to disarm the opponent and thus to subdue him. The U.S. campaigns in late 2001 against the Taliban and in 2003 against Iraq may be seen as a prototype for future military engagements waged with highly advanced weaponry capable of selectively targeting specific high-value military or economic objects.

Convulsive and percolating strife is becoming far more likely than organized, sustained, formal wars. War as a formally declared state of affairs has already become a thing of the past. The last solemn notifications that a state of war was about to ensue were issued to the Nazi government in Berlin by the British and French ambassadors on September 3, 1939, following the Nazi attack (without a declaration of war) on Poland. Since the end of World War II, the United States has engaged in two major wars involving nearly 100,000 American fatalities, about half a dozen relatively significant military operations with minor U.S. losses, and unilateral air strikes against at least three foreign capitals, without once declaring a formal state of war. India and Pakistan fought three bloody conflicts also without declaring war. Israel launched its preemptive 1967 attack against adjoining Arab states, and was itself attacked by them in 1973, similarly without any formal declaration. Iraq and Iran fought a bloody and protracted war in the 1980s without formally acknowledging the fact.

In contrast to the traditional international age, when they were formally declared and formally terminated, wars today are viewed as aberrant behavior much like domestic crime. That in itself represents a measure of progress. Nonetheless, in the era of globalization, "war" has given way to informal, pervasive, and often anonymous strife. This violence may be the result of geopolitical instability, such as that which broke out following the fall of the Soviet Union. In other cases, it is the consequence of ethnic and religious hostility, expressing itself through orgiastic mass violence as seen in Rwanda, Bosnia, and Borneo. Whatever its sources, such strife is currently widespread.[4] The response to it sometimes involves reactive "police" actions such as in Kosovo in 1999.

In time, demographic pressures from the overpopulated poor regions against the richer areas may also transform illegal immigration into more violent migrations. In other cases, acts of organized violence could be the product of fanaticism fostered by non-state groupings and directed at the most obvious focus of their hatred, as has been the case with some terrorist organizations targeting America. Much of the foregoing might also be mobilized by some new integrative ideology, stimulated by resentments of global inequality and likely directed against the perceived bastion of the status quo, the United States (more on this in Part II).

In brief, America's security dilemmas in the twenty-first century are coming to resemble the messy and diverse criminal challenges that large urban centers have been confronting for years, with percolating underworld violence both pervasive and normal. The risk inherent in this condition, however, is magnified by the technological potential of lethal violence to suddenly get out of hand and then massively escalate. Moreover, America's ability to respond may be handicapped by the absence of an easy-to-define and self-evident source of threat. In essence, America's isolated national security of the nineteenth century, which became defense through overseas alliances during the second half of the twentieth, is transmuting into shared global vulnerability today.

Under such circumstances and especially in the wake of 9/11, the rising inclination in America to seek enhanced national security is understandable. The quest for self-protection against existing, anticipated, suspected, and even imagined threats is justifiable, not only because of the unique global security role that the United States has assumed since the end of the Cold War, but also because of the degree to which America's global sociocultural celebrity makes it the world's center of attention. It follows that America has reason to seek more security for itself than most other nations require.

Even if we grant this point, to what extent is a narrowly defined national security conception feasible, in an age in which interstate wars are giving way to widespread strife? At what point does even a justifiable national preoccupation with domestic security cross the invisible line dividing prudence from paranoia? How much of America's security is dependent on multilateral cooperation and how much of it can be—or should be—sought unilaterally? These simple questions pose extraordinarily complex and difficult national security choices, with far-reaching domestic constitutional implications. Ultimately, given the rapidly changing and dynamic character of both modern technology and the international setting, any answers will have to be contingent and temporary.

National Power and International Strife

The notion of total national security is now a myth. Total security and total defense in the age of globalization are not attainable. The real issue is: with how much insecurity can America live while promoting its interests in an increasingly interactive, interdependent world? Insecurity, while uncomfortable, has been the fate of many other nations for centuries. For America there is no longer a choice: even if socially disagreeable, its insecurity has to be politically manageable.

In reflecting on the security implications of this new reality, it is important to bear in mind the points made earlier. America is the world-transforming society, even revolutionary in its subversive impact on sovereignty-based international politics. At the same time, America is a traditional power, unilaterally protective of its own security while sustaining international stability not only for its own benefit, but for that of the international community as a whole. The latter task compels U.S. policymakers to concentrate on the more traditional U.S. role as the linchpin of global stability. Despite the new realities of global interdependence and the mounting preoccupation of the international community with such new global issues as ecology, global warming, AIDS, and poverty, the argument that American power is uniquely central to world peace is supported by a simple hypothetical test: What would happen if the U.S. Congress were to mandate the prompt retraction of U.S. military power from its three crucial foreign deployments—Europe, the Far East, and the Persian Gulf?

Any such U.S. withdrawal would without doubt plunge the world almost immediately into a politically chaotic crisis. In Europe, there would be a pell-mell rush by some to rearm but also to reach a special arrangement with Russia. In the Far East, war would probably break out on the Korean Peninsula while Japan would undertake a crash program of rearmament, including nuclear weapons. In the Persian Gulf area, Iran would become dominant and would intimidate the adjoining Arab states.

Given the foregoing, the long-term strategic alternatives for America are either to engage in a gradual, carefully managed transformation of its own supremacy into a self-sustaining international system, or to rely primarily on its national power to insulate itself from the international anarchy that would follow a disengagement. The instinctive response of most Americans to these choices is to favor some combination of unilateralism and internationalism. Concentration on the preservation of U.S. supremacy is evidently the preferred choice of the more conservative segments of American society and its elites, reflecting basically the interests of the traditional power structures and of the defense-oriented sectors of the U.S. economy. A willingness to devolve some power to like-minded partners in the construction of a global security system tends to be favored by those elements of American society usually identified with liberal causes, for whom the quest for domestic social justice can be empathetically projected onto its international equivalents.

Preponderance, however, is not omnipotence. Whatever the preferred formula, America still needs to consider carefully what regions of the world are most central to its security, how its interests can best be defined and effectively pursued, and what degree of world disorder it can tolerate. The task of making these judgments is rendered all the more difficult not only by the duality of America's own global role, but also by the ongoing transformation of international politics. While the nation-state is still formally the primary actor on the world scene, international politics (with emphasis on the hyphen) is increasingly becoming a seamless, messy, and often violently percolating global process.

Certain conclusions specific to America's security flow from the above argument. The first of the principal threats to international security listed earlier (p. 12)—namely, a central strategic war—still poses a grave ultimate threat, but is no longer the most likely to occur. For years to come, maintaining stable mutual nuclear deterrence with Russia will remain a major security responsibility of U.S. policymakers. Within a decade or so, it is likely that China will also become able to inflict unacceptable damage on American society in the event of a central strategic war.

This security challenge is well understood by the American political elite. Thus we may expect that the United States will continue to make major and costly efforts to improve its own strategic capabilities. At the very least, these will involve improving the reliability, accuracy, and penetrability of U.S. strategic and tactical nuclear weaponry and various related support systems.

We should also expect, however, that the U.S.-pioneered, technologically driven revolution in military affairs will place increasing emphasis on combat versatility below the nuclear threshold, while seeking more generally to de-emphasize the centrality of nuclear weapons in modern conflict. The United States is likely to implement, unilaterally if necessary, significant reductions in its nuclear arsenal while deploying some form of missile defense. The inclusion of both Russia and China, in addition to traditional allies, in a serious dialogue regarding defense against fringe missile attacks from countries that otherwise lack a strategic capability might mitigate their fear that America is seeking through missile defense to regain the strategic superiority it enjoyed in the early 1950s.

The next threats to peace—significant regional wars, fragmenting ethnic wars, and revolutions from below—do not necessarily pose a direct threat to the United States. Even a nuclear war between, say, India and Pakistan or Iran and Israel, however horrible, is unlikely to precipitate a serious threat to the U.S. homeland. In any case, the United States would presumably use its political and even military leverage to prevent or contain such conflicts. The American ability to do so would depend in large measure on how energetic its preventive diplomacy was and how assertive and credible its threats to intervene to terminate regional violence.

The need to play that assertive role provides a major reason for the United States to maintain forces that are able—under the U.S. strategic umbrella—to engage in rapid and decisive intervention in local wars, no matter how distant from the United States. The key words here are "rapid" and "decisive." In fact, the capacity to intervene rapidly and decisively is more important to U.S. security than the somewhat theoretical insistence of some military planners on maintaining a U.S. capability to wage two local wars (of unspecified duration) simultaneously. Being able to win a local war quickly provides a more credible deterrent against the eruption of another local conflict elsewhere than a costly effort to maintain the force levels required to engage in two local wars at the same time.

The essential formula for making decisive intervention possible is to combine the technological advantages of the revolution in military affairs, especially in precision weaponry and massive firepower, with airlift sufficient for rapid deployment of troops capable of heavy combat. Such a standby capability would go a long way in giving the United States, which already controls the oceans, the means to react to almost any local conflict deemed threatening to significant American interests.

This capability is certainly within U.S. reach—and it is noteworthy that no other power in the world can even aspire to such a global-reach capability. That disparity in itself defines the uniqueness of America's current preponderance, and the geopolitical advantages to the United States of having such a decisive capability are self-evident.

The security challenges facing the United States in its own homeland are less clear-cut and much more complicated. On the one hand, such threats are less direct and less self-evident than the ones already noted; on the other hand, they are elusive and could become more pervasive. It is in this murky area that the boundary between prudence and paranoia becomes more difficult to delineate, and the domestic implications for America become more complex.

Prior to 9/11, national concern was heavily focused on the possibility that "rogue" states such as Iran or North Korea might launch, or threaten to launch, a missile attack on the United States.[5] The Clinton administration in late 2000 even named the date by which it thought the nuclear-armed intercontinental ballistic missile (ICBM) threat from North Korea would become real—2005—and announced plans to begin construction of a radar site to support an eventual missile defense deployment designed to offset that threat. Subsequently, the George W. Bush administration made clear its determination to proceed with an even more robust national missile defense system, though the decision regarding its technological characteristics and coverage was to be discussed with the principal U.S. allies, as well as Russia and possibly China.

Both the Clinton administration and the subsequent Bush administration were responding to a genuine public worry that, at some point, hostile nations may acquire weapons of mass destruction as well as the means for their delivery. Both administrations were also sensitive to the political benefits of any scheme that seemed to revive America's traditional sense of special security. Technologically innovative defenses that would mitigate the grim reality of mutual vulnerability were inherently appealing. There were also specific domestic interests advocating the merits of missile defense, ranging from the aerospace industry to constituencies concerned that Iraq or Iran might pose a serious missile threat to Israel. Missile defense was thus an idea whose time had come.

The potential security benefits of any missile defense system, however, have to be weighed against the benefits of offsetting other vulnerabilities. Every dollar spent on missile defense means one less dollar for coping with other threats to the United States. By itself, this is not a case against the development and eventual deployment of some missile defenses, given the synergistic relationship between offensive and defensive weaponry. It is, however, to argue that any missile defense deployment has to follow from a careful weighing of alternative U.S. security needs. This is especially so since some of the other threats could prove more troublesome.

For example, covert attacks from unknown sources pose a particularly difficult and politically disorienting challenge. It is far from evident that even a so-called "rogue" state with missile capability would be so foolhardy as to strike at America in a manner that conveys the attacker's return address—as would clearly be the case with a missile launch. A missile attack would almost certainly provoke a devastating U.S. retaliation, which would also make any second strike against the United States less likely.

In contrast, a sudden nuclear explosion in some U.S. port, detonated aboard an obscure vessel—perhaps one of the more than 1,000 ships that ply the Atlantic on any given day—could annihilate the adjoining city without any perpetrator claiming credit or being available to receive blame. Such an undertaking would be less complex than the construction of a reliable warhead on an accurately guided ICBM, and would present a far graver challenge to American morale. Selecting a target for retaliation would not be as easy, while the fear of repetition would probably precipitate panic in every American city.

Much the same can be said of a terrorist act by a group determined to hurt, disorganize, and intimidate American society. The concentration of urban dwellers into congested spaces offers a particularly tempting target for an attack. If delivered anonymously, it would spark panic, perhaps precipitate overreactions directed at other states or religious and ethnic groups, and also threaten U.S. civil liberties. As the anthrax scare dramatized in the wake of 9/11, a large-scale release of bacteriological agents could unleash lethal epidemics and widespread hysteria while overwhelming existing U.S. disease controls. Similarly, a comprehensive cyber-attack on the computerized U.S. power grids, communications systems, and airlines could literally paralyze American society, provoking a social as well as economic breakdown. In brief, the highly congested and technologically interdependent character of modern society offers lucrative targets for anonymous but extremely damaging acts that are particularly difficult to forestall.

All of these threats—from the strategically familiar to the most unconventional—must be the objects of intensified contingency planning and maybe even preventive action. National security readiness has to be across the board, and it would be a mistake to over-dramatize one threat to the exclusion of others. The security enhancements that are urgently needed include, among others, the

upgrading of domestic emergency readiness to cope with a significant attack on an urban center, improvements in the effectiveness of
border controls against the insertion into the United States of components of weapons of mass destruction, and increased security of
the nation's economically and militarily vital computer systems.[6]

But for the real upgrading of homeland defense—rather than the
mere shuffling of bureaucratic boxes—the top priority must be the
acquisition of effective intelligence. Ultimately, it is impossible to
make every national facility and every football game and shopping mall
safe against terrorist attack. At some point, efforts to make them so
will bog down under the weight of burdensome controls and excessive
costs. Terrorists could have a field day simply by repeatedly unleashing
false alarms—and they may already be doing just that, precipitating
America's unsettling color alerts.

A far more productive security posture would involve a major
organizational and financial commitment to enhance national intelligence capabilities. That enhancement should focus on upgrading the
technological means for surveillance and prompt detection of suspect
activities, on more effective and widespread use of human recruitment
to penetrate hostile foreign governments and terrorist organizations,
and on aggressive covert activities designed to disrupt and terminate,
at an early stage, plots aimed at America. Every dollar spent on active,
preventive intelligence is probably worth more than ten dollars spent
on across-the-board but essentially blind upgrading of security at
potential terrorist targets.

Moreover, genuine national security readiness should foster
public recognition that some degree of vulnerability is a fact of modern life. Scaremongering by interested domestic parties, with periodic
media campaigns targeting particular "rogue" countries as America's
"enemy of the year"—Libya, Iraq, Iran, North Korea, and even
China—risks creating a paranoid vision of America's place in the
world, rather than prompting a broadly gauged national strategy
designed to channel global strife in a more stable and controllable
direction.

Defining the New Threat

The dilemmas inherent in America's new insecurity suggest that the United States is on the cusp of its third historically significant grand debate regarding its national defense. The first, which raged shortly after independence, was about whether the newly emancipated American state should even have a regular peacetime army, and what precautions should be adopted to counter the danger that its very existence could lead to despotism. The U.S. Congress was initially reluctant to approve a standing army, prompting Alexander Hamilton to warn (in the Federalist Papers) that without such an army "The United States would then exhibit the most extraordinary spectacle which the world has yet seen, that of a nation incapacitated by its Constitution to prepare for defense before it was actually invaded."[7]

The second protracted debate, equally far-reaching in its consequences, was precipitated after World War I by America's rejection of membership in the League of Nations. It culminated in the decision reached almost three decades later, after World War II, to undertake an open-ended U.S. commitment to the security of Europe, as expressed in Article 5 of the North Atlantic Treaty. This treaty's approval by Congress involved a fundamental redefinition of the meaning and scope of U.S. national security: the defense of Europe was henceforth to be the front line in the defense of America itself. Alliance became the cornerstone of U.S. defense policy.

The third debate is also likely to be protracted and divisive—at home as well as abroad. In essence, it involves the question of how far the United States should go in maximizing its own security, at what financial and political costs, and at what risk to strategic ties with its allies. Though it erupted into the open after 9/11, the third debate was already foreshadowed in the mid-1980s by the sharp domestic and international clash of opinions precipitated by President Reagan's proposed Strategic Defense Initiative. That project reflected an early recognition that technological dynamics were changing the relationship between offensive and defensive weaponry, and that outer space was becoming the perimeter of national security. The SDI proposal, however, was largely focused on a single threat, the Soviet Union. The issue faded when the threat itself faded.

A decade later, the third major redefinition of U.S. national security focuses increasingly on the broader issue of societal survivability in a setting of almost inevitable diffusion and diversification of weapons of mass destruction, percolating global turbulence, and increased fear of terrorism. These conditions cumulatively create a much more intimate interdependence between the security of the American homeland and the overall state of global affairs.

Although America's role in ensuring the security of its allies and, more generally, in sustaining global stability justifies it in seeking more security for itself than is practically attainable by other states, the fact nonetheless remains that total security has become a thing of the past. The defense of the territory of U.S. allies across the oceans no longer offers a distant shield for America itself. While this emerging reality has long been a source of concern to defense specialists, for the public at large it was the events of 9/11 that drove the truth home.

America's security henceforth has to be seen as inexorably tied to the global condition. Not surprisingly, public priorities after 9/11 show a marked drop in idealistic concerns and a considerable increase in concern for one's own safety. Nonetheless, readiness and planning for domestic and international security by themselves will not provide enduring security. The maintenance of a peerless and comprehensive U.S. military capability and enhanced domestic survivability must be reinforced by systematic efforts to enlarge the zones of global stability, to eliminate some of the most egregious causes of political violence, and to promote political systems that place central value on human rights and constitutional procedures. America from now on will be more vulnerable when democracy abroad is on the defensive, and democracy abroad, in turn, will be more vulnerable if America is intimidated.

A key issue in the third grand debate over America's national security is how to define the threat. How one defines a challenge largely determines the response. Hence, the issue of definition is not just an intellectual exercise, but a strategically important undertaking with several dimensions. The definition of the threat has to provide the springboard for national mobilization. It has to define the stakes involved. It has to not only grasp the essence of the threat, but capture some of its complexity. It has to distinguish between immediate and longer-term tasks. It has to differentiate among long-term allies, opportunistic partners, covert opponents, and open foes.

Given that America is a democracy, the definition of the threat must also be easily understood by the public, so that it can sustain the material sacrifices needed to address the threat. That puts a premium on clarity and specificity, but it also creates the temptation of demagogy. If the threat can be personalized, identified as evil, and even stereotyped visually, social mobilization for a long-haul effort becomes easier. In human affairs, and especially in international affairs, hate and prejudice are much more powerful emotions than sympathy or affinity. They are also easier to express than a more authentic appraisal of the inevitably complex historical and political motives that influence the conduct of nations and even of terrorist groupings.

The public discourse in the United States after 9/11 highlights these considerations. The public reaction—as reflected in speeches by leading politicians as well as in editorials in the leading publications—has tended to focus primarily on terrorism as such, emphasizing its evil character and concentrating attention on the notorious personality of Osama bin Laden. President Bush was inclined (probably because of his religious propensities) to treat the threat almost in theological terms, viewing it as a collision between "good and evil." He even embraced the Leninist formula that "he who is not with us is against us," a notion that is always congenial to an aroused public mood, but whose black-and-white view of the world ignores the shades of gray that define most global dilemmas.

Intellectually more ambitious analyses of the events of 9/11 most often pointed, in a vaguely generalized fashion, at the Islamic mindset, which was interpreted as religiously and culturally hostile to Western

26

(especially American) notions of modernity. To be sure, the administration wisely eschewed identifying terrorism with Islam as a whole and has been careful to stress that Islam as such is not at fault. Some of the administration's supporters, however, have been less careful about such distinctions. They quickly launched a campaign suggesting that Islamic culture as a whole is so hostile to the West that it has created fertile soil for terrorist violence against America. This argument carefully avoided identifying any pertinent political impulses behind the terrorist phenomenon.

President Bush's largely theological approach, in addition to its politically mobilizing effect, had the added tactical advantage of conflating into one simple formula several sources of the threat, irrespective of whether they were interconnected or not. The famous presidential reference to the "axis of evil," made in early 2002, rhetorically lumped together the separate challenges posed by North Korea to the stability of Northeast Asia, by Iran's longer-range ambitions in the Persian Gulf region, and by the unfinished legacy of the 1991 campaign against Iraq's Saddam Hussein. The increasingly ominous dilemmas inherent in these states' efforts to acquire nuclear weaponry were thus encapsulated by the moral condemnation of three specific but not allied regimes (two of them in fact mutual enemies) and were linked to the American people's painful and immediate experience with direct terrorism.

For the American people, the "axis of evil" will probably suffice for a while as a rough definition of the threat. The problem that arises, however, is twofold: First, since America's security is now linked to global security and the campaign against terrorism requires global support, it is important that others, outside America, share this definition. Will they? Second, is such a definition adequate in its diagnosis, and does it provide an effective basis for a long-term and successful strategic response to the challenge posed both separately as well as jointly by terrorism and the proliferation of weapons of mass destruction?

The difficulty is that the administration's definition of what or whom Americans are being asked to fight in "the war on terrorism" has been articulated in a remarkably vague fashion. Matters have not been made clear by the president's reduction (or elevation, depending on one's vantage point) of terrorists to "evildoers," otherwise unidentified, whose motivations are said to be simply satanic. Identifying terrorism itself as the enemy also blithely ignored the fact that terrorism is a lethal technique for intimidation employed by individuals, groups, and states. One does not wage a war against a technique or a tactic. No one, for instance, would have declared at the outset of World War II that the war was being fought against "blitzkrieg."

As a technique of warfare, terrorism is used by specific people generally for decipherable political purposes. Thus behind almost every terrorist act lurks a political problem. Terrorism purposely relies on brutal and morally outrageous strikes against civilians, symbolic persons, or physical objects to achieve a political effect.[8] The weaker and more fanatical the political extremists, the greater their inclination to adopt the most outrageous forms of terrorism as their preferred means of warfare. Their ruthless calculus is to instigate such massive retaliation by the stronger party that they themselves will gain increasing support and even legitimacy. To paraphrase Clausewitz, terrorism is politics by other means.

Accordingly, coping with terrorism requires a deliberate campaign not only to eliminate terrorists as such but to identify them and then to address (in whatever fashion may be appropriate) the political impulses that underlie their actions. To assert that is neither to excuse terrorism nor to urge its propitiation. Almost all terrorist activity originates from a political conflict and has been spawned as well as sustained by it. That applies to the Irish Republican Army (IRA) in Northern Ireland, the Basques in Spain, the Palestinians in the West Bank and Gaza, the Chechens in Russia, and to all other groups.[9]

While new for America, terrorism is not a novelty elsewhere. It was widespread in Europe and Tsarist Russia from the middle of the nineteenth century to approximately the beginning of World War I. It involved thousands of violent attacks, including high level assassinations and the dynamiting of buildings. Perhaps as many as 7,000 officials and policemen were its victims in Russia alone, including even the Tsar. Elsewhere, its most spectacular manifestation, the assassination of Austro-Hungarian archduke Franz Ferdinand in Sarajevo, sparked World War I.

In more recent times, the British have been victimized by IRA terrorism over several decades, and civilian losses from IRA bombings in Britain number in the hundreds, including even senior members of the royal family. Top officials have been assassinated in recent years in several European states—notably in Spain, Italy, and Germany—and other examples could be cited at length.[10] Both left-wing and right-wing terrorists have been active in Latin America, generating casualties in the tens of thousands.

Terrorism rooted in ethnic, national, or religious resentments is the most enduring and the least susceptible to simple extirpation. Generally speaking, terrorism derived from social grievances, even if ideologically reinforced by a dogma such as radical Marxism, tends to fade if the societies in question fail to embrace the terrorists' cause. Social isolation eventually demoralizes some of the terrorists and exposes others to capture. Terrorism based more specifically on the support of an alienated and geographically remote social class, such as the peasantry, has shown greater endurance (as the experiences of China and Latin America demonstrate), particularly if backed by a guerrilla movement. But terrorism derived from shared ethnicity backed by historic myths and fired by religious zeal has proven to be the most resistant of all to simple physical suppression.

The terrorists themselves are doubtless irredeemable, but the conditions that foster them may not be so. This is an important distinction. Terrorists tend to live in a world of their own, cocooned within their pathological self-righteousness. Violence becomes not just the means to an end but also their *raison d'être*. That is why their elimination is necessary. To make certain their ranks are not replenished, however, a careful political strategy is needed in order to weaken the complex political and cultural forces that give rise to terrorism. What creates them has to be politically undercut.

In the case of 9/11, it is evident that the political history of the Middle East has much to do with the terrorists' outrage, and especially with the focus of their outrage on America. That political history need not be dissected too precisely because terrorists presumably do not delve deeply into historical texts before embarking on a violent career. Rather, it is the emotional context of felt, observed, or recounted political grievances that shapes their hatreds and eventually their actions.

In the Middle East, Arab political sentiment has been shaped by the region's encounter with French and British colonialism, by the defeat of the Arab effort to prevent the appearance of Israel, by Israel's subsequent treatment of the Palestinians, and by the direct as well as indirect projection of American power into the region. The last has been perceived by the region's politically and religiously more extremist elements as a sacrilege against the sacred purity of Islam's holy places (first in Saudi Arabia, now in Iraq), as hurtful to the welfare of the Arab people, and as biased in support of Israel against the Palestinians. The extremists' political zeal has been fueled by religious fervor, but it is telling that some of the 9/11 terrorists led notably non-religious lifestyles. Their attack on the World Trade Center, the second within five years, thus had an evident political cast to it.

There is no escape from the historic reality that American involvement in the Middle East is clearly the main reason why terrorism has been directed at America—just as, for example, English involvement in Ireland has precipitated the IRA's frequent targeting of London and even of the royal family itself. The British have recognized that basic fact and have tried to react to it on both military and political levels. In contrast, America has shown a remarkable reluctance to confront the political dimensions of terrorism and to identify terrorism with its political context.

To win the war against Middle Eastern terrorists, one must implement the two key dimensions of the effort: the terrorists must be extirpated, but simultaneously a political process must be promoted that confronts the conditions that lead to the terrorists' emergence.

This is precisely what the British have been doing in Ulster and the Spaniards in Basque country. It is what the Russians have been urged to do in Chechnya. Addressing these political conditions is not a concession to terrorists but an imperative component of a strategy to eliminate and isolate the terrorist underworld.

Hence, the American reluctance to recognize a connection between the events of 9/11 and the modern political history of the Middle East—with its strong political passions, nurtured by religious fanaticism and zealous nationalism, unstably coexisting with political weakness—is a dangerous form of denial. The U.S. inclination, in the spring of 2002, to embrace even the more extreme forms of Israeli suppression of the Palestinians as part of the struggle against terrorism is a case in point. The unwillingness to recognize a historical connection between the rise of anti-American terrorism and America's involvement in the Middle East makes the formulation of an effective strategic response to terrorism that much more difficult.

Initial global support for America after the 9/11 outrage was, as noted earlier, both an expression of genuine empathy and an expedient affirmation of loyalty. It was not, however, an endorsement of the American interpretation of the nature of the threat. As that interpretation rhetorically took shape and was articulated in increasingly sharper language, culminating in the "axis of evil" formulation, the American perspective on terrorism increasingly came to be viewed as divorced from terrorism's political context.

Not surprisingly, within six months of 9/11, the nearly unanimous global support for America gave way to increasing skepticism regarding the official U.S. formulations of the shared threat. That poses the risk that America could find itself increasingly isolated in coping with the political dimensions of the dangers that it faces. The threat, in the meantime, could even worsen as various means of inflicting massive lethality become more and more accessible not only to states but to underground organizations.

The linkage between terrorism and proliferation is a truly menacing prospect. But it, too, cannot be addressed on the basis of abstract formulations about "evil," or by American power alone. Complicating the matter is the fact that the American record on nuclear proliferation is not that pure. The United States assisted Great Britain's efforts to acquire nuclear weapons; it surreptitiously aided France's; it winked at Israel's and perhaps even more than winked; it acquiesced to China's, India's, and Pakistan's; and it has been promiscuously unvigilant regarding its own nuclear secrets. When critics charge that the recent U.S. concerns with proliferation have been late in coming, they have a point.

America's motives are also being challenged by the widespread suspicion abroad, especially in Western Europe, that America's suddenly intense concern about proliferation is due only in part to the shock of 9/11. America's preoccupation with Iran's and Iraq's potential acquisition of deliverable weapons of mass destruction, in contrast to its indifference to Israel's possession of nuclear weapons, is seen as partly fueled by Israel's understandable interest in disarming these states and in keeping them so. The inclusion of North Korea in the "axis of evil" was widely interpreted as a deliberate effort to obscure the narrower, one-sided American preoccupation with proliferation specifically in the Middle Eastern region.

Efforts by foreign states to link their own pursuits to the American war on terrorism have further blurred the definition of the threat, thereby posing the additional risk that the American war on terrorism may be politically hijacked by foreign powers. Notably, Prime Minister Ariel Sharon of Israel, President Vladimir Putin of Russia, and former president Jiang Zemin of China have all seized upon the word "terrorism" to promote their own agendas. For each of them, the vague American definition of "terrorism with a global reach" has been both expedient and convenient in their efforts to suppress the Palestinians, the Chechens, and the Uighurs, respectively.

The point of departure, therefore, for an effective response to the threat of terror plus proliferation is to recognize that both are connected to specific regional issues. All the talk about "terrorism with a global reach" cannot erase the national origins of the terrorists, the specific focus of their hatreds, or their religious roots. Similarly, the threat of proliferation, and especially its linkage with state-sponsored terrorism, is predominantly regional and not global.

It follows, then, that North Korea's increasingly dangerous pursuit of nuclear weapons and its propensity to proliferate can be effectively addressed only in a Northeast Asian regional context, with the interests of South Korea, China, and Japan individually as well as collectively taken into account. The "axis of evil" formula notwithstanding, any attempted solution will have to recognize and respond to the special interests of the region's key countries. Indeed, America's insistence on engaging North Korea—in striking contrast to Iraq and Iran—in a regional multilateral dialogue about proliferation reinforces the point.

The answers to both terrorism and proliferation cannot come without America, but they clearly cannot come from America exclusively. The war on Middle Eastern terrorism will bring the actual elimination of terrorist organizations only when they lose their social appeal and therefore their recruitment ability, and when their financial backing dries up. This victory is likely to be apparent only retroactively. Proliferation will be brought under control when suspect national efforts are either subjected to effective international controls or halted by the duress of outside force. The active involvement of America will be critical to both outcomes, but achieving them will be much easier if American initiatives command genuine international support.

To be sure, the United States has the power to crush North Korea or any Middle Eastern state, to help Israel maintain its security as well as territorial control over the entire West Bank and Gaza, to support punitive antiterrorist military actions against Syria, to deter the Egyptians or Saudis from committing hostile acts against itself or Israel. Any additional military operation against Iran could be confined to selective strikes against any Iranian facilities engaged in WMD production, thereby limiting the scale of the required military effort.

Steps of that kind might deal with the issue of proliferation, at least in the short run. Whether they would cure the terrorist impulse is more doubtful. They would certainly foster intensified resentment of

America and be viewed as a manifestly colonial effort to impose a new order on the region. Moreover, they would very likely breed strong international repudiation, especially in Europe, not to mention the Islamic world. America's position in Europe could thereby be jeopardized, while the "war on terrorism" would become an exclusively American and largely anti-Islamic enterprise. Samuel Huntington's vision of a "clash of civilizations" could thus become a self-fulfilling prophecy.

Last but not least, a policy of unilateral compulsion would breed an international state of mind in which the surreptitious acquisition of WMD would become a high priority for states unwilling to be intimidated. Such states would then have an additional incentive to assist terrorist groups, which, fueled by a thirst for revenge, would be even more likely to anonymously unleash weapons of mass destruction against America. Survival of the fittest, always inherent to some degree in international politics (though gradually mitigated by international conventions guiding the conduct of states), would thereby become the law of the global jungle. In the long run, that could prove to be the fatal undoing of America's national security.

That is why one argument made in the course of the third grand debate about America's security—that it should denigrate the Atlantic Alliance in favor of a new "coalition of the willing"—is so misguided. Though not stated openly, it involves an attempt by a highly motivated group within the Bush administration and within the more conservative political circles to execute a strategic "coup de main" to alter America's fundamental geopolitical priorities. In effect, this group seeks to provide the rationale, the motivation, and the strategy for a new American-led global coalition, replacing the one that America shaped after 1945 during the Cold War.

The cement of the Cold War coalition was opposition to Soviet power, based on shared values and a rejection of Communist dictatorship. The coalition's critical expression was the Atlantic Alliance (formalized through NATO), followed by a separate defense treaty with Japan, and its purpose was to contain any further Soviet expansion.

The eventual collapse of the Soviet Union, in 1991, signaled the historic triumph of this democratic alliance, but it also raised the question of the alliance's future mission. The answer, for the last decade or so, has been to enlarge the alliance itself while gradually seeking to widen its outreach beyond Europe.

The terrorist strike of 9/11 has created the opening for those who feel strongly that the states that are somehow in conflict with Muslims—be they Russia, China, Israel, or India—should now be viewed as America's natural and primary partners. Some even argue that America's goal should be to reorder the Middle East, using America's power in the name of democracy to subordinate the Arab states to its will, to eliminate Islamic radicalism, and to make the region safe for Israel. That perspective is shared domestically in America by various right-wing, neoconservative, and religiously fundamentalist groups. Fear of terrorism gives this orientation a powerful public appeal.

Unlike the earlier coalition, however, this strategic formula offers little prospect of political endurance. The partnership would be opportunistic, organized around tactical goals rather than lasting common values. At best, it is likely to be a short-term arrangement—one that could only destroy, rather than replace, the grand democratic alliance that America successfully promoted for more than forty years.

The risks of such a realignment could be compounded by a rhetorically exuberant redefinition of America's strategic doctrine. President Bush signaled a growing inclination to do just that in his speech of June 1, 2002, at West Point. The White House press office distributed it by email to various members of the foreign policy community with a note stating that the speech "articulates a new doctrine for American foreign policy (preemptive action when necessary to defend our liberty and defend our lives). ... The West Point speech represents the convictions and cast of mind of the President and his Administration...."

In the speech, the president dismissed traditional deterrence as irrelevant to the post-Cold War dangers of terrorism and proliferation, and declared his determination to "take the battle to the enemy, disrupt his plans, and confront the worst threats before they emerge." It is noteworthy that he left "the enemy" unidentified, thus reserving the widest possible latitude for an arbitrary choice of target. The newly proclaimed doctrine of preemptive intervention did not specify what criteria would be used to determine what is terrorism, nor did it clarify under what conditions proliferation would be viewed as an evil justifying preventive military action by the United States.

In essence, the United States was arrogating the right to identify the enemy and to strike first without seeking international consensus on a shared definition of the threat. It was replacing the established doctrine of mutual assured destruction (known as MAD) with the new concept of solitary assured destruction (which might be labeled SAD). Not surprisingly, the shift from MAD to SAD was seen by many as strategically regressive.

The conflation of two distinct concepts, preemption and prevention, did not help matters. In Chapter 5 of the 2002 National Security Strategy document issued by the National Security Council, entitled "Prevent Our Enemies from Threatening Us, Our Allies, and Our Friends with Weapons of Mass Destruction," the two terms are used interchangeably. The Deputy Secretary of Defense further blurred the issue by stating to the International Institute for Strategic Studies (IISS) on December 2, 2002, that "Anyone who believes that we can wait until we have certain knowledge that attacks are imminent has failed to connect the dots that led to September 11."

Yet the distinction between preemption and prevention is significant for international order, and it should not be obscured. It involves the difference, for example, between Israel's decision in June 1967 to *preempt* the Arab attack for which Arab forces were completing their deployment, and Israel's 1981 air attack on the Osiraq nuclear reactor in order to *prevent* Iraq from eventually acquiring nuclear weapons. The former responded to an imminent threat; the latter prevented a threat from arising. Similarly, the U.S. attack on Iraq in 2003 was perhaps *preventive* against some future "grave and gathering threat" (as President Bush put it) but certainly not *preemptive* of an imminent Iraqi strike.

Preemption can be justified on the grounds of supreme national interest in the face of an imminent threat, and thus almost by definition it is likely to be unilateral. It requires extraordinarily good intelligence to justify (at least retroactively) such an arbitrary act. Prevention, in contrast, should be preceded if possible by the mobilization of political pressure (including international support) in order to forestall the undesirable from occurring, and should involve a recourse to force only when other remedies have been exhausted and deterrence is no longer a credible alternative. Failure to discriminate—especially on the part of the superpower, which has the greatest means for deterrence—could precipitate a contagion of unilateral "preventive" wars masquerading as "preemptive."

Ultimately, the worst effect of any such far-reaching alteration in alliances and doctrine could be on America itself. It would transform both America's historical role in the world and the way the world views it. Rather than continue as the beacon of liberty for the politically awakening peoples of the world, America would come to be seen as the leader of a new "Holy Alliance" that lacks a balanced concern for order and justice, security and democracy, national power and social progress. It could produce hegemonic isolation, with old friends cavalierly antagonized and new ones neither truly sharing America's basic values nor capable of becoming genuinely comprehensive partners in coping with the sources of global violence. An isolated America, despite its might, would then be prey to various hostile constellations, comprising not only its enemies but its former but forlorn allies as well as its new but fickle friends.

The fundamental threat facing both America and the world is increasingly violent political turmoil that could end in global anarchy. Terrorism is one of its ugliest manifestations. Proliferation of weapons of mass destruction is one of its greatest dangers. But both are symptoms of a basic global malady. Only the persistent pursuit of a global strategy that addresses the underlying causes of global strife can reduce America's current national insecurity. That calls for the mobilization of worldwide support on a scale that dwarfs even the alliance that defeated the totalitarianisms of the twentieth century. American global power is this strategy's necessary point of departure, but it cannot be its historical destination.

NOTES

1 After Pearl Harbor, the war with Japan was fought on the distant Pacific Ocean islands.

2 "And the seventh angel poured out his vial into the air; and there came a great voice out of the temple of heaven, from the throne, saying, It is done.
And there were voices, and thunders, and lightnings; and there was a great earthquake, such as was not since men were upon the earth, so mighty an earthquake, and so great.
And the great city was divided into three parts, and the cities of the nations fell....
And every island fled away, and the mountains were not found.
And there fell upon men a great hail out of heaven, every stone about the weight of a talent: and men blasphemed God because of the plague of the hail; for the plague thereof was exceeding great. (King James Version)

3 For example, the very success of America's RMA has spurred China to pursue its own "RMA with Chinese characteristics"—described as "people's war under high-tech conditions"—in what some Chinese military leaders and experts consider to be "a major strategic transformation." See Kung Shuang-yin, "Achieving Development by Leaps and Bounds in National Defense," *Ta Kung Pao*, May 31, 2003. (*Author's Note: Throughout book, all quotations from non-English titles are translations.*)

4 According to the annual report on world conflicts prepared in 2002 by the Interdisciplinary Research Programme on Causes of Human Rights Violations (PIOOM), Leiden, Netherlands, there were twenty-three ongoing "high-intensity conflicts" in the year 2001, which consumed some 125,000 human lives, in addition to seventy-nine "low-intensity conflicts" (which consumed from 100 to 1,000 lives each) and thirty-eight "violent political conflicts" (ranging from 25 to 100 fatalities each). Only about thirty-five countries were listed as relatively free of violent political strife.

5 In general, a great deal of vigilance is warranted in regard to so-called intelligence information about the development of weaponry by other countries, especially when such information originates from foreign sources. A case in point is the story

headlined, "Iran May Be Able to Build an Atomic Bomb in 5 Years, U.S. and Israeli Officials Fear," which appeared in *The New York Times*, datelined from Tel Aviv January 3, 1995. It quoted "a senior official" as asserting that "If Iran is not interrupted in this program by some foreign power, it will have the device in more or less five years." Seven years later, on March 19, 2002, the Director of Central Intelligence testified before Congress that "most Intelligence Community agencies project that by 2015 the US most likely will face ICBM threats from North Korea and Iran.... Tehran may be able to indigenously produce enough fissile material for a nuclear weapon by late this decade." Moreover, the experience of all existing nuclear powers is that numerous tests are needed to acquire a reliable nuclear warhead and a reasonably accurate delivery system. Such tests are nearly impossible to conceal. The only exception may have been Israel, which is said to have acquired a covert nuclear arsenal, but Israel has been the informal beneficiary of the technological know-how acquired by tests conducted by the United States and, in earlier years, also by France. Even so, Israel is widely suspected of having conducted in the late 1970s at least one joint nuclear test with the then-white-supremacist government of South Africa.

6   Two citations from Stephen E. Flynn's article, "America the Vulnerable," *Foreign Affairs* (January/February 2002), 63–64, illustrate the scale of the problem: "most of the physical plant, telecommunications, power, water supply, and transportation infrastructure on U.S. territory lies unprotected or is equipped with security suffi- cient to deter only amateur vandals, thieves, or hackers.... In 2000 alone, 489 million people, 127 million passenger vehicles, 11.6 million maritime containers, 11.5 million trucks, 2.2 million railroad cars, 829,000 planes, and 211,000 vessels passed through U.S. border inspection systems."

7   Gregory J.W. Urwin, "The Army of the Constitution: The Historical Context," in ...*to insure domestic Tranquility, provide for the common defence...*, ed. Max G. Manwaring, 45 (Carlisle, PA: Strategic Studies Institute, 2000).

8   Another way of putting it: "terrorism and its associated asymmetry emerge when fragments of a marginalized self-appointed elite are frustrated to the point of violence by what they perceive as injustice, repression, or inequity.... These individ- ual men and women are prepared to kill and to destroy—and perhaps to die in the process—to achieve their self-determined objectives." Max G. Manwaring, *The Inescapable Global Security Arena*, (Carlisle, PA, Strategic Studies Institute, 2002), 7.

9   In a study of suicide terrorism from 1980 to 2001, University of Chicago polit- ical scientist Robert Pape found that, of the 188 separate attacks he identified, "179 could have their roots traced to large, coherent political or military campaigns." He also noted that "there is little connection between suicide terrorism and Islamic fun- damentalism, or any religion for that matter. In fact, the leading instigator of suicide

attacks is the Tamil Tigers in Sri Lanka, a Marxist-Leninist group whose members are from Hindu families but who are adamantly opposed to religion (they have committed 75 of the 188 incidents)." See Robert A. Pape, "Dying to Kill Us," *The New York Times*, September 22, 2003.

10   To cite the case of Italy alone: Franco Ferracuti, "Ideology and Repentance: Terrorism in Italy," in *Origins of Terrorism*, ed. Walter Reich, 59 (Washington, DC: Woodrow Wilson Center Press, 1998), counted no less than 14,569 acts of terrorism in Italy between 1969 and 1986, with a total of 415 deaths. The peak year, 1979, experienced 2,513 terrorist incidents.

2

THE DILEMMAS OF
THE NEW GLOBAL DISORDER

Since the last decade of the twentieth century, conflict in Eurasia has become the world's central security concern. The southeastern rim of Eurasia is the arena for dangerous ethnic and religious interstate wars, the locus of extremist regimes seeking weapons of mass destruction, and the source of the most fanatical creeds and militant movements with whom some states might at some point share their weapons. It encompasses more than half of the world's population (including the two most populous states) as well as about three quarters of the world's poor, it is a principal generator of the world's demographic explosion, and it is the major source of the increasingly tension-charged international migratory pressures.[1]

During the four decades of the Cold War, the central geostrategic challenge facing America was that a hostile totalitarian ideology that controlled some two-thirds of the Eurasian mega-continent might gain dominion over the rest. Eurasia was both the grand arena and the principal stake in the contest because it contains most of the world's politically assertive and dynamic states, as well as two of the world's three most economically advanced regions: Western Europe and the Far East. Complete domination of Eurasia would have been tantamount to global supremacy.

American commitment to prevent the domination of Eurasia by a hostile power carried with it the risk of an apocalyptic nuclear war. Hence, the primary preoccupation of U.S. security policy had to be with the arms race, with the competitive accumulation of nuclear arsenals, and even with the planning of a full-scale nuclear war itself. Deterrence was the organizing principle for the avoidance of war, and containment was the formula for the prevention of a hostile takeover of Eurasia's western and far eastern extremities.

Coping with the new global disorder calls for a more versatile strategy than was required for waging the Cold War, and for a wider-ranging approach than the post-9/11 campaign against terrorism. The war on terrorism cannot be the central organizing principle of U.S. security policy in Eurasia or of U.S. foreign policy in general. It involves too narrow a focus, it is too vague in its definition of the enemy, and most important, it is not responsive to the basic causes of the intense political turmoil in the crucial swathe of Eurasia between Europe and the Far East. Heavily inhabited by Muslims, we might term this crucial subregion of Eurasia the new "Global Balkans."[2]

Especially in the wake of 9/11, America needs to examine, carefully and calmly, its complex relationship with the highly volatile world of Islam. That is the prerequisite to any effective long-term American engagement in pacifying the volatile new Global Balkans in response to the twin dangers of terrorism and proliferation. However, U.S. policymakers must also anticipate the wider risks to America of overextension and of rising anti-American political and religious hostility produced by solitary American intervention.

In addition, the contemporary world disorder stems more broadly from a new reality: The world is now politically awakened to the inequality in the human condition. Until relatively recent times, the vast majority of mankind was fatalistically acquiescent to social injustice. Though peasant rebellions from time to time disturbed the popular resignation to what seemed to be an ordained state of affairs, they erupted mainly when local circumstances became altogether unbearable. Even then, they did so in basic ignorance of the world at large, in relative isolation, and without a transcendental consciousness of injustice.

That state of affairs has been dramatically altered. Spreading literacy and especially the impact of modern communications have produced an unprecedented level of political consciousness among the masses, making them much more continuously susceptible to the emotional appeals of nationalism, social radicalism, and religious fundamentalism. These appeals are fueled by a heightened awareness of the disparities in the material well-being of mankind, prompting understandable envy, resentment, and hostility, and are intensified by self-gratifying cultural and religious contempt for the perceived hedonism of the privileged. In that setting, the demagogic mobilization of the weak, the poor, and the oppressed becomes increasingly easy.

THE POWER OF WEAKNESS

September 11, 2001, was a seminal event in the history of power politics. Nineteen fanatics, not all of whom had western education, with scant financial resources, plunged the world's mightiest and most technologically advanced power into panic and precipitated a global political crisis.

The aftereffects of their act militarized U.S. foreign policy, accelerated Russia's western reorientation, eventually prompted growing fissures between America and Europe, intensified America's economic malaise, and altered the traditional American definition of civil rights. The weapons with which they accomplished all that were merely some box-cutters and a willingness to forfeit their own lives. Never before had so much pain been inflicted on so powerful many by so impotent few.

Therein lies the dilemma for the world's only superpower: how to cope with an enemy that is physically weak but endowed with a fanatical motivation. Unless the sources of the motivation are diluted, attempts to thwart and eliminate the enemy will be to no avail. Hatred will breed replenishment. The foe can be eliminated only through a sensitive recognition of motives and passions that are not precisely defined but are derived from a shared quest of the militant weak to destroy—at all cost—the object of their resentful zeal.

In their quest—in which terrorism in fact is a ruthless tool of the weak against the powerful (a characterization that does not endow it with any moral legitimacy)—the weak have one great psychological advantage: they have little to lose and, they believe, everything to gain. They can find sustenance in religious zeal or utopian fanaticism, and they express their conviction with an intensity derived from the depravity of their condition. Some of the weak are willing to sacrifice themselves because their lives are defined as worthy when they transcend their miserable existence through suicidal acts designed to destroy the object of their hatred. Their desperation generates their fervor and drives their terror.

The dominant, by contrast, have everything to lose—especially that which they value most, their own well-being—and their anxiety disperses their power. The more powerful husband their lives and cherish the good life. Panic among the privileged, once unleashed, tends to exaggerate the actual potential of the unseen and basically weak foe, magnifying his alleged reach while undermining the collective sense of security so necessary for comfortable social existence. Once they slide into panicky overreactions, the dominant unwittingly transform themselves into the hostages of the weak.

The fanatical weak cannot transform themselves, but they have the power to make the lives of the dominant increasingly miserable. The power of weakness is the political equivalent of what military strategists have labeled asymmetrical warfare. In effect, the revolution in military affairs (RMA)—which maximizes the physical power of the technologically dominant—is being offset by a quantum leap in social vulnerability, increasing the fear that the powerful have of the weak.

The power of weakness allows the exploitation of four novel realities of modern life. The first is that access to the means of inflicting large-scale lethality is no longer restricted to organized and powerful states. As already noted in Chapter 1, the capacity to inflict massive social damage, and especially to prompt widespread anxiety, is increasingly accessible to relatively small but determined groupings. Second, worldwide mobility—facilitated not only by rapid travel but also by increased migrations that have broken down barriers between discrete societies—and worldwide communications both facilitate coordination and planning by otherwise dispersed underground cells. Third, democratic permeability facilitates penetration and submersion in open societies, making detection of threats extremely difficult while ultimately damaging the fabric of democracy itself. Fourth, the systemic interdependence of a modern society tends to set off chain reactions. If even a single key element of the system is disrupted, it prompts escalating social disruption and wildfire panic.

In brief, the shock and awe tactic hailed by the strategists of the RMA finds its counterpoint in the paralyzing panic that the weak at low cost can unleash among the powerful. A case in point is the vastly overestimated public perception of the terrorist group al-Qaeda as a highly organized, tightly disciplined, globally pervasive underground army of technologically skilled terrorists directed from an efficient command and control center. Frequent public references after 9/11 to al-Qaeda's "50,000 trained terrorists" reinforced the notion that America, and the West generally, was permeated by hidden cells of technically proficient warriors ready to unleash a series of coordinated and devastating blows designed to disrupt social life. Periodic color-code alerts in the United States reinforced that perception, magnifying the specter's power and endowing its leader, Osama bin Laden, with fearsome reach.[3]

The more accurate estimate is that al-Qaeda is a loose confederation of fundamentalist Muslim cells that for a while enjoyed a secure haven for its chief plotters under the umbrella of the primitively fundamentalist Taliban regime in Afghanistan. Spawned by the Soviet destruction of Afghan society and spurred by a sudden burst of supranational Muslim reaction to the Soviet invasion, the Muslim fundamentalists subsequently focused their already aroused hostility on America, which they came to scorn for supporting Israel, for protecting the region's unpopular regimes, and most of all for defiling the holiest lands of Islam by its military presence. Al-Qaeda provided the prophetic inspiration, the ideological platform, the fundraising for seeding nascent groups elsewhere, the basic operational training, and the broad strategic planning for various terroristic offshoots eager to strike out against "the Great Satan."[4]

The result has been a series of sporadic terrorist attacks against American assets around the world, of which 9/11 was obviously the most daring, dramatic, and devastating. Yet the coordinated scale of the simultaneous strikes against targets in New York and Washington was also atypical in its ambitiousness and in its unanticipated results (since it is most unlikely that even its planners could have foreseen that the World Trade Center towers would totally collapse after being struck). That this attack was not followed, even long afterwards, by a different but equally ambitious attack—such as the much feared "dirty bomb" explosion in an urban center—is a reminder of al-Qaeda's physical and organizational limitations, which were compounded by the U.S. operation against its leaders and haven in Afghanistan.

Nonetheless, the 9/11 strike demonstrated how a single psychologically stunning blow, originating from an invisible source, can alter the outlook and even the conduct of the world's superpower. It is difficult to imagine that the United States would have launched its war in the spring of 2003 against Iraq without the earlier psychological shock that America experienced in the fall of 2001. America's definition of its role in the world was altered not by the challenge of a mighty rival but by the suicidal act of a few unknown fanatics inspired and supported by a remote but zealous underground group lacking any of the attributes of modern state power.

Al-Qaeda's attack signaled yet another important paradox inherent in the power of weakness: The weak become strong by oversimplifying the focus of their hatred, whereas the strong become weak by doing the same. The weak, by demonizing what they despise, gain adherents who are infused with self-sacrificial determination. "The Great Satan" suffices as both explanation and motivation. It replenishes the ranks and fosters acts of brutality in which violence against innocents provides the perpetrators with a self-fulfilling sense of triumph. Victory is defined less by the outcome than by the act itself. Unlike the weak, the powerful cannot afford the luxury of oversimplification. They become weak by oversimplifying their fears. Because their interests are broad, because their stakes are interdependent, and because for them the definition of the good life is subjectively and objectively wide-ranging, the powerful must not simply demonize the challenge posed by the weak or reduce it to a unidimensional scale. To do so is to risk focusing only on the superficial manifestations of the challenge, while ignoring its more complex and historically rooted impulses.

There is thus a practical dimension to the seamless dilemmas of global disorder that America now faces. Power and force alone are not sufficient to preserve American hegemony because America's foes are zealous, less attached to their lives, and ready to exploit America's democratic principles without compunction. Coercion creates new antagonists but does little to prevent them from slipping through the crevices of democracy and attacking from within. If the United States wants to retain the life and liberty it cherishes inside the country, it must maintain the legitimacy of its predominance outside the country. That means nothing less than genuine cooperation with allies, not merely the support of supplicants, and it means above all else a sustained cooperative effort to grasp the complicated nature of the contemporary global disorder.

The weak can fight "the Great Satan" because simplicity of focus helps to compensate for their weakness. The powerful, rather than simply demonizing the enemy, must understand and confront the enemy's complexity.

TURBULENT ISLAM

The immediate challenge this poses for America is the volatile state of its relationship with the world of Islam. That relationship is complicated by strong emotions and a great deal of reciprocal prejudice. The terrorist outrages and, before that, the explicitly anti-American revolution in Iran led many Americans to perceive Islam as almost a mirror image of the Islamic fundamentalist view of America as "the Great Satan."

That specter has even been personalized. Osama bin Laden is projected frequently on the television screens of American homes as the embodiment of evil, his appearance and dress conveying the symbolic message that Islam, the Arabs, and terrorism are organically interwoven.[5] The entertainment industry has tended to provide the public with stereotyped versions of the Islamic, and specifically Arab, connection with terrorism. Even back in 1995, the terrorist bombing in Oklahoma City prompted a widespread focus on Arab-Americans as the primary suspects. The mass media's broad hints at Muslim culpability allegedly prompted some 200 ugly incidents before the real perpetrator was identified.

The inclination to view the security implications for America of the ferment in the Islamic world through an alarmist perspective and to lump diverse policy problems under oversimplified formulas has been almost inescapable. As a result, it has become increasingly difficult for the United States to pursue stable long-term policies based on a careful and detached assessment of the current mood of doctrinal/cultural passion in the Islamic world and of the actual threat it poses to global security. Yet without such a discriminating assessment, America can neither manage the complex and varied forces at work in the Islamic regions, nor effectively counter the deliberate fostering of religiously fueled animus toward the United States within a significant and increasingly politically awakened portion of the world's population.

Dar al-Islam—the House of Islam—is a complex world unto itself. Its basic condition involves existential diversity, political fragility, and explosive potential. Geographically, the bulk of the Islamic world can be encircled by a line running roughly along the shores of the Indian Ocean from Indonesia west to the Persian Gulf, and then south to Tanzania, then continuing west across Africa through mid-Sudan to Nigeria and north along the Atlantic shoreline to the coast of the Mediterranean Sea. From northern Africa, the line crosses the Mediterranean Sea eastward to the Bay of Bosporus at the entrance to the Black Sea and all the way to the northern frontier of Kazakhstan, and then curves southward again through western China and parts of India before rejoining its point of departure by curving around Borneo. Within that half moon live most of the world's Muslims, about 1.2 billion people—or approximately the same as China's total population. Of these, roughly 820 million are located in Asia and 315 million in Africa, with close to 300 million concentrated in the geopolitically sensitive Levantine, Persian Gulf, and Central Asian zone. Contrary to the frequent American mass-media caricature of Muslims as semitic Arabs, the largest concentration of them is actually to be found in South and Southeast Asia: Indonesia, Malaysia, Bangladesh, Pakistan, and the predominantly Hindu India. Other large Muslim concentrations with a distinctive ethnic identity include the Persians of Iran, the Turks (with Turkic ethnicity extending also to Azerbaijan and to several of the Central Asian peoples), and the Egyptians and Nigerians.

By latest count, thirty-two member-states of the UN have populations that are at least 86 percent Muslim, and another nine are in the range of 66 percent to 85 percent Muslim, for a total of forty-one predominantly Muslim countries. Of these, not one is listed in the annual Freedom House *Freedom in the World* assessment as genuinely "free," i.e., fundamentally respectful of both political rights and civic liberties. Eight are listed as "partly free," all the others as "not free"; of the latter, seven are included among the eleven most "repressive" states. In addition, nineteen states have Muslim populations that range from small majorities to significant minorities (of at least 16 percent), like India, with its roughly 120 to 140 million Muslims. Up to 35 million Muslims live in China, somewhere around 20 million in Russia, about 11 million in western and southeastern Europe, 5 to 8 million in North America, and about 2 million in Latin America.

Because of high rates of birth and conversion, Islam is currently the world's fastest growing religion. In recent years, the Middle East has surpassed all other regions in population growth, growing at an annual rate of 2.7 percent, compared to 1.6 percent in the rest of Asia and 1.7 percent in Latin America. Similarly, the Muslim states situated in a belt just south of Russia, which currently have a population of about 295 million, are likely to number no less than 450 million by 2025. Muslim states already are, and increasingly will be, populated in large part by younger people. How successfully these people are absorbed into the economic system and how they are socialized will largely determine their political orientation and conduct.

Almost every state with a predominantly Muslim population, whether it labels itself Islamic or not, confronts some form of religious challenge, often accompanied by a demand for imposition of the Sharia (the strict Islamic code of behavior). Even such formally secular states as Egypt, Algeria, and Indonesia find themselves in the throes of religiously inspired populist ferment. In Egypt, this has fueled years of effort to suppress the Muslim Brotherhood in which executions of Brotherhood leaders were matched by dramatic assassinations of top national figures, such as President Anwar al-Sadat. In Algeria, a secular military regime has been the target of a bloody guerrilla war waged by Islamic activists whose aspirations to create an Islamic republic through popular elections were frustrated by governmental fiat. In Indonesia, the two large but competitive religious parties command the loyalty of an estimated 70 million supporters, many of them educated in the religiously oriented (and often linguistically Arabic-reliant) schools that the parties have established throughout the country.

Because of the fragility of secular political institutions, the weakness of civil society, and the stifling of intellectual creativity, much of the Islamic world faces widespread social stagnation.[6] That condition is partially a legacy of recent decolonization, which left behind no viable constitutional structures; partially the consequence of the continued difficulties of relating religion to politics in the context of a religiously inspired mass political consciousness; partially the product of intensifying but unsatisfied socioeconomic aspirations; and partially an aftereffect of specific regional or even global political conflicts. But it is a problem that varies in gravity from country to country, and hence no sweeping or deterministic prejudgments are justified regarding the political future of the Islamic world as a whole.

Furthermore, even if religion appears to be the paramount catalyst of political ferment, such secular causes as corruption and the unequal distribution of wealth are also major sources of the political volatility. Some Muslim countries suffer from desperate poverty. Afghanistan's GNP hovers under $200 per capita and Pakistan's barely around $500, while in nearby Kuwait it exceeds $20,000 per capita. Differentials of living standards are pronounced not only between countries, but within them, with some ruling elites unabashed in their quest for wealth (and its often covert enjoyment) despite pervasive social deprivation.

Moreover, highly visible examples of personal enrichment by the rulers of several Muslim states—Saudi Arabia, Pakistan, and Indonesia provide the most egregious examples—have dramatized the degree to which the exercise of political power has become synonymous with the acquisition of wealth, conduct not quite in keeping with strict Islamic preaching. Coupled with the pervasive weakness of civil society, in which bloated and inefficient state bureaucracies act as social parasites that stifle economic dynamism and perpetuate mass poverty, such spectacular cases of voracious self-gratification inevitably stimulate popular resentments and intensify the appeal of Islamist populism. Strict implementation of the Sharia, the people are told by certain clerics, would eradicate such elite hypocrisy.

Admittedly, corruption is endemic to a majority of developing states, and especially in the so-called "petro-economies." In that regard, Nigeria, which was rated ninetieth in bureaucratic honesty among ninety-one countries listed by Transparency International in its 2001 Corruption Perceptions Index, Indonesia (ranked eighty-eighth), and Pakistan (ranked seventy-ninth) fall into the same category as such non-Muslim states as Russia (tied with Pakistan for seventy-ninth place), India (ranked seventy-first), and some of the narco-states of Latin America.

In any case, the almost certain prospect is that the majority of Muslim states will continue to be weak, ineffective, frequently wracked by political ferment, resentful of the West, but mostly preoccupied with internal problems or conflicts with their neighbors. Their condition will foster international insecurity, generate periodic bursts of terrorism, and create a climate of pervasive tension. With weakness breeding social distress, anti-American passions will tend to be as much the result of a generalized religious animus as the byproduct of national grievances or regional conflicts.

Of these political grievances, the most evident is Arab resentment of U.S. support for Israel.[7] That resentment has spread gradually also to non-Arab Muslims in Iran and Pakistan. Lately, suspicion has also surfaced among the Afghans and Muslims in Central Asia that America is supporting Russian efforts to contain the spread of Islam among Russia's new southern neighbors. All of this is generating a transnational Muslim political identity that is both explicitly and subconsciously anti-American.

From the standpoint of international security, the key question for the future is how the percolating ferment within *Dar al-Islam* will define itself politically. Is religious fundamentalism the wave of the future? Or will radicalism with an Islamic veneer prevail? Are Muslim societies, because of their religious tradition and teachings, unable to evolve into democratic political systems? Is there a fundamental incompatibility between Islam and modernity—with the latter defined largely by the contemporary (and globally contagious) experience of the increasingly secular America, Europe, and Far East? The issue becomes increasingly complex as one progresses through the above questions.

During the last two decades—since the onset of the theocratic seizure of power in Iran—Islamic fundamentalism has greatly preoccupied the West. With the recent decline in terrorism by the secular PLO but the increased reliance on terrorism by Iranian-backed Shiite organizations and their Wahhabi-supported Sunni counterparts (of which Osama bin Laden has become the most notorious symbol),

Western mass media have tended to stress religious fundamentalism as a rising and increasingly pervasive force in the Islamic world. Ferment within even the more established Muslim countries has often been presented as foreshadowing a fundamentalist takeover.

In fact, however, until the U.S. occupation of Iraq in 2003 and its resulting boost to Shiite theocratic aspirations, the fundamentalist phenomenon appeared to be losing momentum. Even in Iran, the more moderate elements within the theocracy have become more assertive and critical of the rigid dogmatism and social censorship imposed by the imams. Twenty years after the fundamentalist revolution, public discourse in Iran is increasingly predominated by political/theological reformers. The theocratic political-theological nexus still defines the context in which debates over Iran's future occur, but the thrust of the debates is in the direction of narrowing the religious domain and expanding the sphere of free choice. Throughout 1999 and 2000, Iranian public life was dominated by the spectacular public trials of several leading politically active clerics who had openly advocated a retraction in the scope of religious control over political life, including calls for the civic right to criticize the theocracy. Their views evoked widespread support among the Iranian intelligentsia.

How Iran will evolve is unclear, but the days of its fundamentalist theocracy are numbered. It is in its "Thermidorian" phase. And without Iran, fundamentalism elsewhere will tend to lack staying power. It can pose challenges (as in Pakistan), it can exacerbate internal conflicts (as in Sudan), it can engage in isolated external acts of terrorism (as in Indonesia), or it can be the focus of resistance to foreign occupation (as first in Lebanon and lately in Iraq). But it lacks the momentum and historical relevance required of an enduring political attraction for the hundreds of millions of young Muslims who are becoming politically conscious.

Islamic fundamentalism is essentially reactionary—that is the source of both its short-term appeal and its long-term weakness. It is strongest in the most isolated and primitive portions of the Muslim world—be they in Soviet-pulverized Afghanistan or in the Wahhabi strongholds of Saudi Arabia. But even when driven by bitter resentments against external enemies or angered by the hypocrisy of their rulers, the younger generation of Muslims is not immune to the seduction of television and films. Withdrawal from the modern world can attract only fanatical minorities; it is not a long-term option for the many, who are not inclined to forfeit the benefits of modernity. The majority wants change, but change that also addresses its aspirations.

To be sure, Islamic fundamentalism feeds off anti-Western xenophobia, which has been the main source of its political vitality. It is noteworthy that, beyond the very specific conditions of Shiite Iran and Israeli-occupied southern Lebanon, only Soviet-devastated Afghanistan and a part of Sudan fell into the hands of intensely anti-Western and reactionary fundamentalists. If the United States is not careful, that could also happen in some parts of Iraq. Efforts to take power in secular Muslim states such as Egypt, Algeria, and Indonesia have largely been suppressed, while the relatively conservative governments with an ostensibly religious Islamic self-definition—such as the Moroccan or the more dogmatically traditional Saudi Arabian governments—have been able to contain the political appeal of religious fundamentalism.

The more lasting political challenge, especially in the predominantly Sunni Muslim countries, is more likely to come from populist movements that espouse "Islamism"[8] as a comprehensive political ideology, but do not advocate a theocracy as such. Usually led by secular intellectuals, these movements combine militant populism with a religious gloss. The Islamists are often explicitly critical of religious fundamentalism, which they see as reactionary and ultimately self-defeating, and they seek to formulate a Muslim response to modern social and political dilemmas that they believe have been largely ignored by the theocratic fundamentalists. Not surprisingly, the populist case—fusing religious intensity with sociopolitical doctrine—tends to resonate more with the restless younger generation.

In almost every Muslim country, a modern, often Western-trained intelligentsia is actively debating the relationship of Islam, democracy, and modernity. This debate is often inchoate, suffused with Islamic invocations, and politically contradictory. Islamist political rhetoric is often laced with lingering resentment of Western domination. The more Western-minded elements in the Muslim intelligentsia tend to be particularly suspicious of concepts like "the clash of civilizations." To them, such notions are a confirmation of European, American, or Israeli feelings of superiority. One should bear in mind that most of *Dar al-Islam* has been free of colonial control only for the last two generations. The memory of this history inevitably colors the debates and makes them more passionate.

Given the fashion of the times, Islamist ideologues often invoke "democracy." Just as often, however, this term pertains to an essentially plebiscitary populism guided by religious principles. The economic dilemmas facing the Muslim countries, made more acute by their rapidly growing populations, also tend to be slighted in the Islamist political discourse, though the evident failure of the statist economic system has lately jolted some proponents of Islamism—who on religious grounds had generally favored nationalization of the economy—into a grudging recognition that a measure of economic freedom, based on private ownership and the market mechanism, is a prerequisite of economic growth.

The relationship of political freedom to religion is even more complicated. Western secular democracy is a particularly troublesome concept for the Islamists, for it implies to many of them an essentially atheistic society. They interpret the secularizing trends in the West as signifying the fading of religious preeminence. The West's prevailing tendency to deem unethical or immoral only that which is confirmed to be illegal, they believe, deprives it of its capacity to make moral judgments. The Islamists' commitment to the Sharia is thus reinforced by their perception that the separation of church and state means the elimination of the religious domain by the secular. As a result, where to draw the line in an Islamic state between civic liberty and religious content remains for them a perplexing dilemma. On this issue, the Islamist dialogue is intense and basically inconclusive.[9]

In some respects, the religiously-based social radicalism of the Islamist political movements is reminiscent of the early phases of the mass populist parties, both of the left and of the right, that were spawned in Europe a century and a half ago by the onset of the Industrial Revolution and the resulting social iniquities. The reaction to these iniquities included the notion that the state should play the central role in society's economic life in order to promote greater social justice. It also involved an analogous argument: that even a modern society needs a religious value system, and it is the duty of the state to instill it. In Europe, the often painful church-state dilemma was easier for the Christian Democratic parties to resolve, given the gradual subordination of both society and state to a religiously neutral rule of law. The Islamist proposition that a state infused with Islamic values would be inherently more just, and that a society subjected to the Sharia would be morally cleansed, reinforces political appeal with much more intense religious fervor.

Given the potential mass attraction of such views, Islamist radical populism represents a potent challenge both to conservative, ostensibly religious governments such as Saudi Arabia's and to the more secular (often military-based) regimes of such states as Algeria, Egypt, and Indonesia. More cautiously and indirectly, it is also a challenge to Turkey. But Islamism may be more than just a successful rival to Islamic fundamentalism. It may signal that a once vital but lately dormant civilization is beginning to stir again.

The Western, and particularly American, inclination to focus on the egregious and reactionary manifestations of Islamic fundamentalism, especially in Iran and in Afghanistan under the Taliban, reflects widespread ignorance of the intensity and intellectual scope of the ongoing debates among politically minded Muslim intellectuals. These debates do not quite fit the stereotypical notion of Islam as frozen in a medieval mold, inherently hostile to modernity and incapable of assimilating democracy.

These debates, however, do not exclusively take the form of a peaceful dialogue. Islamic fundamentalism as well as Islamist populism both involve extremist manifestations, including reliance either on conventional violence to seize power or on terrorism. Much of that extremism has been turned inward, producing episodic bloodshed within individual Muslim states. The absence of democratic traditions within the majority of Muslim countries has helped to spawn a variety of secret societies or movements that have become engaged in assassinations of their opponents. The increased presence of Muslims in Western Europe has also had the effect in recent decades of exporting terrorism, notably to France, the United Kingdom, Germany, and Spain.

Nonetheless, peaceful political change has taken place in some Muslim countries ranging from Indonesia to Bahrain, Tunisia, Morocco, and even fundamentalist Iran, not to mention Turkey—thereby demonstrating that a more moderate political culture can gradually take hold even among the restless Muslim masses. In that volatile context, Islamist populism and Islamic fundamentalism should be seen as dialectically related, reflecting the intellectual ferment within the Muslim world. Islamic fundamentalism (the "thesis") represents an essentially pre-modern but post-colonial Islam in reaction against the dominant and secular West; Islamist populism (the "antithesis") is an effort to overcome the legacy of that Western domination by assimilating some of its modern elements while dogmatically and often demagogically counter-symbolizing them through an Islamic framework.

The "synthesis" is yet to come. Most probably it will come in many manifestations, with few of them, if any, genuinely democratic at first. Nevertheless, the diverse world of Islam is not immune to the impact of global communications and mass education. Gradually, and in some cases quite painfully, the Muslim countries one by one will likely make their individual adaptations of the precepts of Islam to increasingly modern politics based on more participatory social mobilization.

The adaptations will vary because Islamism, unlike Marxism, is not a comprehensive ideology providing guidance and direction on all aspects of societal existence. Its economic vacuity has already been noted. Its desire to assimilate technological modernity for the sake of national power is bound to have unintended consequences. Even its lip service to democracy, in time, will work to legitimize civic rights and separate them from the religious sphere. Thus the range of the secular dimension will progressively widen, with Islamist populism propelling, even if not ultimately defining, social and political change.

The process will certainly be uneven. At times, Islamist populism will be fanatically extremist, especially when it is ignited by a specific ethnic or xenophobic grievance. Nonetheless, Islam theologically cannot be said to be more hostile to democracy than Christianity, Judaism, or Buddhism. Societies subscribing to each of the foregoing have experienced their versions of fundamentalist sectarianism, but in each case the dominant trend has been in the direction of political pluralism, through a progressive accommodation between the secular and the religious.

Hence the United States should avoid conveying the impression that it views Islam as so culturally distinct as to be incapable of progressing through the same stages of political development as both the Christian and the Buddhist worlds did. That Germany and Japan would today be stalwart democracies was certainly not self-evident sixty years ago. That South Korea and Taiwan would be such was not self-evident even twenty years ago. That Indonesians would be able to peacefully remove two presidents from office for malfeasance did not seem likely five years ago. That Iran would be able to stage relatively free elections seemed altogether improbable even very recently. Politically sensitive ecumenism is needed, not only to overcome anti-Western sentiments within many Muslim countries but also to overcome the public stereotypes in America that limit U.S. flexibility in the pursuit of its national security.

Ultimately, it is in America's national security interest that the Muslim believers come to see themselves as just as much a part of the emerging global community as the currently more prosperous and democratic non-Islamic regions of the world. It is equally important that the politically active elements in the Islamic world not view the United States as the principal obstacle to Islam's civilizational rebirth, as the main sponsor of their socially regressive and economically self-serving political elites, or as the supporter of foreign states that seek to perpetuate or restore a quasi-colonial subordination of various Muslim peoples. It is even more essential that Muslim extremists be isolated by Muslim moderates. A more peaceful world is simply not attainable without the constructive participation of the world's 1.2 billion Muslims. Only a highly differentiated U.S. policy, responsive to the reality of Muslim diversity, can promote that desirable, if still distant, objective.

THE HEGEMONIC QUICKSAND

For the next several decades, the most volatile and dangerous region of the world—with the explosive potential to plunge the world into chaos—will be the new Global Balkans. It is there that America could slide into a collision with the world of Islam while American-European policy differences could even cause the Atlantic Alliance to come unhinged. The two eventualities together could even put the prevailing American global hegemony at risk.

It is therefore essential to recognize that the ferment within the Muslim world must be viewed primarily in a regional rather than a global perspective, and through a geopolitical rather than a theological prism. The world of Islam is disunited, both politically and religiously. It is politically unstable and militarily weak, and likely to remain so for some time. Hostility toward the United States, while pervasive in some Muslim countries, originates more from specific political grievances—such as Iranian nationalist resentment over the U.S. backing of the Shah, Arab animus stimulated by U.S. support for Israel, or Pakistani feelings that the United States has been partial to India—than from a generalized religious bias.

The complexity of the challenge America now confronts dwarfs what it faced half a century ago in Western Europe. At that time, Europe's dividing line on the Elbe River was the strategically critical frontline of maximum danger, with the daily possibility that a clash in

Berlin could unleash a nuclear war with the Soviet Union. Nevertheless, the United States recognized the stakes involved and committed itself to the defense, pacification, reconstruction, and revitalization of a viable European community. In doing so, America gained natural allies with shared values. Following the end of the Cold War, the United States led the transformation of NATO from a defense alliance into an enlarging security alliance—gaining an enthusiastic new ally, Poland—and it has supported the expansion of the European Union (EU).

For at least a generation, the major task facing the United States in the effort to promote global security will be the pacification and then the cooperative organization of a region that contains the world's greatest concentration of political injustice, social deprivation, demographic congestion, and potential for high-intensity violence. But the region also contains most of the world's oil and natural gas. In 2002, the area designated as the Global Balkans contained 68 percent of the world's proven oil reserves and 41 percent of the world's proven natural gas reserves; it accounted for 32 percent of world oil production and 15 percent of world natural gas production. In 2020, the area (together with Russia) is projected to produce roughly 42 million barrels of oil per day—39 percent of the global production total (107.8 million barrels per day). Three key regions—Europe, the United States, and the Far East—collectively are projected to consume 60 percent of that global production (16 percent, 25 percent, and 19 percent, respectively).

The combination of oil and volatility gives the United States no choice. America faces an awesome challenge in helping to sustain some degree of stability among precarious states inhabited by increasingly politically restless, socially aroused, and religiously inflamed peoples. It must undertake an even more daunting enterprise than it did in Europe more than half a century ago, given a terrain that is culturally alien, politically turbulent, and ethnically complex.

In the past, this remote region could have been left to its own devices. Until the middle of the last century, most of it was dominated by imperial and colonial powers. Today, to ignore its problems and underestimate its potential for global disruption would be tantamount to declaring an open season for intensifying regional violence, region-wide contamination by terrorist groups, and the competitive proliferation of weaponry of mass destruction.

The United States thus faces a task of monumental scope and complexity. There are no self-evident answers to such basic questions as with whom, and how, America should be engaged in helping to stabilize the area, pacify it, and eventually cooperatively organize it. Past remedies tested in Europe—like the Marshall Plan or NATO, both of which exploited an underlying transatlantic political/cultural solidarity—do not quite fit a region still rent by historical hatreds and cultural diversity. Nationalism in the region is still at an earlier and more emotional stage than it was in war-weary Europe (exhausted by two massive European civil wars fought within just three decades), and it is fueled by religious passions reminiscent of Europe's Catholic-Protestant forty-year war of almost four centuries ago.

Furthermore, the area contains no natural allies bonded to America by history and culture, such as existed in Europe with Great Britain, France, Germany, and lately even Poland. In essence, America has to navigate in uncertain and badly charted waters, setting its own course, making differentiated accommodations while not letting any one regional power dictate its direction and priorities. To be sure, several states in the area are often mentioned as America's potential key partners in reshaping the Global Balkans: Turkey, Israel, India, and—on the region's periphery—Russia. Unfortunately, every one of them suffers serious handicaps in its capability to contribute to regional stability, or has goals of its own that collide with America's wider interests in the region.

Turkey has been America's ally for half a century. It earned America's trust and gratitude by its direct participation in the Korean War. It has proven to be NATO's solid and reliable southern anchor. With the fall of the Soviet Union, it became active in helping both Georgia and Azerbaijan consolidate their new independence, and it

energetically promoted itself as a relevant model of political development and social modernization for those Central Asian states whose
people largely fall within the radius of the Turkic cultural and linguistic traditions. In that respect, Turkey's significant strategic role has
been complementary to America's policy of reinforcing the new independence of the region's post-Soviet states.

Turkey's regional role, however, is limited by two major offsetting considerations stemming from its internal problems. The first pertains to the still uncertain status of Atatürk's legacy: Will Turkey
succeed in transforming itself into a secular European state even
though its population is overwhelmingly Muslim? That has been its
goal since Atatürk set his reforms in motion in the early 1920s. Turkey
has made remarkable progress since then, but to this day its future
membership in the European Union (which it actively seeks) remains
in doubt. If the EU were to close its doors to Turkey, the potential for
an Islamic political/religious revival and consequently for Turkey's
dramatic (and probably turbulent) international reorientation should
not be underestimated.

The Europeans have reluctantly favored Turkey's inclusion in
the European Union, largely in order to avoid a serious regression
in the country's political development. European leaders recognize
that the transformation of Turkey from a state guided by Atatürk's
vision of a European-type society into an increasingly theocratic
Islamic one would adversely affect Europe's security. That consideration, however, is contested by the view, shared by many Europeans,
that the construction of Europe should be based on its common
Christian heritage. It is likely, therefore, that the European Union
will delay for as long as it can a clear-cut commitment to open its
doors to Turkey—but that prospect in turn will breed Turkish
resentments, increasing the risks that Turkey might evolve into a
resentful Islamic state, with potentially dire consequences for southeastern Europe.[10]

The other major liability limiting Turkey's role is the Kurdistan
issue. A significant proportion of Turkey's population of 70 million is

composed of Kurds. The actual number is contested, as is the nature of the Turkish Kurds' national identity. The official Turkish view is that the Kurds in Turkey number no more than 10 million and that they are essentially Turks. Kurdish nationalists claim a population of 20 million, which they say aspires to live in an independent Kurdistan that would unite all the Kurds (claimed to number 25–35 million) currently living under Turkish, Syrian, Iraqi, and Iranian domination. Whatever the actual facts, the Kurdish ethnic problem and the potential Islamic religious issue tend to make Turkey—notwithstanding its constructive role as a regional model—also very much a part of the region's basic dilemmas.

Israel is another seemingly obvious candidate for the status of a preeminent regional ally. As a democracy as well as a cultural kin, it enjoys America's automatic affinity, not to mention intense political and financial support from the Jewish community in America. Initially a haven for the victims of the Holocaust, it enjoys American sympathy. As the object of Arab hostility, it triggered American preference for the underdog. It has been America's favorite client state since approximately the mid-1960s and has been the recipient of unprecedented American financial assistance ($80 billion since 1974). It has benefited from almost solitary American protection against UN disapprobation or sanctions. As the dominant military power in the Middle East, Israel has the potential, in the event of a major regional crisis, not only to be America's military base but also to make a significant contribution to any required U.S. military engagement.

Yet American and Israeli interests in the region are not entirely congruent. America has major strategic and economic interests in the Middle East that are dictated by the region's vast energy supplies. Not only does America benefit economically from the relatively low costs of Middle Eastern oil, but America's security role in the region gives it indirect but politically critical leverage on the European and Asian economies that are also dependent on energy exports from the region. Hence good relations with Saudi Arabia and the United Arab Emirates—and their continued security reliance on America—is in the U.S. national interest. From Israel's standpoint, however, the resulting American-Arab ties are disadvantageous: they not only limit the degree to which the United States is prepared to back Israel's territorial aspirations, they also stimulate American sensitivity to Arab grievances against Israel.

Among those grievances, the Palestinian issue is foremost. That the final status of the Palestinian people remains unresolved more than thirty-five years after Israel occupied the Gaza Strip and the West Bank—irrespective of whose fault that actually may be—intensifies and in Arab eyes legitimates the widespread Muslim hostility toward Israel.[11] It also perpetuates in the Arab mind the notion that Israel is an alien and temporary colonial imposition on the region. To the extent that the Arabs perceive America as sponsoring Israeli repression of the Palestinians, America's ability to pacify anti-American passions in the region is constrained. That impedes any joint and constructive American-Israeli initiative to promote multilateral political or economic cooperation in the region, and it limits any significant U.S. regional reliance on Israel's military potential.

Since 9/11, the notion of India as America's strategic regional partner has come to the forefront. India's credentials seem at least as credible as Turkey's or Israel's. Its sheer size and power make it regionally influential, while its democratic credentials make it ideologically attractive. It has managed to preserve its democracy since its inception as an independent state more than half a century ago. It has done so despite widespread poverty and social inequality, and despite considerable ethnic and religious diversity in a predominantly Hindu but formally secular state. India's prolonged confrontation with its Islamic neighbor, Pakistan, involving violent confrontations with guerrillas and terrorist actions in Kashmir by Muslim extremists benefiting from Pakistan's benevolence, made India particularly eager to declare itself after 9/11 as co-engaged with America in the war on terrorism.

Nonetheless, any U.S.-Indian alliance in the region is likely to be limited in scope. Two major obstacles stand in the way. The first pertains to India's religious, ethnic, and linguistic mosaic. Although India has striven to make its 1 billion culturally diverse people into a unified nation, it remains basically a Hindu state semi-encircled by Muslim neighbors while containing within its borders a large and potentially alienated Muslim minority of somewhere between 120 and 140 million. Here, religion and nationalism could inflame each other on a grand scale.

So far, India has been remarkably successful in maintaining a common state structure and a democratic system—but much of its population has been essentially politically passive and (especially in the rural areas) illiterate. The risk is that a progressive rise in political consciousness and activism could be expressed through intensified ethnic and religious collisions. The recent rise in the political consciousness of both India's Hindu majority and its Muslim minority could jeopardize India's communal coexistence. Internal strains and frictions could become particularly difficult to contain if the war on terrorism were defined as primarily a struggle against Islam, which is how the more radical of the Hindu politicians tend to present it.

Secondly, India's external concerns are focused on its neighbors, Pakistan and China. The former is seen not only as the main source of the continued conflict in Kashmir but ultimately—with Pakistan's national identity rooted in religious affirmation—as the very negation of India's self-definition. Pakistan's close ties to China intensify this sense of threat, given that India and China are unavoidable rivals for geopolitical primacy in Asia. Indian sensitivities are still rankled by the military defeat inflicted upon it by China in 1962, in the short but intense border clash that left China in possession of the disputed Aksai Chin territory.

The United States cannot back India against either Pakistan or China without paying a prohibitive strategic price elsewhere: in Afghanistan if it were to opt against Pakistan, and in the Far East if it allied itself against China. These internal as well as external factors constrain the degree to which the United States can rely on India as an ally in any longer-term effort to foster—let alone impose—greater stability in the Global Balkans.

Finally, there is the question of the degree to which Russia can become America's major strategic partner in coping with Eurasian regional turmoil. Russia clearly has the means and experience to be of help in such an effort. Although Russia, unlike the other contenders, is no longer truly part of the region—Russian colonial domination of Central Asia being a thing of the past—Moscow nevertheless exercises considerable influence on all of the countries to its immediate south, has close ties to India and Iran, and contains some 15 to 20 million Muslims within its own territory.

At the same time, Russia has come to see its Muslim neighbors as the source of a potentially explosive political and demographic threat, and the Russian political elite are increasingly susceptible to anti-Islamic religious and racist appeals. In these circumstances, the Kremlin eagerly seized upon the events of 9/11 as an opportunity to engage America against Islam in the name of the "war on terrorism."

Yet as a potential partner, Russia is also handicapped by its past, even its very recent past. Afghanistan was devastated by a decade-long war waged by Russia, Chechnya is on the brink of genocidal extinction, and the newly independent Central Asian states increasingly define their modern history as a struggle for emancipation from Russian colonialism. With such historical resentments still vibrant in the region, and with increasingly frequent signals that Russia's current priority is to link itself with the West, Russia is being perceived in the region more and more as a former European colonial power and less and less as a Eurasian kin. Russia's present inability to offer much in the way of a social example also limits its role in any American-led international partnership for the purpose of stabilizing, developing, and eventually democratizing the region.

Ultimately, America can look to only one genuine partner in coping with the Global Balkans: Europe. Although it will need the help of leading East Asian states like Japan and China—and Japan will provide some, though limited, material assistance and some peacekeeping forces—neither is likely at this stage to become heavily engaged (further discussion in Chapter 3). Only Europe, increasingly organized as the European Union and militarily integrated through NATO, has the potential capability in the political, military, and economic realms to pursue jointly with America the task of engaging the various Eurasian peoples—on a differentiated and flexible basis—in the promotion of regional stability and of progressively widening trans-Eurasian cooperation. And a supranational European Union linked to America would be less suspect in the region as a returning colonialist bent on consolidating or regaining its special economic interests.

America and Europe together represent an array of physical and experiential assets with the capability to make the decisive difference in shaping the political future of the Global Balkans. The question is whether Europe—largely preoccupied with the shaping of its own unity—will have the will and the generosity to become truly engaged with America in a joint effort that will dwarf in complexity and scale the earlier, successful joint American-European effort to preserve peace in Europe and then end Europe's division. European engagement will not occur, however, if it is expected to consist of simply following America's lead. The war on terrorism can be the opening wedge for engagement in the Global Balkans, but it cannot be the definition of that engagement. This the Europeans, less traumatized by 9/11, understand better than the Americans. It is also why any joint effort by the Atlantic community will have to be based on a broad strategic consensus regarding the long-term nature of the task at hand.

Somewhat the same considerations apply to Japan's potential role. Japan, too, can and should become a major if somewhat less central player. For some time to come, Japan will eschew a major military role beyond that of direct national self-defense. But despite its recent stagnation, Japan remains the globe's second-largest national economy. Its financial support for efforts designed to enlarge the world's zone of peace would be crucial and ultimately in its own interest. Hence Japan—in conjunction with Europe—has to be viewed as America's eventual partner in the long-term struggle against the many forces of chaos within the Global Balkans.

In brief, America will need a broadly cooperative strategy for coping with the region's explosive potential. As the successful experience of shaping the Euroatlantic community has shown, burdens cannot be shared without shared decision-making. Only by fashioning a comprehensive strategy with its principal partners can America avoid becoming mired, alone, in hegemonic quicksand.

STRATEGIC BUT NOT SOLITARY ENGAGEMENT

Given that the area's problems involve an almost seamless web of overlapping conflicts, the first step in a comprehensive response is to define priorities. Three interrelated tasks stand out as central: (1) resolving the Arab-Israeli conflict, which is so disruptive to the Middle East; (2) transforming the strategic equation in the oil-producing region from the Persian Gulf to Central Asia; and (3) engaging key governments through regional arrangements designed to contain WMD proliferation and the terrorist epidemic.

Arab-Israeli peace is the most urgent need, because it is essential to the pursuit of the other two. Immediately at issue is the Israeli-Palestinian conflict, whose specific resolution has to be the proximate goal. But there is also the larger reality of Arab hostility toward Israel, which breeds tension in the Middle East and ricochets Muslim hostility *against* America.[12] That condition can only be ameliorated by a fair and viable peace that eventually fosters constructive Israeli-Palestinian cooperation, thereby diluting Arab animus and inducing Arab acceptance of Israel as a permanent fixture on the Middle Eastern scene.

Adding urgency to the issue is the risk that the Euroatlantic alliance could split asunder on the Middle Eastern rock. Although America is the dominant external power in the Middle East, its relations with Europe could come under severe duress as transatlantic views diverge over how best to engage the region. For decades since the abortive Franco-British Suez adventure of 1956, the area from the Suez to the Persian Gulf has effectively been an American protectorate. Gradually, the protector shifted from a pro-Arab to a pro-Israeli preference while successfully eliminating any significant

European and, later, Soviet political influence from the region. The decisive military victories in the 1991 and the 2003 campaigns against Iraq firmly established the United States as the sole external arbiter in the area.

After 9/11, the more conservative elements in the American political establishment, particularly those with strong sympathies for the Likud side of Israel's political spectrum, have become tempted by the vision of an altogether new order imposed by the United States on the Middle East as a response to the new challenge of terrorism plus proliferation. The pursuit of that vision has already involved the forcible termination of Saddam Hussein's dictatorship in Iraq, and it could portend action against the Baathist regime in Syria or the Iranian theocracy. In the name of democracy, there have also been calls for the United States to distance itself from the current rulers of Saudi Arabia and Egypt and to press for internal democratization, even at cost to America's interests in the region.

It is already evident that the European Union, as it begins to identify its own foreign policy interests, will not remain merely a passive observer or compliant supporter of whatever the American policy is in the Middle East. In fact, it is precisely with regard to the Middle East that the European Union is beginning not only to shape its first truly joint and comprehensive strategy but also to challenge America's monopoly in regional arbitration. In the Seville Declaration of June 22, 2002, the EU took the important step of formulating a concept of a peaceful solution to the Israeli-Palestinian conflict that is significantly at variance with America's.[13] Intensifying U.S.-EU disagreements over the aftermath of the war against Iraq and possible political change in Iran may further encourage European assertiveness.

In the short run, America has the power and the will to disregard Europe's views. It can prevail by using its military might and temporarily prompt reluctant European accommodation. But the European Union has the economic resources and financial means to make the critical difference to the region's long-run stability. Thus no truly viable solution in the area will be possible unless the United

States and the EU increasingly act in common. The Middle East is at least as vital for Europe as Mexico is for America, and the EU—as it slowly defines itself—will increasingly attempt to assert its position. Indeed, it is in the Middle East that European foreign policy, for the first time since the Suez debacle of 1956, could explicitly define itself *against* America.

Nevertheless, the Euroatlantic community's emerging cleavage over the Middle East is reversible. There is remarkable international consensus regarding the substance of an eventual Israeli-Palestinian peace treaty. There are even drafts of the likely peace treaty that go considerably beyond the vague "roadmap" that the Bush administration reluctantly endorsed in the spring of 2003. The real issue, how to get the Israelis and the Palestinians to cross the t's and dot the i's, will be a challenge despite the actual support for a compromise peace among the Israeli and Palestinian peoples. Left to themselves, they have proven unable to bridge their lingering differences or transcend their embittered suspicions.

Only the United States and the European Union together can decisively accelerate the process. To do so, they will increasingly have to spell out in substance, and not just in procedural terms, the out-lines of an Israeli-Palestinian peace. Broadly speaking, there is international consensus that its basic framework will include two states, territorially defined by the 1967 lines but with reciprocal adjustments to permit incorporation into Israel of the suburban settlements of Jerusalem; two capitals in Jerusalem itself; only a nominal or symbolic right of return for the Palestinian refugees, with the bulk of returnees settling in Palestine, perhaps in vacated Israeli settlements; a demilitarized Palestine, perhaps with NATO or other international peace-keepers; and a comprehensive, unequivocal recognition of Israel by its Arab neighbors.

The internationally sponsored adoption of a viable formula for the coexistence of Israel and Palestine would not resolve the wider region's manifold conflicts, but it would have a triple benefit: it would somewhat reduce the focus of Middle Eastern terrorists on America;

it would disarm the most likely trigger for a regional explosion; and it would permit a more concerted effort by the United States and the European Union to address the region's security problems without seeming to embark on an anti-Islamic crusade. The resolution of the Arab-Israeli conflict would also facilitate American efforts to promote the progressive democratization of the adjoining Arab states without appearing, in Arab eyes, to exploit the democratization issue as yet another pretext for delaying a comprehensive Israeli-Palestinian accommodation.

Similarly, creating a stable Iraq after the 2003 military intervention is a formidable and prolonged task that can only be made easier by U.S.-EU collaboration. The fall of the Iraqi regime could reopen latent border issues with Iran, Syria, and Turkey. These could be dynamically complicated by the Kurdish issue, while the internal animus between Iraqi Sunni and Shiite believers could unleash protracted and increasingly violent instability. Moreover, Iraq's 25 million people, generally considered the most nationalistically self-conscious of all the Arab peoples, may prove less pliant to external domination than expected. A long, costly, and difficult recovery program will have to be managed in a volatile and potentially hostile environment.

More broadly, American-European cooperation in promoting a stable and democratic Iraq and in advancing Israeli-Palestinian peace—in effect, a "regional roadmap"—would create more favorable political preconditions for addressing the unsatisfactory strategic equation that prevails in the oil- and natural-gas-producing areas of the Persian Gulf, Iran, and the Caspian Basin. Unlike energy-rich Russia, the states of this zone—from Kazakhstan and Azerbaijan all the way down to Saudi Arabia—are almost entirely exporters, but not major consumers, of the energy that is extracted from their ground. They have by far the world's largest reserves of oil and natural gas. Since reliable access to reasonably priced energy is vitally important to the world's three economically most dynamic regions—North America, Europe, and East Asia—strategic domination over the area, even if cloaked by cooperative arrangements, would be a globally decisive hegemonic asset.

From the standpoint of American interests, the current geopolitical state of affairs in the world's principal energy-rich zone leaves much to be desired. Several of the key exporting states—notably Saudi Arabia and the United Arab Emirates—are weak and politically debilitated. Iraq faces a prolonged period of stabilization, reconstruction, and rehabilitation. Another major energy producer, Iran, has a regime hostile to the United States and opposes U.S. efforts on behalf of a Middle Eastern peace. It may be seeking WMD and is suspected of terrorist links. The United States has sought to isolate Iran internationally, but with limited success.

Just to the north, in the southern Caucasus and Central Asia, the newly independent energy-exporting states are still in the early stages of political consolidation. Their systems are fragile, their political processes arbitrary, and their statehood vulnerable. They are also semi-isolated from the world energy markets, with American legislation blocking the use of Iranian territory for pipelines leading to the Persian Gulf and with Russia aggressively seeking to monopolize international access to Turkmen and Kazakh energy resources. Only with the completion, several years from now, of the U.S.-sponsored Baku-Çeyhan pipeline will Azerbaijan and its trans-Caspian neighbors gain an independent link to the global economy. Until then, the area will be vulnerable to Russian or Iranian mischief.

For the time being, the powerful and exclusive U.S. military presence in the Persian Gulf region and the effective U.S. monopoly of significant long-range warfare capabilities give America a very considerable margin for unilateral policymaking. If it should become necessary to cut the potential nexus between the proliferation of WMD and conspiratorial terrorism, the United States has the means to act on its own, as it proved in bringing down the recent Iraqi regime. The problem becomes more complex, however, and the chances of a solitary American success more ephemeral, when the longer-range consequences of a violent strategic upheaval are taken into account.

It is difficult to envisage how the United States alone could force Iran into a basic reorientation. Outright military intimidation might work initially, given the gaping disparity of power between the two states, but it would be a gross error to underestimate the nationalist and religious fervor that such an approach would likely ignite among the 70 million Iranians. Iran is a nation with an impressive imperial history and with a sense of its own national worth. While the religious zeal that brought the theocratic dictatorship to power seems to be gradually fading, an outright collision with America would almost certainly reignite popular passions, fusing fanaticism with chauvinism.

While Russia has not stood in the way of any decisive U.S. military efforts to alter the strategic realities of the region, the current geopolitical earthquake in the Persian Gulf could jeopardize America's efforts to consolidate the independence of the Caspian Basin states. American preoccupation with the upheaval in Iraq, not to mention increased American-Iranian tensions, could tempt Moscow to resume its earlier pressure on Georgia and Azerbaijan to abandon their aspirations for inclusion in the Euroatlantic community, and to step up its efforts to undermine any enduring U.S. political and military presence in Central Asia. That would make it more difficult for the United States to engage the Central Asian states in a larger regional effort to combat Islamic fundamentalism in Afghanistan and Pakistan. A resurgence of Muslim extremism of the Taliban variety could then even acquire a regional scope.

These risks could be lessened by closer U.S.-EU strategic collaboration with regard to Iraq and Iran. That may not be easy to achieve, given divergent American and European perspectives, but the benefits of cooperation outweigh the costs of any compromise. For the United States, a joint approach would mean less freedom of unilateral action; for the European Union, it would mean less opportunity for self-serving inaction. But acting together—with the threat of U.S. military power reinforced by the EU's political, financial, and (to some degree) military support—the Euroatlantic community could foster a genuinely stable and possibly even democratic post-Saddam regime.

Together, the United States and European Union would also be better positioned to deal with the broader regional consequences of the upheaval in Iraq. Significant progress in the Israeli-Palestinian peace process would reduce the Arab concern that U.S. actions directed at Iraq's regime were inspired by Israel's desire to weaken all neighboring Arab states while perpetuating its control over the Palestinians. Moreover, strategic collaboration between the United States and the EU would make it easier for Turkey to avoid a painful choice between its loyalty as a U.S. ally and its hopes for EU membership.

Active strategic partnership between the United States and the European Union would also make it more likely that Iran could eventually be transformed from a regional ogre into a regional stabilizer. Currently, Iran has a cooperative relationship with Russia, but otherwise either wary or hostile relations with all of its neighbors. It has maintained a relatively normal relationship with Europe, but its antagonistic posture toward America—reciprocated by restrictive U.S. trade legislation—has made it difficult for European-Iranian and Iranian-Japanese economic relations to truly prosper. Its internal development has suffered accordingly, while its socioeconomic dilemmas have been made more acute by a demographic explosion that has increased its population to 70-odd million.

The entire energy-exporting region would be more stable if Iran, the region's geographic center, were reintegrated into the global community and its society resumed its march to modernization. That will not happen as long as the United States seeks to isolate Iran. More effective would be an approach in which the Iranian social elite sees the country's isolation as self-imposed and thus counterproductive, instead of something enforced by America. Europe has long urged the United States to adopt that approach. On this issue, American strategic interests would be better served if America were to follow Europe's lead.

In the longer run, contrary to the image projected by its ruling mullahs—that of a religiously fanatical society—Iran stands the best chance, of all the countries in the region, of embarking on the path traced earlier by Turkey. It has a high literacy rate (72 percent), an established tradition of significant female participation in the professions and political life, a genuinely sophisticated intellectual class, and a social awareness of its distinctive historical identity. Once the dogmatic rule imposed by Ayatollah Ruhollah Khomeini wears thin and the Iranian secular elites sense that the West sees a regionally constructive role for Iran, Iran could be on the way toward successful modernization and democratization.

Such a progressive alteration of the region's prevailing strategic equation would permit implementation of the Caucasus Stability Pact proposed by Turkey in 2000, providing for various forms of region-wide cooperation.[14] To make it effective, not only Turkey's and Russia's involvement would be needed, but also Iran's. Iran's reorientation would also permit wider economic access to the energy resources of Central Asia. In time, pipelines through Iran to the Persian Gulf could also be matched by parallel pipelines from Central Asia through Afghanistan and Pakistan to the Indian Ocean, branching out also to India. The result would be of major economic (and potentially political) benefit not only to south-central Asia but to the increasingly energy-ravenous Far East.

Progress along these lines, in turn, would help advance the third strategic priority for this region, the need to contain both the proliferation of WMD and the terrorist epidemic. Neither issue is susceptible to a quick resolution. But tangible movement on the first two priorities—Israeli-Palestinian peace and the remaking of the region's strategic landscape—would undercut some of the popular support for anti-Western, and especially anti-American, terrorism. It could also make it easier to concentrate on the struggle against Middle Eastern terrorists while reducing the risks of a more comprehensive religious and cultural clash between the West and Islam.

Further to the east, the continuing conflict between Pakistan and India poses wider regional security and proliferation challenges. These have to be more directly addressed. Under present circumstances, neither India nor Pakistan has any incentive to limit the buildup of its nuclear arsenal—in fact, both have compelling, even if not completely reciprocal, reasons for continuing their buildup.[15] For Pakistan, nuclear weapons are the great leveler against its otherwise much more militarily powerful neighbor; for India, they offset any potential threat from China, Pakistan's regional friend, while countering any Pakistani nuclear blackmail. Both Pakistan and India also feel symbolically gratified by their new status as nuclear powers.

For the time being, the key U.S. interest is to prevent a nuclear war from erupting between Pakistan and India and to discourage any further regional proliferation, especially since there can be little doubt that the once-imperial and nationally ambitious Iran looks with understandable envy at its nuclear-armed neighbors. Of the two goals, the prevention of a nuclear war may be somewhat easier to pursue because the very possession of nuclear weaponry is forcing both the Indian and the Pakistani militaries to calculate more cautiously the potential consequences of their periodic border clashes.

Nonetheless, the unresolved issue of Kashmir is bound to produce repeated collisions, each of which inflames the volatile and religiously conflicted Muslim and Hindu masses. Pakistan could then even become a fundamentalist Muslim state (thus probably determining Afghanistan's fate as well), while India might be seized by fanatical Hindu passions. Irrationality might then overwhelm the strategic restraint inherent in the nuclear calculus.

Just as the West for years has been relatively indifferent to the unresolved Palestinian issue, so it has also neglected Kashmir. India has been able to insist formally that there is no Kashmir issue, either between India and Pakistan or for the international community as a whole—that it is an internal matter. Pakistan in turn has relied on thinly camouflaged official support for guerrilla and terrorist actions against India's control of the province as a way of keeping the issue alive—thereby also precipitating increasingly heavy-handed Indian repression of Kashmiris suspected of disloyalty. Once both countries acquired nuclear weapons, the Kashmir issue inevitably gained wider international significance.

The question of Kashmir has now become part of the larger problem of instability in the Global Balkans. Its peaceful resolution is likely to be at least as difficult as that of the Arab-Israeli conflict. The conflict involves two major states that jointly have a population approaching 1.2 billion people—roughly one-fifth of the world—and much of that population is still pre-modern, semiliterate, and susceptible (even among the elites) to demagogic appeals. Fostering a compromise in that setting will require sustained outside engagement, considerable international pressure, major political and financial inducements, and a great deal of patience.

Here again, political solidarity between the United States and the European Union, perhaps tangibly backed by Japan, would make eventual success more likely. Great Britain, for historical reasons, can play an important diplomatic role, especially in concert with the United States. Both Russia and China may be supportive, since neither would benefit from a nuclear war in its immediate proximity, and each can subtly influence the major purchaser of its arms exports (India in the case of Russia, Pakistan in the case of China). The reality, however, is that a major collective international effort is likely only in the face of an imminent threat of war, with international concern rapidly fading once the threat recedes.

The absence of a concerted international commitment also impedes the emergence of any effective regional arrangement to contain the acquisition and proliferation of WMD within the new Global Balkans. Only a region-wide solution, made possible by the progressive resolution of particular conflicts, would be likely to endure: i.e., only when both India and Pakistan, as well as Israel and all its Arab neighbors, have resolved their respective conflicts.[16] Even then, Iran—given its resources and size, and given that Russia's help has already endowed it with a potential nuclear weapons capability—is likely to insist on co-equality with the nuclear states in its vicinity: Pakistan, India, and Israel, not to mention Russia and China.

An effective halt to further nuclear proliferation in this conflict-ridden region will ultimately have to be based on a regional arrangement.

If nations are to forsake the acquisition of nuclear weapons, they must have alternative sources of security: either a binding alliance with a nuclear-armed ally or a credible international guarantee. A region-wide agreement banning nuclear weapons—on the model of the convention adopted some years ago by South American states—would be the preferable outcome. But in the absence of regional consensus, the only effective alternative is for the United States, or perhaps the permanent members of the UN Security Council, to provide a guarantee of protection against nuclear attack to any state in the region that abjures nuclear weapons.

The effort to stabilize the Global Balkans will last several decades. At best, progress will be incremental, inconsistent, and vulnerable to major reversals. It will be sustained only if the two most successful sectors of the globe—the politically mobilized America and the economically unifying Europe—treat it increasingly as a shared responsibility in the face of a common security threat.

NOTES

1   The illustrative data below speak for themselves:

The world's most widespread social deprivation. As much as 85 percent of South Asia's populace live on less than $2 per day. In parts of Eurasia paralyzed by regional or domestic strife—North Korea, Afghanistan, Iraq, the Occupied Territories—poverty can be even more extreme. Early in 2002, unemployment had reached more than 38 percent in the West Bank and more than 46 percent in the Gaza Strip; in Chechnya, it surpasses 90 percent.

The world's most concentrated demographic congestion. No matter how the demographic data are spun, their trends are daunting. The collective population of four countries alone in this stretch of Eurasia—India, Pakistan, China, and Bangladesh, respectively—will increase by 1.05 billion people by 2050. Measuring population growth over that same period as a percentage, six of the top nine countries growing most rapidly—including the top three—form a solid block from Palestine through the Persian Gulf.

The world's potentially most explosive ethnic time bombs, including the partition of about 25 million Kurds by Turkey, Iraq, Iran, and Syria; the domination of more than 4.5 million Arab Palestinians by 5 million Jewish Israelis; the separation of some 15–25 million Azerbaijani Turks in Iran from Azerbaijan; the corralling of at least 8 million Kashmiris by India and Pakistan; and Russia's gradual genocide of the Chechen nation, to mention only a few.

The world's most intense religious violence. Bloodthirsty retribution between Muslims and Hindus in Gujarat, India, and between Christians and Muslims in Indonesia; violent rancor between Jews and Muslims in the Middle East, and perhaps also between Iraq's Shiite Muslim majority and its Sunni minority—all reflect the pervasiveness and visceral intensity of religious antagonisms across Eurasia.

Some of the world's politically most despotic regimes. In the 2001–2002 edition of Freedom House's *Freedom in the World*, of the ten countries rated worst for political rights and civil liberties, seven of them fall between the Suez Canal and the China Sea. Fifty-nine percent of the countries in that swathe of Eurasia are classified as "Not Free." Of the remainder, 28 percent are rated "Partly Free"; only 13 percent are considered "Free."

2   The reference to "Global Balkans" is meant to draw attention to the geopolitical similarity between the traditional European Balkans of the nineteenth and twentieth centuries and the unstable region that currently extends from approximately the Suez Canal to Xinjiang and from the Russo-Kazakh border to southern Afghanistan, almost like a triangle on the map. In the case of both areas, internal instability has served as a magnet for external major power intervention and rivalry. (For fuller discussion, see Brzezinski, *The Grand Chessboard*, chap. 5.)

3   The near panic set loose in Washington, DC, by the "sniper" shootings perpetrated by two criminals in the fall of 2002—including the widespread speculation at the time that it may have been a terrorist undertaking—is symptomatic of the degree to which fear of the unknown combined with mass-media hype can produce a state of mind that unintentionally helps to accomplish what the terrorists actually intend.

4   For a sober appraisal of al-Qaeda's capabilities, see Paul J. Smith, "Transnational Terrorism and the al Qaeda Model: Confronting New Realities," *Parameters* (U.S. Army War College Quarterly) 32, no. 2 (Summer 2002), 33–46. Al-Qaeda's transnational appeal, as reflected in its captured archives, is vividly summarized in a report published in *The New York Times*, March 17, 2002. In their article, "A Nation Challenged; Qaeda's Grocery Lists And Manuals of Killing," David Rohde and C. J. Chivers note that "From the mid-1990's on, recruits came to Afghanistan from more than 20 countries, as varied as Iraq and Malaysia, Somalia and Britain. The young men arrived in Afghanistan under the auspices of several different militant groups, each of which ran training camps. But once there, they received strikingly similar courses of religious indoctrination and military training. ...Diverse Muslim groups joined Mr. bin Laden's global jihad. Sometimes, they also came seeking help in pressing their own causes back home."

5   Even reputable American papers contributed to such stereotyping. Professor Ervand Abrahamian of the City University of New York noted that, in reaction to 9/11, "Quality papers, such as *The New York Times*, ran one article after another with such titles as 'This is a Religious War,' 'Yes, This is About Islam,' 'Islamic Rage,' 'Muslim Rage,' 'Islamic Anger,' 'Muslim Anger,' 'The Core of Islamic Rage,' 'Jihad 101,' 'The Deep Intellectual Roots of Islamic Terror,' 'Faith and the Secular State,' 'The Force of Islam,' 'Kipling Knew What the US May Now Learn,' 'Al-Jazeera: What the Muslim World is Watching,' 'The Real Cultural Wars,' 'The Revolt of Islam,' 'The One True Faith,' 'The First Holy War,' and 'Feverish Protests Against the West Trace to Grievances Ancient and Modern'…. Contemporary politics got left out—a strange absence for daily newspapers." *Middle East Report*, no. 223 (Summer 2002), 62.

6   This severe appraisal is reinforced and acknowledged specifically in relationship to the Arab world by the remarkably candid "Arab Human Development Report 2002," prepared by a team of prominent Arab public figures and intellectuals and cosponsored by the Arab Fund for Economic and Social Development (Kuwait City) and the UN Development Program. They included Thoraya Obaid (executive director of the UN Population Fund), Clovis Maksoud (former representative of the Arab League at the UN), Mervat Tallawy (head of the Economic and Social Council for West Asia), Nader Fergany (director of the Almishkat Center for Research in Cairo) as the lead author, and a cluster of leading academics. While noting some positive elements (such as that the level of abject poverty among Arabs is the world's lowest), the report was scathing in its criticism of intellectual and social creativity in, as well as the intellectual self-isolation of, the Arab world. In a telling statistic, the report noted the meager number of translations of foreign books into Arabic, noting that the annual total of about 330 books is roughly one-fifth of the number that are translated in nearby Greece into Greek alone. The report denounced the reliance on nostalgia for past glories as a counterproductive evasion of the challenges of modernity.

7   According to numerous public opinion polls, this issue gives rise to the most intense anti-American emotions. Reputable journalistic reports reinforce that conclusion. In the early fall of 2002, Jane Perlez reported in some detail that "Anger at the United States, embedded in the belief that the Bush administration lends unstinting support to Israel at the expense of the Palestinians, is at an unparalleled high across the Arab world." See "Anger at U.S. Said to Be at New High," *The New York Times*, September 11, 2002. She was echoed by Karen DeYoung, who reported that Arab dislike of America "focused largely on what they saw as a general unfairness toward and lack of understanding of the region, and a particular bias toward Israel in the Israeli-Arab conflict." See "Poll Finds Arabs Dislike U.S. Based on

Policies It Pursues," *The Washington Post*, October 7, 2002. Arabs have also tended to interpret U.S. hostility toward Saddam's Iraq as driven by one-sided U.S. support for Israel, according to Zogby International polls conducted in mid-March 2003 in several Arab countries.

8   Islamism is used here to denote a political ideology derived from Islam and thus to be differentiated from Islamic religious teachings as such. Islamists are the proponents of politics based on Islam, in contrast to Islamic fundamentalists who favor a direct theocracy. It should be noted that a differing assessment, namely that Islamism—especially its radical variant—is already declining, is argued by French scholar Gilles Kepel in his *Jihad: The Trail of Political Islam*, trans. Anthony F. Roberts (Cambridge, MA: Harvard University Press, 2002).

9   Only a limited number of Western scholars have been paying attention to the impact of the innovative and often courageous debates that have been redefining the terms of the political discourse within the world of Islam. Western, especially American, mass media have almost entirely ignored them. Even the increasingly controversial role of Qatar's al-Jazeera satellite TV—which has been staging debates on the most sensitive issues ranging from women's rights to democracy and its relationship to the faith—has been hardly noted. That is even more the case with the writings and speeches of the currently most active and significant Islamist thinkers/ideologues. In very summary form, brief reference might be made here to the teachings of the influential Iranian philosopher Abdul Karim Soroush, who argues that faith should be a free choice; or to the highly popular work of Muhammad Shuhrur of Syria, whose title, *al-Kitāb wa-al-Qur'ān (The Book and the Qur'an)*, seeking to adapt Islamic religious imperatives to a modern society, is being widely read; or to the teachings of Yusuf al-Qaradawi, an Egyptian living in Qatar, or of Rashid al-Ghannushi on religion and politics. It is noteworthy that two leading and popular Islamist ideologues, Sheikh Muhammed Hussein Fadlallah of Lebanon and Hassan Abdallah al-Turabi of Sudan have distanced themselves from the Iranian theocracy (as well as from terrorism), while also denouncing the religious hypocrisy of the Saudi regime. Like the others, they seem to be groping for a definition of some sort of a populist political system infused with religious values, with the Sharia substituting for a secular constitutional framework.

10   How far the latter in such circumstances could go was dramatically conveyed in a speech on March 7, 2002 at the Ankara War Academy by General Tuncer Kilinc, the secretary-general of the National Security Council, who bluntly stated that "Turkey hasn't seen the slightest assistance from the EU" in its efforts to become part of Europe and that in seeking allies Turkey might hence do well "to begin a new search that would include Iran and the Russian Federation" (as reported by Nicholas Birch, "Once Eager to Join EU, Turkey Grows Apprehensive," *The Christian Science*

Monitor, March 21, 2002; see also the analysis of the speech's import by Hooman Peimani, "Turkey Hints at Shifting Alliance," *The Asia Times*, June 19, 2002).

11 Demographics play a role as well: The fact that somewhat more than 5 million Jewish Israelis dominate the somewhat less than 5 million Arab Palestinians (of whom about 1.2 million are Israeli citizens) and that the latter are increasing much more rapidly intensifies Israeli insecurity and Arab resentments.

12 See endnote 7.

13 The Seville Declaration was much more explicit in formulating the specific parameters of a peace agreement between Israel and Palestine—notably on such matters as the sharing of Jerusalem, the 1967 frontiers, and the right of the Palestinians to chose their own leaders, including Arafat—than the corresponding U.S. formulations at the time, which made concrete demands of the Palestinian side while not addressing the more contentious immediate issues.

14 In January 2000, President Suleyman Demirel of Turkey proposed a "Caucasus Stability Pact," based on the successful experience of the "Stability Pact for South Eastern Europe" founded in June 1999. The latter—with strong U.S. and EU backing and under their security umbrella—was subsequently able to raise substantial amounts of money to promote the recovery of the Balkans. A similar initiative for the Caucasian region, involving its three newly independent states as well as the United States, the EU, Russia, and Turkey (at some point also Iran) could become an important vehicle for multilateral efforts to stabilize the volatile Caucasian region, to help resolve its various ethnic conflicts, and to facilitate a peaceful solution to such tragic conflicts as the Russian war in Chechnya.

15 In general, professional military establishments have a preference for nuclear weapons with reliable means for their delivery over either chemical weapons, which are less efficient, or bacteriological weapons, which are less controllable. Since it is easier to detect the production and deployment of nuclear weapons and to monitor the likely range of their delivery systems, and since any use of them can be traced to their source, the strategy of deterrence may continue to provide some reassurance of stability even in the face of regional nuclear proliferation. That cannot be said with regard to bacteriological weapons, which are likely to become the WMD of choice for terrorist groups whose targeting is less discriminating than that of the military. In the more immediate future, therefore, the more complex issue of bacteriological weapons will deserve special international attention.

16 It is noteworthy that Israel does not exclude the eventual possibility of a WMD-free zone (WMDFZ) in the Middle East. "In 1991, Israel and the Arab

states held unprecedented direct discussions on arms control issues in general and on establishing a WMDFZ in the Middle East in particular" once formal peace and peaceful relations have been established in the region. See Chen Zak, *Iran's Nuclear Policy and the IAEA* (Washington, DC: The Washington Institute for Near East Policy, 2002), 63–64.

3

THE DILEMMAS OF ALLIANCE MANAGEMENT

International affairs were significantly affected by 9/11, but more because 9/11 altered America than because it altered the world. America was shaken into a sudden awareness of its vulnerability. The prompt U.S. military reactions expanded the direct scope of America's post-Cold War hegemony all the way through Iraq and Afghanistan to Central Asia. They also reflected America's intensifying societal insecurity. Both the enlarged worldwide engagement and the growing insecurity highlight America's need for a strategic consensus with Europe and East Asia over a long-term strategy for managing the mercurial, complex Global Balkans.

The 9/11 attacks accelerated several basic international trends that were already visibly underway, notably: (1) the widening gap in military capabilities, not only between the United States and its former Communist rivals, but also between America and its principal allies; (2) the significant lagging of Europe's politico-military unification behind its economic integration; (3) the growing realization within the Kremlin that, to survive with its territory intact, Russia has no choice but to realign itself as the West's junior partner; (4) the emerging consensus among Chinese leaders that China needs an internationally quiescent pause in order to manage the next phase of its difficult domestic transition; (5) the increasing inclination of Japan's political elite to transform their country into an internationally serious military power; and (6) the spreading apprehension worldwide that a unilateralist America, because it is the linchpin of collective stability, could become unintentionally a menace to all.

In this setting, America enjoys some new options, but it must also be alert to some new temptations. It would be unwise to focus predominantly on the campaign against terrorism while losing sight of America's enduring interest in shaping a world governed by common rules and infused with genuinely shared—and not only rhetorically proclaimed—democratic values. The war on terrorism cannot be an end in itself. Ultimately, the key strategic question is: With whom, and how, can the United States more effectively shape a progressively better world? The answer calls for historically enduring trans-Atlantic and trans-Pacific strategies.

It was almost inevitable that 9/11 would provoke speculation in America about the need for a strategic realignment. Frustration with the Europeans, the desire to inflict a crippling blow against the elusive agents of terrorism, the fixation on Iraq, and the fear of renewed strikes against the U.S. homeland generated calls for an international divorce and remarriage. Why not align America with regimes that will more unequivocally and decisively strike at "terrorism," even if they do so for self-serving ends? As briefly noted in Chapter 1, the case for such a coalition can be discerned in the rhetoric of the more militant American commentators on foreign affairs, notably those on the extreme right of the political spectrum. In their view, America's traditional allies have become flabby, self-serving, and unwilling to confront the grimmer and more muscular realities of global power politics.

The unifying theme of these arguments is the proposition—most often assumed but sometimes explicitly stated—that Islam as a whole is intrinsically anti-Western, anti-democratic, and tainted by an in-built propensity toward fundamentalist extremism. The root problem, the argument goes, is culture and philosophy writ large, not the historical and political dilemmas of complex, interconnected, but still discrete regions. America's recent confrontation with terrorism is thus to be viewed not primarily as a political challenge derived from recent Middle Eastern history but as part of a larger, global Islamic threat to Western civilization that calls for an equally global anti-Islamic response. (The reader should note that Chapter 2 presented a quite different view of Islam.)

Yet any seriously pursued strategic realignment, if it is to be more than just a temporary tactical accommodation, must be based on wider, more enduring common goals and shared values. Tactical expediency in politics is sometimes necessary, but—derived from momentary preoccupations—it is also inimical to a long-term commitment. Eventually it can become self-defeating, prompting instability and unpredictability, both of which undercut stable international acquiescence to American leadership. To be viewed as legitimate, that leadership has to reflect comprehensive global interests; to be effective, it must be backed by allies with similar popular convictions and societal values.

Therefore, it is more than doubtful that America's long-term interests would be well served by the replacement of the established alliance of democracies by some sort of new grand coalition designed for anti-Islamic or anti-terrorist repression. At best, such a realignment could serve only as a short-term remedy. It would lack the staying power required for a concerted and broadly gauged response to the myriad problems faced by the politically awakened world. For example, although deeper cooperation with Russia is strategically desirable and historically timely (fuller discussion follows in the next section), Russia still lacks the economic, financial, and technological means for addressing the growing risks of large-scale social turmoil and political turbulence in the new Global Balkans. So does India. Neither of the two can replace Europe or Japan as America's partner in the long-haul effort to sustain a modicum of global order.

Any such realignment would also run the risk of compromising America's moral standing in the world. American hegemony is palatable to many because America has been viewed as a genuinely democratic state, committed to the enhancement of human rights. Indiscriminate American willingness to accept repressive states as allies based simply on their claims that they are conducting their own wars on terrorism would entail a tacit American endorsement of their particular definitions of terrorism, irrespective of any causal connection between their state-sponsored ethnic, religious, or racial oppression and the rise of morally abhorrent terrorism. Our acceptance of allies during the Cold War was sometimes just this indiscriminate, and this habit seriously diminished our moral standing in the fight against communism.

Moreover, even toying with the idea of such a realignment—even if merely for the tactical purpose of stirring America's traditional allies to greater engagement—runs the risk of becoming a self-fulfilling prophecy. It could stimulate a reciprocal move by the Europeans and Japanese to loosen established ties and explore yet undefined options. The consequences could be globally destabilizing while altogether depriving America of the wealthy partners it needs in order to cope with the dynamic and wide-ranging problems of the Eurasian landmass.

In this context, three sets of broad but centrally significant geostrategic questions need to be addressed:

1. Given the intense collision in 2003 between the United States on one hand and France and Germany on the other over war with Iraq, can Europe remain America's key ally? If so, what is the most effective formula for a meaningful, if still asymmetrical, security partnership between America and the emerging but far from politically united Europe? Moreover, how deeply can Russia be absorbed into the Euroatlantic community, and how can it help to stabilize Eurasia?

2. How can America maintain an equilibrium among an increasingly powerful China, a Japan that is dependent on the United States but is poised for a rapid takeoff as a military power, an unstable Korean Peninsula that is becoming nationalistically restless, and an internationally ambitious India?

3. Finally, can the expanding scope of European stability, driven by the enlarging Euroatlantic community and Russia's potential inclusion in it, eventually be linked to Far Eastern security issues?

Responses to these questions may determine whether a more coherent framework for coping with the new global disorder is feasible.

THE GLOBAL CORE

Together, the United States and the European Union represent the core of global political stability and economic wealth. Acting together, America and Europe would be globally omnipotent. Yet they are often at odds. Even before the vociferous disagreement in 2003 over Iraq, the most frequently voiced American complaint about Europe was that it did not do "enough" in the area of collective defense. The most frequent European complaint about America was that it acted too much on its own. A good point of departure for an appraisal of the Atlantic relationship is thus to ask: What if the Europeans were to do "enough," and what if the Americans were to act less on their own?

The American complaint is statistically justified. With a collective GDP roughly equivalent to America's, the European Union, currently fifteen states with 375 million people (versus America's 280 million), spends somewhat less than half what America spends on defense. Moreover, for the last fifty years, U.S. forces have been deployed on European soil for the purpose of protecting Europe from the Soviet threat. The reality is that during the entire Cold War, Europe was de facto an American protectorate. Even after the Cold War, it was American forces that spearheaded the military effort to repress violence in the European Balkans. Europe is also the economic beneficiary of the politically and militarily stabilizing role that the United States has played both in the Middle East (on whose oil Europe depends even more than America) and in the Far East (with whom Europe's trade is steadily increasing). To the average American, Europe is indeed a freeloader.

But what if Europe were to cease being one? Would America be better off? Would the Atlantic relationship be healthier and closer? To answer, one needs to imagine what circumstances would have to prevail for Europe to develop the political will to double its spending on defense and acquire military capabilities matching America's. Such an effort would require dramatically increased political unity among the various European states and widespread popular yearning for Europe to be—like America—self-sufficient in defense. With the Soviet threat gone and Russia reduced to a medium-level power, the impulse for both conditions could only come from the pervasive conclusion that America's own security policies gravely threaten Europe's and from an intense European public desire to free Europe from its security dependence on America.

With the EU's economic potential already matching America's and with the two entities often clashing on financial and trade matters, a militarily emergent Europe could become a formidable rival to America. It would inevitably pose a challenge to America's hegemony. To form a truly equal partnership between the two superpowers would not be easy, because any such adjustment would require a dramatic contraction of America's preeminence and an equally dramatic expansion of Europe's. NATO would have to cease being an American-led alliance, or maybe even cease being. If America has been occasionally discomfited by France's posturing as a great power—and has been able to dismiss it as a quirky but inconsequential manifestation of vain ambitions—a Europe that actually did do "enough" in defense would inescapably give America an acute case of post-hegemonic discomfort.

A militarily self-reliant Europe, a comprehensive global political-economic power like America, would confront the United States with a painful choice: either to disengage from Europe altogether or to fully share with it the responsibilities of worldwide policymaking. Disengagement of American power from the western periphery of the Eurasian continent would be tantamount to an abandonment of Eurasia to new and unpredictable conflicts among the principal Eurasian competitors. But power-sharing in a symmetrical global partnership would be neither easy nor pain-free.

A politically powerful Europe, able to compete economically while militarily no longer dependent on the United States, would inevitably contest American preeminence in two regions that are strategically vital to America: the Middle East and Latin America. The rivalry would be felt first in the Middle East, given not only its geographic proximity to Europe, but especially Europe's greater dependence on its oil. Given Arab resentment of U.S. policies, European overtures would find a sympathetic reception while Israel would stand to lose the privileged position it has enjoyed as America's favored client state.

A European challenge in Latin America would likely come next. The Spaniards, Portuguese, and French have long-standing historical and cultural connections with Latin American societies. Latin American nationalism would be quite responsive to intensified political, economic, and cultural ties with an assertive Europe, which would diminish the traditional U.S. domination of the region. Thus a Europe that became simultaneously an economic giant and a militarily serious power could confine the scope of U.S. preeminence largely to the Pacific Ocean.

A serious American-European rivalry would obviously be destructive for both Europe and America. As of now, however, the Europeans lack the unity and motivation to make themselves into a serious military power. Until that happens, American-European quarrels are not likely to become major geopolitical contests. Complaints and criticisms that lack teeth have no bite. Nonetheless, given the reciprocal bitterness generated by the transatlantic disagreements over

Iraq, it might be wise for Americans to become less persistent in their charge that, in the military area, Europe is not doing "enough."

The Europeans also need to weigh more carefully their complaints about America. Leaving aside the European elite's tradition of cultural pretentiousness (which actually flies in the face of American mass culture's widespread appeal in Europe), the main European criticism is that America has become increasingly unilateralist in its international conduct. That criticism is not new: During the Cold War, America was often taken to task for its allegedly simple-minded anti-Communism, its unwillingness to compromise with the Soviet Union, and its excessive emphasis on military readiness. More than two decades ago, German chancellor Helmut Schmidt was as disdainful of the U.S. human rights policy and as ready to endorse the Communist suppression of dissidents as France's president Valéry Giscard d'Estaing was subsequently contemptuous of Reagan's militancy and his successor, François Mitterrand, dismissive of Bush's efforts to reunify Germany.

Since the end of the Cold War, the European criticism of America as a global bull in the international china shop has become more pervasive and elaborate. The disappearance of the Soviet threat has made such criticism rather risk-free, while the progressive integration of Europe's economy has pushed transatlantic economic clashes of interest to the forefront. One-sided U.S. congressional legislation, new farm subsidies, and the imposition of tariffs on steel imports have strongly reinforced the European view that America's commitment to an open global economy is disingenuous.

That perspective was reinforced by the widespread European belief that, on the global issues that affect the long-term quality of mankind's existence, and therefore should prompt the emergence of broadly shared supranational rules of conduct, America is dramatically delinquent. The Europeans were especially incensed by the abrupt and unexpected U.S. rejection of the UN's Framework Convention on Climate Change (the Kyoto Protocol), a decision that, for now, has scuttled any effective action on the internationally sensitive and politically inflammatory issue of global warming. They also viewed the American refusal to accept the International Criminal Court as inconsistent with the oft-proclaimed U.S. commitment to human rights, not to mention the strong U.S. pressure in favor of international war crimes trials in the wake of the several Yugoslav conflicts. American economic sanctions against Iran, Iraq, Libya, and Cuba were similarly seen as evidence of arbitrary American caprice, with successive U.S. administrations acquiescing—even against their better judgment—to domestic political pressure groups.

Criticism of America's unilateralism and indifference to European concerns predates the Iraqi issue. Even normally pro-American Germany at times succumbed to the spreading perception of America as one-sided and arbitrary in its conduct—and that view did not emerge only after the election of President George W. Bush. The normally moderate *Frankfurter Allgemeine Zeitung* (in an article entitled "The American Fist," March 2, 2000) flatly condemned America for its non-acceptance of "Europe's political weight," declaring the reason to be that "the two continents function according to a different political system of values; the laws of globalization are written by the hegemonic power. Only America can put up with growing societal discrepancies and the glaring gap between rich and poor. The Continent's political understanding, in contrast, demands more control and regulation, the reconciliation of conflicting interests and the limitation of power. European politics is based on consideration and mutual support by partners." A week later the leading German liberal weekly, *Die Zeit*, accused Americans of preferring "the law of the jungle" and of getting "lost in their search for new enemies."

Such critical views of America did not stem entirely from greater global sensitivity in contrast to selfish American arrogance, as the Europeans were occasionally inclined to suggest. Given Europe's military weakness and political disunity, the condemnations of America provided the Europeans with much-needed compensation for the asymmetry of power between the two sides of the Atlantic. By placing America on the moral and legal defensive, the Europeans created a somewhat more level playing field while arming themselves with reassuring self-righteousness.

But pretense can only go so far. The Europeans know, even better than the Americans, that a really serious rupture in the Atlantic relationship would be fatal for the emerging Europe. It not only would make Europe again vulnerable to internal rivalries and external threats but would likely also endanger the entire European architecture. Traditional fears of German power and historically rooted national animosities would be quickly rekindled. Without the American presence, Europe would indeed be Europe again, but not in the way European visionaries have been hoping.

In the final analysis, strategically minded Europeans—even despite the controversy that surfaced over the arbitrary U.S. decision to unseat Saddam Hussein—do realize that American unilateralism is partly a function of America's unique security role, and that reluctant tolerance of it is a price others must pay to preserve the American "can-do" attitude in a world in which economic, legal, moral, and security motivations cannot be easily compartmentalized. That attitude is derived from America's historic vision of itself as the world's standard bearer of freedom. An America that is scrupulously deferential to international rules, studiously avoids flexing its muscle in economic areas of special interest to major segments of its electorate, is obediently ready to limit its own sovereignty, and is prepared to place its military under international legal jurisdiction might not be the power of last resort needed to prevent global anarchy. In brief, the Europeans would be well advised to weigh prudently the consequences for themselves, as well as for others, of a pliant America that subordinates its leadership to the lowest common denominator of collective consensus.

There is also, however, a more ominous lesson to be drawn from the polemics over Iraq that pitted Washington against Paris and Berlin in 2003. The spat should serve as a warning signal of the potential vulnerability of transatlantic relations, should reciprocal recriminations and lack of mutual sensitivity ever provide an anti-American motive for a truly serious European effort to gain independent military power.

A Europe that seeks political unity by defining itself explicitly as a (de facto anti-American) "counterweight" to the United States would be a Europe that destroys the Atlantic Alliance.

For the time being, neither the dreams nor the nightmares of either side are likely to come to pass. Neither side will satisfy the hopes of the other, but neither will justify the other's worst fears. For at least a decade and probably longer, Europe will not attain sufficient political unity and motivation to undertake the financial sacrifices necessary to become a globally significant military power.[1] Europe will not threaten America's primacy for the basic reason that European political unity will be achieved, at best, very slowly and grudgingly. The forthcoming expansion of the EU to twenty-seven members will further complicate the already overly complex and highly bureaucratized structures of European integration, which are reminiscent of a giant economic conglomerate.

Conglomerates do not have historic visions; they have tangible interests. The impersonal bureaucratic structures of the European Union cannot evoke the popular sentiment necessary for a political vocation. As a French commentator scathingly put it, "Europe's original sin, of which it has not yet cleansed itself, is to have been conceived in offices. And of having prospered there. A common destiny cannot be built on such foundations, any more than it is possible to fall in love with a growth rate or milk quotas."[2] The overriding European interest is global stability, without which the European architecture would crumble. Hence the European Union will eventually acquire the attributes of political-military power, just as huge multinational corporations often develop their own armed security personnel to protect their vital interests. But even then, Europe's military efforts for some time to come will be largely supplementary to, and not competitive with, America's military capabilities.

Moreover, the unlikelihood of any eventual European military prowess being motivated by a transnational European chauvinism is all to the good. It will mean that even a politically and militarily more powerful Europe will be guided in its international conduct by self-restraint, derived from the limits inherent in the complex nature of its continental unity and from the dilute character of its political identity. Imbued with neither missionary zeal nor self-righteous fanaticism, the Europe of tomorrow could become the example of, as well as the impulse for, the responsible multilateralism the world ultimately needs.

The intense transatlantic disagreements that surfaced about Iraq should not obscure the fact that an essentially multilateralist Europe and a somewhat unilateralist America make for a perfect global marriage of convenience. Acting separately, America can be preponderant but not omnipotent; Europe can be rich but impotent. Acting together, America and Europe are in effect globally omnipotent. Both sides of the Atlantic know this. America—even given its current one-dimensional preoccupation with terrorism, its impatience with allies, its unique global security role, and its sense of historic mission—is nevertheless grudgingly accommodating to the progressive expansion of regional as well as international consultative frameworks. Neither America nor Europe would do as well without the other. Together, they are the core of global stability.

The vitality of that core depends on a relevant agenda for both America and Europe that transcends the issues dividing them. Such an agenda does exist, the bitterness of the spring of 2003 notwithstanding. Most immediately, it involves urgently needed transatlantic cooperation in stabilizing the Middle East. As argued in Chapter 2, without such a joint strategic undertaking, both American and European security interests in the Middle East will suffer. A joint effort would help to infuse the Atlantic relationship with a common geopolitical purpose.

For the longer run, the enlargement of Europe will remain a central common interest, best promoted through the political and geographical complementarity of the EU and NATO frameworks. Enlargement is the best guarantee that the security landscape of Europe will continue to evolve in a manner that expands the world's central zone of peace, promotes the absorption of Russia into the enlarging West, and engages Europe in joint American-European efforts to advance global security.

The expansion of the EU and the enlargement of NATO are the logical and inevitable consequences of the favorable outcome of the Cold War. With the Soviet threat gone and with Central Europe free of Soviet domination, maintaining NATO as a defensive alliance against a vanished Soviet threat would have made no sense at all. Moreover, failure to expand to Central Europe would have left to its own devices a truly unstable belt of less privileged and less secure European states squeezed between the prosperous West and the tumultuous post-Soviet Russia, with potentially unsettling consequences for all concerned.

The EU and NATO thus have no choice: they have to expand lest their success in the Cold War be undone, even though each addition dilutes the political cohesion of the former and complicates the military interoperability of the latter. In the case of the EU, the split between the so-called "old Europe," which largely opposed the Bush administration's rush to war against Iraq, and "new Europe," which supported Washington, has dramatized the increasing difficulty of defining a common European foreign policy. In response, France and Germany may try to organize an informal inner cluster within the EU to speak and act on behalf of "Europe," but for some time to come, the EU as such will be much more a reality economically than politically.

In NATO, the quest for military interoperability and integration will also have a different meaning. Integrating standing national armies for territorial defense made sense when Western Europe was facing a potential Soviet attack. Integrating twenty-six national armies makes no sense when territorial defense is no longer the central need. NATO will therefore concentrate on specialized contributions and on the development and enhancement of a genuinely capable and integrated rapid reaction force for missions outside its members' territory.

The enlargement of both the EU and NATO will continue. After each expansion, as the east recedes and the west expands, the dangers of a geopolitical no-man's-land simply move eastward. At the same time, the West's evolving relationship with Russia and Ukraine's proclaimed desire to eventually join the Euroatlantic community give salience to the merits of continued expansion. It follows that neither an EU of twenty-seven members (following the likely additions of new states by 2005) nor a NATO of twenty-six (in the wake of the enlargement decisions made in late 2002 at the NATO summit in Prague) is likely to be the last word.

Expansion, however, need not involve an endless, mechanical addition of new members right up to the Chinese border. In the area of security, it could involve much longer periods of growing cooperation between prospective states and NATO, of deepening military and political cooperation, and of intensified NATO involvement in the enhancement of regional security arrangements. In some cases, that may then lead to additional memberships; other cases may involve some NATO members and closely associated non-members jointly participating in NATO-led security arrangements. A good example is Ukrainian participation in 2003 in the Polish-led sector in Iraq backed logistically by NATO.

In any case, NATO will not be able to draw a final line after the second major enlargement of its membership. The evolving NATO-Russia cooperation, spurred by the creation of the Joint NATO-Russia Council, has made it more difficult for Moscow to object to Ukraine's desire to join NATO. In May 2002, shortly after the decision to create the Council was formalized, Ukraine announced its firm intention to seek eventual NATO membership (and at some point EU membership as well). Though it is unlikely that Ukraine can soon meet the criteria, it certainly would be strategically unwise for NATO to rebuff Ukraine's aspirations, thereby potentially rekindling Russia's imperial ambitions. Accordingly, a purposeful process of encouraging Ukraine to prepare itself for NATO membership (perhaps attainable within this decade) will be the logical next step.

Somewhat the same considerations apply to the volatile region of the Caucasus. Formerly under exclusive Russian imperial control, it now includes three independent but insecure states (Georgia, Armenia, and

Azerbaijan), as well as a host of small ethnic enclaves in the still Russian-dominated Northern Caucasus. The region is not only beset by intense internal ethnic and religious hostilities, it has also been the traditional focus of power rivalries among Russia, Turkey, and Iran. In the post-Soviet setting, these long-standing conflicts have been compounded by vigorous competition over the division of the energy resources of the Caspian Sea. Moreover, it is probably only a question of time before the very large Azeri population of northwestern Iran begins to seek reunification with its newly independent and potentially more prosperous homeland, thereby injecting more fuel into the region's wildfires.

None of the three traditional rivals for regional preeminence—Russia, Turkey, and Iran—now has the power to impose its unilateral will on the area as a whole. Even a combination of two against one—say, Russia and Iran against Turkey—would be insufficient, as in the background lurk both the United States (through NATO, of which Turkey is a key member) and the European Union (to which Turkey aspires). Yet without some active external involvement, the internal social, political, ethnic, and religious conflicts of the Caucasus will not only continue to fester but are likely to erupt into periodic violence, as they have already done several times since 1990.

That increasingly self-evident reality may even induce Russia to conclude, albeit reluctantly, that its interests would be best served by some form of collaboration with the Euroatlantic community to promote a more stable, eventually cooperative and prosperous, Caucasian region. The two bloody wars Russia brutally waged against the independence-seeking Chechnya in the decade following the disintegration of its historic empire not only did enormous damage to Russia's moral standing but demonstrated the physical limits of its capacity to wage an imperial war in the post-imperial age.

In the 1990s, NATO assumed a new role by imposing stability on the turbulent and violent Balkans. By the early years of the subsequent decade, it was becoming evident that some sort of a new Stability Pact for the Caucasus—modeled on the Stability Pact for the

Balkans—will be needed. With Russia's eventual concurrence more likely, in view of its wider interest in accommodation with the American-led alliance and also given the expansion of economic and political ties between Russia and Turkey, the stabilization of the Caucasus may become—as it should—increasingly also a NATO responsibility.

In these circumstances, both Georgia and Azerbaijan, whose leaders have already publicly signaled their interest in eventually joining the alliance, will likely intensify their efforts to gain formal membership. It is unlikely that Armenia will then stand aside; redoubled efforts to resolve the Armenian-Azeri ethnic and territorial conflict may then follow, in turn facilitating a normalization of Turkish-Armenian relations and thus opening a door for Armenia to establish a NATO connection. Additional impetus for such geographic expansion of NATO's stabilizing mission is being generated, as already observed, by Russia's own strategic decision to accept the Atlantic community's preeminence in the world's security architecture. Once Russia resigned itself to the inevitability—even if not the desirability—of NATO's continued enlargement, and chose to sugarcoat that bitter pill by claiming friendly co-equality with NATO through the Joint NATO-Russia Council, the obstacles to a widened NATO reach within the former Soviet space crumbled.

Moreover, the U.S. military's post-9/11 leapfrogging into the formerly Soviet Central Asian republics of Uzbekistan, Kazakhstan, and Kyrgyzstan, and Moscow's initially reluctant decision to acquiesce to that reality, made it easier for the various post-Soviet states to explore closer security links with the Euroatlantic community in the name of the joint struggle against terrorism. The states in the region certainly noted that the Russian government, probably with inner resentment but also with considerable realism, not only acquiesced to an American security role in Russia's hitherto sacrosanct "near abroad," but even acknowledged it through the American-Russian "Joint Declaration on the New Strategic Relationship," announced on May 24, 2002, by Presidents Bush and Putin. Its language was unambiguous: "In Central Asia and the South Caucasus, we recognize our common interest in promoting the stability, sovereignty and territorial integrity of all the nations of this region"—a conclusion with obviously major geostrategic implications.

Though the Kremlin's own inclination toward the West predated 9/11, that event made its stance easier to justify in the face of criticism from those elements of the Russian political elite who saw their government as excessively compliant to America's self-assertion. President Putin's strategic decision came from a realistic geopolitical calculus: Given the rise of China to the east (with China's economy already five times larger than Russia's and its population nine times larger), the mounting hostility of the 300-or-so million Muslims to the south (likely to increase to well over 400 million over the next two decades), and Russia's own economic weakness and demographic crisis (with the Russian population already down to 145 million and dropping further), Russia literally had no choice. Rivalry with America was senseless, and an alliance with China would have meant subordination.

To be sure, in the near future—for a decade or so—it is altogether unlikely that Russia could become a member of NATO. Not only will it take time for Russia to meet the democratic criteria for membership, but nostalgic pride as well as Russia's traditional penchant for secrecy stand in the way. The notion that its admission is now contingent on the votes of such former Russian dominions as the Baltic states is also too galling for the current Russian political elite to swallow, while the generals would find it hard to stomach the requirement to let NATO comptrollers examine their defense budgets and NATO experts check their weapons.

Yet in the longer run, Russia may come to realize that NATO membership will give it greater territorial security, especially in its depopulating far east. That consideration may eventually prove to be the most persuasive. At some point, depending on how China evolves, Russia's expanding collaboration with NATO on various specialized threats to global security (as envisaged by the Joint NATO-Russia

Council) may create the basis for a trans-Eurasian security system that would span much of the continent and could include even China (more on this later).

It will take even more time for Russia to qualify for EU membership, if ever.[3] Membership would require a thorough restructuring of the country's socioeconomic and legal structures. There cannot be any shortcuts: the process is both comprehensive and complex, and neither the European Union nor Russia is remotely ready for genuine integration. That, however, need not stand in the way of provisional and partial accommodations to maximize two-way access for trade, investments, and the increasingly free movement of labor—all designed to gradually integrate Russia into the European system. The Kaliningrad region of Russia will soon be entirely surrounded by NATO and EU members. Special arrangements for Kaliningrad, especially regarding freer access of its residents to the neighboring countries, could spearhead the cooperative embrace of Russia by the expanding Euroatlantic community.

The Kremlin doubtless entertained the hope that an accommodation with America—especially with an America that was shell-shocked by 9/11 and hence more likely to be considerate of Russia's interests—could be beneficial materially as well as geopolitically. It could strengthen Russia's position vis-à-vis China, help to generate investment for Russia's economic recovery, and enable Russia to exercise more influence in its former imperial domain, while entangling the United States in a prolonged conflict with Islam that diverts Islamic hostility from Russia. But even such opportunistic calculations could not alter the fact that accommodation with America meant entanglement with America, and the weaker party was bound to be much more entangled than the stronger.

Russia's only choice—even if tactical—thus provided the West with a strategic opportunity. It created the preconditions for the progressive geopolitical expansion of the Western community deeper and deeper into Eurasia. Russia's formerly exclusive "near abroad" became the object of Western, notably American, penetration even as Western ties with Russia widened. Ultimately, however, Russia had little choice if it wished to retain the most important of its territorial possessions. It is the immeasurable natural wealth of Siberia that provides the best promise for Russia's future, and without the help of the West, Russia cannot be entirely certain that its dominion there will endure.[4]

Accordingly, a transnational effort to develop and colonize Siberia could stimulate genuine European-Russian bonding. For the Europeans, Siberia could represent the opportunity that Alaska and California combined once offered the Americans: a source of great wealth, an occasion for profitable investments, an *El Dorado* for its more adventurous settlers. To retain Siberia, Russia will need help; it cannot do so on its own, given its demographic decline and what is emerging next door in China. Through a larger European presence, Siberia could eventually become a common Eurasian asset, exploited on a multilateral basis (it should be recalled that the Volga region was developed by invited German colonists) while challenging the satiated European society with an exciting "new frontier."

Until then, the deliberate support of efforts to consolidate a post-imperial, increasingly democratic Russia will remain a major task of Euroatlantic policy. There may still be serious setbacks, given Russia's lack of a deeply ingrained democratic political culture, the residual imperial ambitions of much of its political elite, and the authoritarian inclinations of its power structures. A turn to a nationalist dictatorship still cannot be ruled out. Europe must be especially careful lest its new "energy partnership" with Russia give the Kremlin new sources of political leverage against its neighbors. Cooperation with Russia must be matched by simultaneous efforts to consolidate geopolitical pluralism in the former Russian imperial space, thereby creating enduring obstacles to any attempts at imperial restoration. NATO and the EU must therefore make certain to include the newly independent post-Soviet states, especially Ukraine, in the Euroatlantic community's expanding orbit.

At stake is the future global security role of the Euroatlantic community. The eventual inclusion of Russia as a normal, middle-ranking European state (though no longer an imperial Third Rome) in the

Euroatlantic system would create a much more solid and comprehensive basis for coping with the rising conflicts in the Global Balkans of west and central Asia. The consequent worldwide primacy of the Euroatlantic institutions would finally end the bitter struggles for supremacy waged for so long and with such destructive intensity among the European nations.

But the enhancement of Europe's role in ensuring global security will not wait. Though the new threats to global security currently point more at America than at Europe, especially given America's deepening and increasingly one-sided involvement in the rancorous Middle East, nevertheless, in the final analysis the threat is indivisible: an endangered America would mean an increasingly vulnerable Europe. The response, therefore, must be a joint one, and America and Europe possess a joint instrument: NATO. The issue is how to make use of it, taking into account NATO's primary mission, the respective American-European political concerns, and Europe's desire to acquire some measure of autonomous military power.

During the Cold War, the two sides of the Atlantic agreed on the nature of the threat and recognized the interdependence of their vulnerabilities. The defense of Western Europe was tantamount to the defense of America, and vice versa. After 9/11, the same sentiments prevailed on both sides of the ocean, but only for a while. The immediate European reaction to the attack was total solidarity with America. NATO, for the first time ever, invoked Article 5, declaring unanimously that all its members were engaged in a common defense against a shared threat. Though the United States chose not to rely on NATO forces in the military campaign it waged in Afghanistan, preferring to use its own forces and some selected and highly interoperable units from allied Anglo-Saxon states, deployments from NATO countries securing the peace in post-Taliban Afghanistan subsequently came to outnumber the U.S. troops there.

In the months that followed 9/11, America's European allies also endorsed the Washington view that terrorism and proliferation were the two major (and potentially interconnected) threats to global security. But before long, it became evident that subtle but important differences in the American and European perspectives stood in the way of genuine transatlantic cooperation in the area of global security. Two key issues define the difference: the nature of the threat, and the scope of the required response.

Perhaps because it is historically rather familiar, Europeans see terrorism less as a manifestation of evil and more as a political emanation. As such, it has to be attacked in a manner that recognizes the connection between direct measures to extirpate terrorism and policies designed to cut its political and social roots. In other words, the struggle against terrorism cannot be the central organizing principle of the West's global security policy; that policy has to have a broader political and social focus, encompassing efforts to address the underlying issues that contribute to the emergence of terrorists and are exploited by them. Perhaps the most pointed divergence between the continental Europeans and the Americans has involved their respective assessments of Palestinian terrorism: many Americans, including some in the administration, see terrorism as an evil largely unrelated to Israeli occupation of the Palestinian lands, while many Europeans tend to view the occupation and especially the settlements as instigating the terrorism.

Secondly, as a leading German commentator on international affairs put it: "The Americans tend to see the whole world as a field of action for the Atlantic community, while the Europeans want to act in and around Europe, which is still pretty vague, but far more limited."[5] The gap in perspectives, which became gradually more marked after the end of the Cold War, emerged in even sharper relief after 9/11. For the United States, the fight against "terrorism with a global reach" had to be worldwide, and it was only natural that NATO should become globally engaged to defend "civilization as such," in the fervent words of President Bush. For the Europeans, that smacked of pressure to subordinate Europe's shared interest in global stability to America's more immediate preoccupation with the "axis of evil" and particularly with Iraq.

With Europe inching toward greater political unity and with European military capabilities gradually (even if very slowly) emerging, the gap between the European and the American perspectives on global security could widen as Europe's own definition of its security perimeter inevitably expands. But even then, Europe's capacity for significant out-of-area combat missions will remain quite limited. For some years to come, Europe's planned 60,000-soldier rapid reaction force—unless significantly upgraded—will still lack the full spectrum of military assets necessary for serious long-range warfare. Hence the essence of Europe's gradually expanding security role can be encapsulated simply: complementarity with, but not autonomy from, America.

The issue most likely to prompt Europe to assume a more significant out-of-area security role and even to develop a distinctive sense of Europe's strategic purpose is the Middle East.[6] Given the Middle East's proximity to Europe and Europe's historic political and economic interests in the Middle East, the European Union will have to assume a more active role in pacifying the region. But to sustain that role, Europe will also have to be willing to assume some of the burdens of paying for and enforcing peace together with America.

In effect, as they have done in Afghanistan and may do soon in the Middle East, the Europeans may take a gradually expanding, though still complementary, role in global security. A joint American-European deployment in the Middle East, even if partly based on the EU rapid reaction corps, would probably still be coordinated and commanded through NATO, which would highlight the widening horizons of the alliance's security mission. The effect of the Europeans' participation, and the resulting pressure on America to consult Europe more closely on the politics of the region, would enhance the role of the expanding Euroatlantic community as the core of global stability, *provided that* both Washington and Brussels learn how to balance burden-sharing with shared policymaking.

EAST ASIA'S METASTABILITY

East Asia is yet to establish whether its geopolitical future will resemble the Europe of the first half of the twentieth century or the Europe of the second half of the twentieth century. In some respects, today's Asia eerily recalls Europe prior to 1914. This is not to say that the region is doomed to a tragic replay of Europe's self-destruction. Perhaps Asia will avoid repeating Europe's failure to cope with its internal power rivalries. But it is to note that the region is metastable— a solid condition until subjected to a sudden impact that sets off a destructive chain reaction.

The rising power of several Asian states threatens the region's stability. The region lacks any restraining cooperative structure of regional security. Strong reciprocal grievances among immediate neighbors exist in a setting of acutely felt national pathologies made more ominous by their respective strategic vulnerabilities. Today's Asian powers operate in a fluid and still largely unstructured regional context, one that lacks the kind of multilateral frameworks for political, economic, and security cooperation now seen in Europe or even in Latin America. Asia is thus at once a rising economic success, a social volcano, and a political hazard.

In it, a rising China competes for regional preeminence with America-allied Japan, Korea is unnaturally divided and at all times potentially explosive, Taiwan's future is a source of contention, Indonesia is internally vulnerable, and India feels menaced by China while seeing itself as China's peer. China and India (as well as India's antagonistic neighbor Pakistan) are overt nuclear powers. North Korea is defiantly seeking to become one, while Japan is poised to make itself into one quickly. As a rising power, China is reminiscent of imperial Germany, which was envious of Great Britain, hostile toward France, and contemptuous of Russia; today's China, though increasingly pragmatic about the American role in the Pacific, is neuralgic about Japan, patronizing toward India, and dismissive of Russia.

Global security will unavoidably be affected by how the international scene in the Far East actually evolves. That, in turn, will depend largely on the conduct of the two leading East Asian states, China and Japan, and on how America influences their behavior. A stable East Asia—ensured by a gradually institutionalized and carefully balanced U.S.-Chinese-Japanese strategic triangle—will provide a critical eastern anchor for dealing with wider Eurasian turmoil. In different ways, India, Russia, and the European Union may also contribute to the interplay of the above, but only peripherally.

The grievances and resentments complicating relations among the Asian states are many. They are historical, territorial, and cultural. The Chinese resent the continued separation of Taiwan, for which they blame America, they fear and closely monitor Japan's rearmament and condemn the Japanese as insufficiently repentant for wartime misdeeds, and they have not forgotten the territories Russia seized from them during their period of historical weakness. The Japanese view China as a potential security threat and a rising rival to Japan's regional economic and political primacy, while Russia's continued retention of the southern Kurile Islands so rankles the Japanese that a formal Russo-Japanese peace treaty is yet to be signed more than fifty-five years after the end of World War II. The Japanese also increasingly view their dependence on the United States as a temporary strategic necessity dictated by the dangerously unresolved World War II partition of Korea, rather than as a desirable long-term condition. The Indonesians are apprehensive of China's rising power, while the Indians resent the arrogant refusal of the Chinese to view India as China's Asian peer and feel threatened by the implicit Chinese-Pakistani alliance.

Matters are not made easier by deep national complexes, intensified by bitter historical memories. The Japanese rose to imperial greatness and fell into the abyss of crushing defeat within a single century. They remain the only victims of atomic weapons. They are conscious of their lack of natural resources and increasingly worried about the social and economic consequences of their rapidly aging population (the second most rapidly aging in the world). The Chinese bitterly resent the prolonged national humiliation inflicted upon them by the

Japanese, the Americans, the Russians, the British, and the French (with some minor participation, during the Boxer Rebellion, by the Germans and Italians). Their intensifying nationalism is likely to become the main source of China's political unity as the ruling communist ideology fades into irrelevance. On the margins, the Indians are preoccupied with growing communal strife at home and are jealous that China is a far greater magnet for foreign direct investment, while the Russians fret that in the longer run they may lose their own far eastern territories to the more powerful and densely populated China.

Compounding this vortex of fears, antagonisms, and complexes is everyone's strategic vulnerability. Each of the major Asian players is uniquely dependent for its economic survival on unfettered access for its maritime commerce to only two or three major ports. It would take only a few magnetic mines blockading Shanghai or Yokohama or Bombay (and one or two more) to cause Japan's, or China's, or India's economy literally to grind to a halt. Their economies are almost exclusively dependent on cargo carried by ships—including oil imports, which for them are absolutely essential. International commercial rail transport is not only inapplicable to island states like Japan and Indonesia, it is also insignificant for China and India. The Strait of Malacca, just off Singapore, is a particularly vital sea lane since the Far East's trade with Europe as well as its oil imports from the Middle East move through this narrow passage.

No wonder, then, that an Asian naval arms race has been quietly gathering steam. The parallel to the European naval rivalry of the last century is quite striking. Without fanfare, all the major protagonists have been expanding their submarine fleets, acquiring surface vessels equipped to carry attack helicopters, exploring the possibility of obtaining aircraft carriers, and striving to extend the range of their air power. China and India have been seeking powerful blue water navies, with each country actively negotiating with Russia to obtain one of the large aircraft carriers the Soviet Union failed to finish building. Both of them have been modernizing their destroyer flotillas (including advanced models acquired from Russia) and expanding their submarine fleets as a key sea denial force. In their strategic literature, Chinese naval planners have argued for China to expand the perimeter of its naval reach southwestward, while their counterparts in India have increasingly been stressing not only India's special naval responsibility in the Indian Ocean but also the need for India to assert itself eastward in the Strait of Malacca.

Nor have the Japanese been laggard. In 2001, the Japanese let it be known that they would start the regular dispatch of armed patrol vessels to the Malacca Strait to help protect the Japanese tankers and cargo ships that have been preyed upon by local pirates. In addition to their modern fleet of highly competent destroyers, the Japanese have sought a longer-range naval capability by acquiring a so-called landing platform dock (LPD) ship equipped to carry attack helicopters and potentially also fixed-wing aircraft. Current Japanese plans for additional 13,500-ton helicopter-carrying destroyers will give Japan vessels bigger than the Italian aircraft carrier *Garibaldi*, which can carry sixteen Harrier jets. Backed by long-range refueling fighter aircraft (their long-range refueling capability is officially described, incredibly, as designed for "humanitarian" purposes) and by a modern submarine fleet, the Japanese naval forces—still modest compared to the American navy—are already the most advanced and potent among the Asian states.

Ultimately, war or peace in the Far East will be determined largely by how China and Japan interact with each other and with the United States. If the United States were to withdraw its forces from the region, a repetition of the twentieth century European scenario would be very probable. Japan would have little choice but to rapidly unveil and accelerate its ongoing rearmament; China would be likely to engage in a rapid buildup of its nuclear forces, which till now have been designed to give China a minimal deterrent; the Taiwan Straits would become the locus of Chinese national self-assertion; Korea would most likely experience a violent end to its partition and perhaps emerge unified as a nuclear power; and the Chinese-Indian-Pakistani nuclear triangle could provide a dangerous umbrella for the resumption of open conventional warfare. A single match could then set off an explosion.

For the next decade or so, however, the most likely pattern will involve the interplay of China's overt rise to regional power, Japan's continued but ambiguous acquisition of increasingly superior military power, and America's efforts to manage both of the foregoing. That management will require careful strategic calibration and genuine sensitivity to the aspirations of both the Chinese and the Japanese. China is moving into its post-communist phase as an increasingly nationalistic power, while Japan (still the number two economy in the world) is becoming uneasy over the degree to which its own security remains dependent on a potentially overstretched and occasionally arbitrary America.

The Chinese view of the world—and of China's own role in it—has become increasingly pragmatic and non-doctrinal, especially after 9/11. Evidently concerned that they were risking international isolation, given Russia's apparent decision to give up its flirtation with a Russo-Chinese coalition against American "hegemonism," the Chinese abandoned their frenetic denunciations of American aggressiveness as well as their drumbeat allegations that the United States was planning war against the People's Republic of China. While such views were still frequent in the Chinese media as recently as the first half of 2001,[7] by 2002 the black-and-white depiction of a global confrontation between peace-loving and warlike states had given way to a much more nuanced interpretation. Quite revealing in that respect was the sensible assessment advanced in the February 4, 2002, edition of *Jiefangjun Bao*, the official organ of the General Political Department of the People's Liberation Army (PLA), which concluded that "The essential pattern of the development of the international situation at present and in the near future will be: overall peace with localized wars, overall calm with localized tension, and overall stability with localized unrest."

The Chinese analysis went on to argue that "The international security issue has become increasingly diversified, traditional security factors and non-traditional ones have become intertwined, and the harm caused by the non-traditional security problems such as terrorism and drug trafficking is becoming more serious." Reflecting a more doctrinal perspective, the PLA organ warned that the above notwithstanding, the United States is increasingly inclined to give its alliances, notably NATO and the defense treaty with Japan, an offensive capability that should be of concern to China. It was the Japanese-American connection, needless to add, that most worried the strategists in Beijing.

That the Chinese have a healthy respect for Japan's potential power is understandable. That they deliberately exaggerate it is also not surprising, since this channels the nationalist emotions of the Chinese masses without complicating the Chinese-American relationship. The Chinese realize that the continued inflow of foreign direct investment and advanced technology into China, as well as access to a major foreign market for exports of Chinese industrial products, depends on non-antagonistic relations with the United States. In contrast, a subdued and carefully managed hostile rivalry with Japan is not only historically natural but politically expedient: it mobilizes national unity without prohibitive international cost.

Thus the Chinese people are repeatedly told by their mass media, and their political elite is repeatedly informed in greater detail by the more specialized PLA journals, that Japan has already become a major military power again and that its military capabilities are both significant and rapidly growing. Its power is said to represent a growing threat to China's as well as to the region's security, especially given Japan's increased acquisition of technologically advanced capabilities for offensive operations. Moreover, bellicose statements by any Japanese politician tend to receive major play in the Chinese media, which also carefully record any Japanese inclination to dilute Japan's formal constitutional commitment to a purely and narrowly defined defensive posture.

According to the Chinese political and military journals, Japan—in addition to its very modern naval and air forces and the second-largest national defense budget in the world—is developing an impressive ballistic missile capability, already qualitatively surpassing that possessed by France and China itself and even comparable to America's. Japan's M-5 rocket, developed in the late 1990s, is said to represent an improvement on America's last and most potent ICBM, the solid-fuel MX missile. A more recent model allegedly designed for space research, the H-2A rocket, has an effective range of 5,000 kilometers, giving Japan the ability to deliver a two-ton conventional warhead to any target within China. At the same time, Japan's evident interest in cooperating with the United States on a guided missile defense system, and its acquisition of the most advanced Aegis air defense destroyers, are viewed as motivated by the desire to gain a strategic advantage over China.[8]

More ominously in the Chinese view, Japan is seen as on the brink of becoming a major nuclear power. The case for that proposition rests on the argument that Japan has a contingent of highly trained scientists capable of producing and rapidly assembling ready-made parts ("within only one week," according to a Chinese report) into atomic bombs; that Japan with its forty-four nuclear reactors is already the third largest nuclear-power-generating nation in the world; that Japan's nuclear fuel-handling capability—which is up to 800-plus tons—ranks third in the world, only after America's (at 2,100 tons) and France's (at 1,200 tons); and that this capability is projected to grow significantly over the next ten years, by which time Japan will possess the largest plutonium reserves in the world, even though its current reserves are sufficient to produce thousands of nuclear warheads. In brief, Japan is presented as "a *de facto* nuclear power on the nuclear threshold."[9]

Given Japan's growing military potential, the Chinese find two scenarios particularly haunting. The first would involve an unleashed Japan (either because it detached itself from dependence on America, or because of a sudden American withdrawal from the

Far East) that relies on its growing naval power and nuclear potential to embark on a policy of open hostility toward China, while forming an offshore alliance with Taiwan. In Chinese eyes, Taiwan would then be transformed into the twenty-first century equivalent of Manchukuo, the early twentieth century protectorate imposed by Japanese militarists over China's Manchuria. A Sino-Japanese military collision could then ensue.

The second scenario envisions that the existing security ties linking the United States with Japan, South Korea, and Taiwan—officially bilateral, and in the case of Taiwan largely unofficial—would be openly redefined by the United States as an anti-Chinese alliance. The political status of Taiwan would be as in the first scenario, even though the United States might be less likely than a nationalist Japan to sponsor Taiwan's formal separation from China. In any case, China would find itself geopolitically hemmed in, with India probably then tempted to take advantage of the opportunity to press China for the return of the territories that India claims were forcibly taken from it in the border conflict of the early 1960s.

That some politically influential circles in Taiwan would be quite receptive to either development has been more than hinted by Taiwanese president Chen Shui-bian, who called in early 2002 for the joint development of missile defenses by the United States, Japan, and Taiwan. Taiwanese mass media have also favorably cited comments by Japanese and Taiwanese defense specialists advocating "a silent alliance" between Japan and Taiwan to deter China. As one Taiwanese defense expert put it, "The most important thing for Japan in treating Taiwan as a silent ally will be to think of Taiwan as a real ally."[10]

Given the foregoing risks, the Chinese will very carefully assess the evolution of the U.S.-Japanese connection and its impact on the historically competitive Chinese-Japanese relationship. It may turn out, paradoxically, that—with the gradual waning in China of the communist ideology, and with the pragmatic recognition of China's stake in a relatively stable relationship with the United States—Japan's growing military potential may actually prompt the Chinese to more highly appreciate continued Japanese dependence on the United States. The practical value of a genuinely stable American-Chinese-Japanese rapprochement would then outweigh the earlier Chinese inclination to view the world in doctrinally influenced dichotomous categories.

There are indications that such a change is already taking place. Lately, some Chinese experts have been arguing in public that a sophisticated Chinese policy, alert to the sensitive realities of the American-Japanese connection, might do more than impede the emergence of the ominous scenarios outlined above. It could foster a broader sense of Asian identity within Japan itself, preventing the permanent American-sponsored detachment of Japan from Asia. Such detachment, the Chinese fear, could result from the ongoing American efforts to transform Japan from an Asian country into a Pacific Ocean equivalent of the United Kingdom: a country guided by a distinctive insular non-continental identity, serving as America's privileged military partner in the Pacific Ocean, with its key mission being to help America contain "the China threat." To encourage Japan to identify its future with Asia instead, as one Chinese foreign affairs specialist put it, "the most ideal result of improving the China-Japan relationship for China is benign, equilateral, and interactive progress in the China-US-Japan relationship."[11]

To that end, Beijing has been making increasing efforts to improve its relations with both the United States and Japan, the latter's military buildup notwithstanding. The important strategic lesson this shift implies is that a gradual, carefully calibrated upgrading of Japan's security role actually increases the Chinese stake in maintaining a stable and cooperative relationship with the United States, in favoring continued American-Japanese ties, and in sustaining a balanced Chinese-Japanese-American triangle.

It would be a mistake, however, for U.S. decision-makers to infer that a similarly significant Taiwanese military buildup would likewise have a positive effect. Unless altogether detached from the United States, a gradually more powerful Japan is unlikely to exploit its increasing military prowess to directly challenge any vital Chinese interest. That is not the case with Taiwan. There is a greater risk that the separatist political forces in Taiwan would be tempted to use any major upgrading of Taiwan's military capability as an opportunity to declare their island's formal independence from China. No Chinese government, not even a highly authoritarian one, could then remain passive, especially in view of the increased role of nationalism in the Chinese mass consciousness. Chinese popular fury could then trigger a regionally destabilizing Sino-American military clash.

The Taiwan issue apart, the main foreign-policy preoccupation of China's leaders will continue to be how dynamic, politically assertive, and internationally ambitious Japan's acquisition of military power will be—and to what degree that acquisition will be restrained by the American-Japanese connection. There are grounds for cautious optimism. Neither the United States nor Japan is likely to engage in a rash strategic reorientation. The occasional campaigns in the American mass media to portray China as America's next superpower rival and principal threat have not generated massive congressional or public pressure to adopt a more antagonistic U.S. stance toward China. Nor have there been calls for an urgent Japanese rearmament reminiscent of West Germany's in the dangerous Cold War 1950s.

The Japanese themselves show considerable sensitivity to Chinese concerns and are likely to maintain a low profile even while steadily enhancing their military capabilities. That enhancement appears to be driven largely by a prudent desire not to be altogether defenseless in the event of some unexpected U.S. disengagement, and not by a national passion for independent military power. On balance, the Japanese goal is more to have a fail-safe option than to plot a sudden breakout.

It is, in fact, to the great credit of the Japanese people and its political elite that democratic values and a strong anti-militarist ethic have become deeply engrained in their outlook. The ongoing debates in Japan regarding the scale and geostrategic scope of the country's military programs, and the continued public support for strict constitutional limits on Japanese military engagement abroad, all reflect a rational and responsible view of Japan's international role. In brief, the Japan of today—a genuine constitutional democracy—is a good global citizen.

To be sure, voices have been raised in Japan in favor of a more assertive international posture, especially in the wake of 9/11. But aside from a strident minority without much popular support, the mainstream case for a more active Japanese posture tends to emphasize Japan's obligation as the world's number two economic power to shoulder its commensurate share of responsibility for global security. By and large, this posture does not involve calls for an altogether independent military status that would de-link Japan from the United States. There may be a growing inclination to reject internationalist pacifism, but that does not signify a desire to embrace nationalist militarism.

The views expressed after 9/11 by the chairman of the Japanese Upper House Standing Committee on Foreign Affairs and Defense are typical. He noted that "a simple pacifist concept that military power is evil has existed in postwar Japan as a result of the nation's tragic experiences in World War II. This idea became exaggerated and developed into the so-called one-country pacifism, and we must do some soul-searching about that." He then went on to argue that "Japan should become capable of serving a role in responding to new threats in the post-Cold War era as a responsible member of the international community. Next, we must establish a system to protect our lives, property, and land from traditional threats (such as armed attacks by other countries)....Finally, we must make adjustments to legal frameworks for smooth functioning of the Japan-US alliance, which is indispensable to maintaining the overall military balance in East Asia."[12]

This and many similar statements reflect growing public support for a more affirmative Japanese political role on the world scene. Japan is clearly moving from a passive and pacifist posture toward a more active engagement that would include not just peacekeeping but direct Japanese military participation in peace-enforcement (as in Iraq). That is a far cry, however, from an independent, nationalistic, and militaristic foreign policy—which is likely to emerge only in the wake of a far-reaching and threatening transformation of Japan's security environment.

Unlike the nations of pre-1914 Europe, neither China nor Japan has been engaging in nationalist bombast regarding its prospects as a great power. Unlike the Soviet leaders who frequently boasted that, before long, Russia would bury the United States, the Chinese have tended to emphasize (correctly) their relative backwardness and the long time needed to overcome it.[13] The Japanese, after a brief and intoxicating flurry in the 1980s generated largely by American anxieties that Japan was becoming "the next superstate," have been similarly modest about their long-term prospects. They are acutely aware not only of their country's vulnerability in the event of a global upset but also of the handicaps created by their prolonged economic doldrums and increasingly aging population.

Most importantly, the Chinese know better than anyone that they lack—and will continue to lack for some time—the power to afford serious military provocations. Any military scenario that generates a collision with the United States would be a calamity for China. The United States could blockade China at will—and thus completely halt China's foreign trade and oil imports.[14] Even short of that, as already noted, a serious conflict in the region could generate yet another nightmare for China: a militarily advanced and politically aroused Japan that is detached from the United States.

By far the better course for China is to husband its strength, promote its own economic growth, patiently foster Taiwan's economic dependence on the mainland, and subtly promote a distinctive Asian political identity through the cultivation of an Asian economic community that eventually entices Japan. China's political interest in promoting such a distinctive community, one not tied to America, has been evidently growing. In it, the Chinese expect that they would have the loudest political voice—and America would have to listen.

The Chinese not only know that they need peace in the Far East to make that possible. They also know that with peace, China stands a good chance of becoming, quite literally, the global factory—the world's center for manufacturing investments and the world's main exporter of finished manufactured products. In that respect, China is already putting out of business some traditional industrial sectors in the highly developed economies—including America's—and even in such economically developing rivals as India. Chinese firms are also beginning to buy out some bankrupt Japanese firms in Southeast Asia. The Chinese sense that over the next two decades or so, the cumulative effect of this trend could make China the dominant trade power as well as the political leader of Asia.

In any case, the year 2008 can serve as a marker for the minimum period of China's continued external prudence. The 2008 Olympics, to be hosted in Beijing, are simply too important to China's self-image and too vital to its socioeconomic success to be jeopardized by an international crisis of China's own making. That applies as much to the Taiwan Straits as to North Korea.

Moreover, the Chinese elite sense that their country's internal political and social tensions are rising, potentially even posing a threat to the stability of the system as a whole. Among the many factors likely to produce political and social unrest, two stand out: the younger generation's increased access to the Internet, and the growing signs of social inequality. The first is breaking down the Communist Party's long-established monopoly on information. Approximately 35 million Chinese are Internet users, and studies show that they are mainly younger, relatively well-off, educated males—and therefore full of social and political aspirations. They tend to rely on the Internet as a primary source of information, and they prefer to seek this information from non-domestic sources. In an interesting comparison, only 4 percent of Japanese Internet users were visiting non-Japanese sites, whereas 40 percent of Chinese users visited non-Chinese sites.[15]

Secondly, growing social inequality is likely to pose an intensifying challenge to the regime's formally egalitarian doctrines. Even the official Communist Party organ has publicly acknowledged that "the gap between the rich and the poor has begun to widen and is widening further, and contradictions in distribution have become increasingly obvious....Contradictions and conflicts are getting more antagonistic."[16] Other Chinese studies report that social inequality has already reached "dangerous levels."[17]

In sum, for the next decade at least, and probably longer, China is unlikely to see itself as ready to pose a serious political challenge to the existing international pecking order. That gives America time to prod East Asia in the direction of a modified replay of Europe's post-1950 success, and away from a replay of Europe's post-1914 disaster. The United States has a decade or so to translate the emerging informal political equilibrium among itself, Japan, and China into a more structured security relationship capable of absorbing the various strains and rivalries inherent in today's politically awakened but institutionally underdeveloped East Asia. But the needed structures and cooperative arrangements will not congeal on their own. Only the United States can promote them and prod others—including the dynamic South Korea—to become engaged.

Perhaps paradoxically, such a triangular equilibrium, to be enduring, requires that Japan become more politically engaged. Japan will gradually have to assume the full range of international security responsibilities, and this implies a wider range of military capabilities. Japanese pacifism need not take the form of an indefinite and one-sided abstention from the realities of regional power. For the long run, peace in the Far East needs a Japan that—while not threatening to China—does not feel itself vulnerable to Chinese power or resentful of its dependence on America. Japan as America's militarily capable ally in the Pacific Ocean, rather than as America's security protectorate, will increase China's stake in a peaceful East Asia while diminishing its ability to exploit pan-Asian sentiments to channel Japanese nationalism in an anti-American direction.

Accordingly, the United States should encourage a cautiously steady Japanese military buildup—integrated in its high-tech dimensions with the U.S. defense establishment, focused on air and naval power and not on a large army designed for mainland operations. Japan should also be prodded to develop an elite strike force for special operations and to use it to participate in direct actions abroad designed to promote global peace. The promotion of that peace should be interpreted as consistent with Japan's constitutional mandate, which limits Japan's military role to self-defense.

At the same time, in addition to intensifying the occasional, rather modest, and mainly informal three way U.S.-Japanese-Chinese security discussions, the three countries should establish a formal process of regular triangular military consultation. With each side free to vent its anxieties and to query the others regarding their strategic ideas, such a process would begin to generate a modicum of reciprocal confidence. In time, it could be expanded to address wider regional security issues and also to include other Asian states.

The issue of security on the Korean Peninsula, for example, could lead to the eventual inclusion of the South Korean and North Korean militaries in such discussions. Progressively, other Asian countries could also be involved in a widening and more formalized security dialogue. The nuclear challenge posed so defiantly by North Korea can be resolved peacefully only through multilateral cooperation in which all the states adjoining the two Koreas take part. In the absence of such a cooperative regional response, the two remaining options are almost equally unappealing: U.S. acquiescence to North Korean demands will strengthen the Japanese inclination to seek their security on their own, while a unilateral American military reaction, already delayed by the U.S. preoccupation with Iraq, could plunge the region into warfare.

One should not underestimate the complicating force of rising Korean nationalism. For decades, that nationalism was subdued by Korea's division into two competing blocs. South Korean nationalism naturally defined itself in pro-American terms while harboring strong anti-Japanese sentiments. But the end of the Cold War and the appearance of a new Korean generation, for which the 1950 North-South war is a remote memory, have stimulated a more intense awareness of a separate Korean identity. To many, America looks less like a protector and more like a power with an interest in the country's continued partition. Though that sentiment is still a minority one, its surfacing indicates that the U.S. military presence in South Korea is becoming an increasingly contentious issue.

In the meantime, the North Korean nuclear challenge has become the litmus test for effective regional cooperation in Northeast Asia. U.S. failure to effectively promote such cooperation will mean a progressive slide into increasing regional tension, not to mention further nuclear proliferation. Obviously, the stakes are high. Failure to deal with the problem could unhinge the American position in Northeast Asia, whereas success in galvanizing China, Japan, and Russia into a collective stand would set precedents for broader security cooperation even on a wider Eurasian scale.

In time, regional cooperation in Northeast Asia could lead to the transformation of the existing Organization for Security and Cooperation in Europe (OSCE) into a body that embraces all of Eurasia. Although its powers are limited, the existing OSCE has played a useful role in monitoring the several peacekeeping arrangements that arose in response to ethnic conflicts in post-Cold War Europe. The expansion of its geographic scope would create an all-Eurasian security forum for dealing with such novel challenges as transnational terrorism and proliferation.

In the much longer term, the foregoing could lead to the emergence of a transcontinental Eurasian security system. As NATO expands, particularly if Russia in some fashion becomes an extension of it, the stage could be set for the establishment of a trans-Eurasian collective security structure that also involves China and Japan. Though inevitably lacking the cohesion of NATO, such a forum could evolve into the central organ for promoting peace in Eurasia. Its key membership could be expanded gradually to include other states, such as India. For quite a while to come, the stabilizing effects of continued American-Japanese and American-South Korean alliances will be needed, but that is a reality that both China and Russia have increasingly recognized.

In the meantime, it would also be productive for a new effort to be made to transform the G-8 annual summit into a consultative political and economic process that more accurately reflects the new global realities. The original G-7 summit was meant to provide an opportunity for the heads of the leading and economically most powerful democracies to consult one another. The inclusion of Russia (and thus the expansion to the G-8) was motivated by the political desire to give the troubled post-Soviet Russia—though it is neither a genuine democracy nor a leading economy—a sense of status and belonging. Given that precedent, the continued exclusion of both China and India makes no sense, and the addition of both would make the ensuing "G-10" into a significant mechanism for Eurasia-wide consultations on both economic and political matters.

In such a gradually widening and increasingly institutionalized cooperative context, the prospects for the constructive resolution of both the Taiwan issue and the Korea issue would be likely to improve. Only a truly post-communist China (at least de facto, even if not formally divorced from its doctrinal roots) will be able to attract Taiwan into reunification. But with the rapid growth of economic links between the island and the mainland, with internal change in China, and with China's gradual involvement in a wider transcontinental security system, some form of reunification under a new formula will become more probable. Similarly, Korea will be reunited only when, first of all, China sees Korean reunification as beneficial to itself, and thus also when the United States and Japan cease to be viewed by China as potential threats.

The United States thus confronts a daunting agenda in the Far East, requiring a sustained American strategic engagement. Nevertheless, the progressive integration of the Far East into a larger Eurasian security framework will in time increase the prospects that both the historically familiar as well as the novel threats to East Asia's security will become more susceptible to effective resolution.

Eurasia's Revenge?

This hopeful scenario is premised on the assumption that America's trans-Atlantic and trans-Pacific strategies will continue to be shaped by a sober definition of both the style and the substance of America's global leadership. Should that cease to be the case, one cannot rule out the risk that America could find itself confronted by continent-wide resentment of its global leadership, and consequently that it could lose its strategic preeminence in Eurasia.

America has played so central a role in world affairs during the last sixty years that currently it is almost impossible either for the Europeans or for the Asians to envisage any international arrangement that does not somehow politically involve America as well. For Europe, that reality has been enshrined in NATO, and in the years to come probably also will be cemented through the overlapping responsibilities of NATO and the EU's own slowly emerging military capabilities. In the Far East, American defense ties with Japan and South Korea, as well as informally with Taiwan, have made these three states' security inseparable from America's. Even China itself, for decades critical of America's military presence in Asia, has in recent years moved to a recognition (as a PRC official put it) that "the purposes of China's policy and that of the United States on maintaining Asian stability are generally identical."[18]

That condition could be undermined if Europe and Asia were to be swept by a populist anti-American movement that defined itself as Pan-Europeanism in the west and as Pan-Asianism in the east. Each has its forerunners, though neither has so far succeeded in mobilizing the hearts and minds of most Europeans or Asians. Both are nascent forms of supranationalist regionalism. In Europe, a Pan-European movement surfaced after the calamities of World War I, but it failed to overcome the nationalistic particularisms of the European peoples. During World War II, Hitler tried, especially during his attack on the Soviet Union, to enlist the loyalties of Fascist-minded Frenchmen, Belgians, Dutchmen, and Norwegians on behalf of the defense of a common "Europa" against the Bolshevist hordes. The effort met with minimal success. In the Far East, the Japanese militarists promoted the "Greater

East Asian Co-Prosperity Sphere," exploiting the idea of Pan-Asianism to appeal to the anti-colonial sentiments of the Chinese, Thais, Javanese, Burmese, and Indians. Again the effort foundered, though it did contribute marginally to the rise of anti-colonial passions.

One cannot entirely dismiss the possibility—remote as it currently may be—of an anti-American reaction that cloaks itself in European and Asianist garbs. It could happen if Pan-Europeanism and Pan-Asianism become the rallying cries for those who view America as a common menace. Anti-Americanism would then be deliberately defined in regionally nationalistic terms, and the effort to reduce or even expel the American presence from the western and eastern extremities of Eurasia would serve as a common platform.

In Europe, a Franco-German alliance—a resurrection of the state of Charlemagne—could become the standard bearer of a Pan-Europeanism that is defined as well as politically energized by resentment of American hegemony in general and of its role in the Middle East in particular. It would thus blend political, strategic, and cultural irritation with America in the larger cause of an autonomous Pan-Europe. Previews of such an extreme orientation surfaced in the European outcries against the war that the United States undertook against Iraq in 2003.[19]

In the Far East, with ideology waning and nationalism intensifying, China is beginning to redefine itself from a "revolutionary" power into Asia's putative leader. China already dominates the trade of most Southeast Asian states and is increasingly making its economic and political presence felt in the formerly Russian-dominated Central Asia. Chinese officials speak of Asia's rising role and link Asia's future with China's. The new president of China selected in March 2003, Hu Jintao, declared when visiting Malaysia as vice president in May 2002 that "Asia cannot become prosperous without China. History has proved and will continue to prove that China is an active force propelling Asian development." References to China's Asian mission have also become increasingly frequent in Chinese foreign policy pronouncements, with an emphasis on China's special role.

A distinctive Asian political orientation may already be emerging from the progressive institutionalization of purely Asian regional cooperation. China, Japan, and South Korea have annually been holding separate trilateral summits; there is movement toward an Asian economic bloc; and security cooperation on an Asian regional basis is under discussion. Some Asian leaders make no secret of the fact that the foregoing points toward emancipation from U.S. domination. The Chinese are quite open about their design. "...setting up a cooperative organization in the East Asian region had become one of China's long-term strategic goals....China has already realized that the integration of a region not only means social and economic integration, but political and security-oriented integration as well. At the same time, it also realized that in order to gain the trust of the nations on the periphery and to play the role that a large nation should assume in the region, then it must blend in with the society of the region in all respects, and together with other nations determine and follow a unified game plan."[20]

This trend has been noted by Japanese observers, some of whom have pointedly described the Chinese efforts as aiming at "a Greater Chinese Economic Sphere." They have also warned that "there is a danger that a Great China region may be created in Asia and in turn could lead to exclusionary regionalism."[21] Japanese discussions of foreign affairs have signaled, furthermore, that the Japanese are becoming increasingly concerned that the existing security arrangements in the Far East may weaken and that Japan may face some basic choices. As noted earlier, the most likely reaction to a major destabilizing jolt to East Asia's metastability—such as an American failure to deal effectively and in a regional approach with the challenge posed by North Korea—would be for Japan to take an abrupt and isolated plunge into remilitarization. That by itself would then intensify China's inclination to assume more explicit leadership of an exclusionary continental Asianism.

The volatile character of Japanese and Korean nationalisms presents a critical element of uncertainty. Both nations were subdued and sublimated in the context of post-World War II dependence on America. That dependence has been rationalized as a historical as well as strategic necessity. Should that acceptance give way to resentment, radical nationalisms in both countries could turn anti-American, igniting a regional Asianist identity that defines itself in terms of independence from American hegemony. The potential for that exists in both countries, and some unexpected but traumatic development could trigger it.[22]

The emergence of anti-American Pan-Europeanism and Pan-Asianism, especially if fueled by U.S. unilateralism, would preclude the shaping of the needed framework for global security. Even if not dominant, they could reverse the global architectural progress of the last several decades. And if dominant, they could push America out of Eurasia. Sensitivity to that risk should further spur U.S. efforts to deepen and expand America's strategic connections with the vital western and eastern regions of Eurasia.

NOTES

1   In fact, the military gap between the United States and the European Union is widening. A systematic comparative assessment of U.S. and West European spending on military research and development (R&D), completed in early 2003 by the French Defense Ministry, concluded that Europe faces "veritable technological disarmament," with cumulative European spending representing only 40 percent of U.S. spending in 1980, 30 percent in 1990, and less than 23 percent in 2000. See Jacques Isnard, "Europe Threatened by Technological Disarmament," Le Monde, April 15, 2003.

2   Bertrand Le Gendre, "Tomorrow's Europe Seeks a Past," Le Monde, November 23, 2002.

3   An unfashionable case against even the eventual membership of Russia in the EU was strongly made in early 2001 by the sitting president of the EU, Swedish prime minister Goran Persson. He bluntly stated that "Russia is not a European country, but a continental country that comprises major parts of Europe and also Asia. ...I can imagine that some day we will have very large-scale economic cooperation with Russia, because both sides need it. ...But to accept Russia would be to alter the EU's fundamental character." See Laurent Zecchini, "Relations with Russia Extremely Important," Le Monde, March 23, 2001.

4   If one were to draw a straight line from the Caspian to Sakhalin, one would divide the Asian portion of Eurasia into the vastly underpopulated Siberia and Russian far east, containing 30–35 million people, and the vastly overcrowded area immediately south of it, containing approximately 3 billion Chinese, Indians, and Muslims.

5   Theo Sommer, "Drafting a Route for the Diplomacy of the Berlin Republic," *Die Zeit*, March 1, 2001.

6   As one French observer put it, "the main weakness of the foreign policy of the Fifteen is above all spinelessness.... What do the Fifteen lack? The response is self-evident: a political project and a common vision." Laurent Zecchini, "The Hang-Ups of 'Europe as a Power,'" *Le Monde*, April 20, 2001. Such complaints became widespread in Europe after 9/11, which highlighted the contrast between America's single-minded focus and Europe's lack of strategic purpose even in the Middle East, a region right next to Europe.

7   Typical was the violent denunciation of the United States in the official organ of the Chinese Communist Party's Central Committee (CCP-CC), *Renmin Ribao*, April 20, 2001, which asserted that "US forces are continually making trouble all over the world, posing a tremendous threat to global peace and stability," while singing "a gangster's tune." Quite revealing of the change was a public polemic about American policy, which appeared in the same official organ almost a year later, on March 23, 2002. When one author made the case that America is exploiting the war against terrorism in order to retain its global supremacy, he was taken to task by another who asserted that the American "mainstream moves toward mutual cooperation and trust" in U.S.-PRC relations. Another example of a sober analysis of the U.S.-PRC relationship, entitled "Five Great Differences between China and the United States Must Be Properly Handled," appeared in *Wen Wei Po*, a PRC-owned daily in Hong Kong, February 21, 2002.

8   It is noteworthy that Japan has resolved to deploy a two-tiered missile defense network, comprising sea-based (SM3) and land-based (PAC3) interceptor missiles and requiring at least eight Aegis destroyers. Its cost could range from 500 billion to more than 1 trillion yen (roughly $4.2 billion to $8.4 billion). Editorial, "Japan Firms Up Policy to Deploy Missile Defense by Fiscal 2006," *Sankei Shimbun*, June 23, 2003.

9   Among the numerous examples of the case being made to the above effect, one may cite *Jiefangjun Bao* of February 12, 1999, discussing Japan's missile technology; *Renmin Ribao*, December 11, 2000, focusing on the overall size of the Japanese defense establishment and its large budget; *Liaowang* (a general affairs weekly journal of the Chinese official news agency) of June 17, 2002, stressing the nuclear issue.

10   As reported by Monique Chu, "Taiwan and Japan 'Silent Allies'," *Taipei Times*, July 24, 2001.

11   See Pang Zhongying, "A Discussion on the U.S. Factor in Sino-Japanese Relations (Part 2)," *Renmin Wang*, (Internet organ of the CCP-CC), April 23, 2002.

12   Keizo Takemi, as quoted by *Sankei Shimbun*, December 27, 2001. A Japanese private sector conference, much in keeping with the foregoing, recommended that a "National Strategy Council" be set up under the Cabinet Office to help develop plans for a more effective Japanese response to international emergencies, and that it be paralleled by a "Japan-US Strategic Conference" of officials and leaders of the private sector "for the purpose of expanding the Japan-US alliance relationship." See Editorial, *Sankei Shimbun*, March 10, 2002. Japanese public opinion polls have also been indicating that, despite support for some changes in the Japanese constitution, a large majority (even among those who support some changes) remains in favor of keeping Article 9, which renounces Japan's right to engage in war.

13   A study by the Chinese Academy of Sciences released to the public in March 2001 concluded that China will become only a "moderately developed" country by 2050.

14   Since 1993, China has become an increasingly significant oil importer, with its current 20 percent reliance on foreign imports likely to rise to over 40 percent by 2010, exceeding Japan's oil imports in volume. See "The Situation Facing China's Petroleum Security," *Ta Kung Pao*, November 10, 2000. The resulting sense of vulnerability has led China to consider the creation of an ambitious national strategic oil reserve system. See "Invest \$100 Billion in Building Strategic Oil System," *Ta Kung Pao*, November 13, 2002.

15   Per reports in *South China Morning Post*, July 27, 2001, and July 8, 2002. To be sure, this might simply reflect a lack of Chinese sites, or a lack of sites of a certain type, such as news outlets, relative to Japan and other countries.

16   According to the lengthy report entitled "A Political Issue that Should Be Seriously Studied," *Renmin Ribao*, May 31, 2001.

17   Reports of Chinese studies reviewed in *South China Morning Post*, June 20, 2001, and January 7, 2002. Using the Gini coefficient, an international measure of income inequality on a scale of 0.0 to 1.0 (the higher the number, the greater the inequality), 0.4 represents a dangerous level; by 2002, urban-rural inequality in China had reached 0.59, a level that poses a threat to societal stability. To put this in perspective, in 2002 Brazil had a Gini coefficient of 0.607. The change in this indicator over the past two decades might correlate with people's discomfort with the emergence of sudden

wealth for a few, in a society with an egalitarian ideology—especially if corruption is known to be widespread.

18   Fu Ying (director of the Asian Affairs Department in the Ministry of Foreign Affairs), "China and Asia in the New Period," *Ta Kung Pao*, January 11, 2003. She also noted that "The U.S. presence in this region is an objective reality formed through history."

19   "The European public, for weeks, has been loudly expressing itself....This public does not speak the same language, though. It speaks Spanish, French, Italian, English, German, or Polish....a large majority comes to the same conclusion: the Iraq war, which is waged and led by the United States, is illegal and dangerous....Perhaps, in 10 or 20 years, people will remember that it was in the spring of 2003 that the preamble for a European Constitution was written in the streets and squares of Europe." See Editorial, "So Students, Come Rally," *Sueddeutsche Zeitung*, March 26, 2003.

20   Zhang Xizhen and Zhuang Jin, "Another Great Move in China's Diplomacy (Specialist Evaluation)," *Renmin Ribao* (official newspaper of the Chinese Communist Party's Central Committee), October 9, 2003.

21   See Editorial, "ASEAN-Plus-Three; Need to Guard against China's Lead Role," *Sankei Shimbun*, November 5, 2002. The editorial went on to call upon Japan "to cooperate with countries outside the region...to prevent Asian regionalism led by China." See also Editorial, "Year to Exercise Major Option – Abandon 'Inactivism,'" *Sankei Shimbun*, January 1, 2003.

22   Though still a minority phenomenon, one senses the rise in both countries of feelings of greater affinity for Asia and some restlessness about the respective country's current status. In South Korea, this nascent mood expresses itself through more explicit affirmations of an all-Korean identity; in Japan, through emphasis on a Japan that should stand more on its own feet and play a more active Asian role. Public opinion polls in Japan, conducted in 2001 by the Cabinet Office and in early 2002 by *Asahi Shimbun*, indicated a strong public preference for Japanese economic aid to be targeted primarily at other Asian nations. The latter polls also reported a high degree of preference among Japanese, South Koreans, and Chinese for closer regional collaboration. E.g., in an Internet survey of fifty-six "New Asian Leaders" (as designated by the World Economic Forum), more than half thought that more economic cooperation in Asia is desirable, and almost two-thirds considered either an ASEAN+3 (China, Japan, Korea) or an ASEAN+4 (China, Japan, Korea, India) configuration to be the most desirable model for integration. See So Chi-yon, "Korea to Become Research Base for Asia," *The Korea Times*, June 21, 2003.

PART II:

AMERICAN HEGEMONY AND THE COMMON GOOD

America's world role is derived from the two new central realities of our time: unprecedented American global power and unprecedented global interaction. The former signals a unipolar moment in the history of international affairs, with American hegemony—whether boastfully declared or subtly exercised—currently a worldwide reality. The latter validates the notion that a universal (though perhaps not entirely benign) process of "globalization" is gradually stripping nation-states of their hallowed sovereignty. The combination of the two is producing a far-reaching transformation of international affairs, prompting not only the death of traditional diplomacy but, more importantly, the birth of an informal global community.

The transformation is both symbolically and visibly expressed by the de facto appearance of the first-ever global capital. That capital city, however, is not New York, the place where the General Assembly of all nation-states periodically convenes. New York might have become the capital if the world's new order had emerged on the basis of comprehensive collaboration among nation-states, based on the legal fiction of equal sovereignty. But such a world did not come to pass, and indeed the very notion has become an anachronism given the new realities of transnational globalization and of the historically unique scope of sovereign American power.

And yet a global capital did emerge, not between the Hudson and East rivers but on the banks of the Potomac. Washington, D.C., is the first global political capital in the history of the world. Neither Rome nor ancient Peking—both the capitals of regional empires—nor Victorian London (except perhaps in international banking) even came close to matching the concentration of global power and decision-making in a few square blocks of downtown Washington. Decisions made within two overlapping but relatively tight triangles project U.S. power worldwide and heavily influence the way globalization evolves. A line drawn from the White House to the monumental Capitol build-ing, to the fort-like Pentagon, and then back to the White House encapsulates the triangle of power. Another line from the White House to the World Bank just a few blocks away, to the State Department, and back to the White House (thus also encompassing the International Monetary Fund and the Organization of American States) demarcates the triangle of global influence. The two triangles together signal the degree to which traditional "foreign affairs" have become inside-the-beltway affairs.

Nowadays, the outstanding political event in the foreign affairs of most states is a visit by their head of state to Washington. This is treated by their national media as a historic occasion, with the visiting dignitary's every step reported in minute detail. A foreign ambassador feels he has scored a lifetime career coup if he gains for his president a half-hour audience with the U.S. president. More often than not, the most that is granted is a five-minute photo opportunity in the Oval Office, which can then be reported in the home media (without any reference to its actual duration) as a historically significant encounter.[1] Since, on average, leaders of foreign governments now visit the global capital at least once a week, the overwhelming majority are altogether ignored by the national U.S. and even local Washington media.

A distinguished Italian friend of America caught the essence of this development when he noted how "The Franco-Belgian writer Marguerite Yourcenar, author of the enchanting novel *Memoires of Hadrian*, has the aging Roman emperor reminisce about a journey to Greece during his youth." Yourcenar wrote:

> In the midst of the studious life of Athens, where all pleasures, too, received their due, I regretted not Rome itself but the atmosphere of that place where the business of the world is continually done and undone, where are heard the pulleys and gears in the machine of governmental power....Compared with that world of immediate action, the beloved Greek province seemed to me to be slumbering in a haze of ideas seldom stirred by change, and the political passivity of the Hellenes appeared a somewhat servile form of renunciation.

The Italian observer adds: "These words used to spring repeatedly to the minds of frequent visitors to Washington, like the author of this article, a European from Rome."[2]

To note the foregoing is not to indulge the arrogance of American power. It is to acknowledge America's centrality in world affairs and the concentration in Washington of global institutions that reflect the historical marriage between U.S. global power and global interdependence in the age of instant communications. Traditional diplomacy, conducted by "ambassadors extraordinary and plenipotentiary," minutely instructed by their respective foreign ministers (often relying on elegant aristocrats with foreign language skills), has been replaced by a globe-spanning and instantly interactive process largely centered on Washington. Direct telephone conversations between heads of state as well as foreign ministers, helped by simultaneous translation, are now a daily occurrence. Consultations by closed-circuit television are becoming frequent. Direct official dialogue with a variety of U.S. or international agencies located in the global capital is now routine for senior foreign government officials all over the world.

This new reality is reflected in the increasing personal bonds that foreign political and business leaders have with America. Many of them have attended American universities. A period of study at a leading American graduate school has lately become almost a social requirement among the elite, even of countries, such as France, with a strong intellectual tradition and high national pride. It is only a matter of time before that practice is also emulated by such until-recently isolated societies as Russia and China. This phenomenon is even more widespread among the international business elite and the officialdom of the large global financial institutions located in the United States. Meetings of such prestigious organizations as the Trilateral Commission (an elite North American, East Asian, and European NGO) are increasingly reminiscent of college reunions.

A concomitant but more general phenomenon is the appearance of a distinct global elite with a globalist outlook and a transnational loyalty. Fluent in English (usually in its American idiom) and using that language to conduct its business, the new global elite is characterized by high mobility, a cosmopolitan lifestyle, and a primary commitment to the workplace, typically a transnational business or financial corporation. Non-native senior executives within such firms are now common, with 20 percent of Europe's largest companies even directed by individuals who once would have been considered foreigners. The annual meeting of the World Economic Forum has become, in effect, a party congress for the new global elite: top politicians, financial tycoons, captains of commerce, media moguls, academic heavyweights, and even rock stars. That elite increasingly displays its own distinctive sense of interest, camaraderie, and identity.[3]

This elite is fostering the emergence of a global community of shared interest in stability, prosperity, and perhaps eventually democracy. Its focus on America is a tacit acknowledgment that even a global community needs a central clearinghouse for ideas and interests, a focal point for crystallizing some form of consensus, a source of consequential initiative, and ultimately of a sense of direction. Even if it does not entail any formal recognition of Washington's special status as the global capital, the focus on America is a bow to the twin realities of our time, that of one nation's power and that of transnational globalization.

This unprecedented combination, however, involves two crucial tensions, maybe even contradictions: first, between the dynamics of globalization and America's self-interest in preserving its political sovereignty, and second, between America's democratic impulses and the imperatives of power. America proclaims the benign and globally shared benefits of globalization but respects its rules mainly when expedient. It rarely acknowledges that globalization expands and cements its own national advantage—even as it breeds a seething and potentially dangerous worldwide resentment. Likewise, America's global power grates against American democracy, both domestic and exported. America's domestic democracy complicates the external exercise of the nation's power, while conversely America's global power could threaten its democracy at home. Moreover, America views itself as the historical champion of democracy, and subliminally exports democratic values through the currents of globalization—but this also generates worldwide expectations of America that do not accommodate the hierarchical demands of hegemonic power. As a result of this dual dialectic, America has still to give a meaningful definition to its role in the world, one that transcends the conflicting pulls of globalization, democracy, and preponderant power.

In the recent past, America's role was easier to define in a politically comprehensible and appealing fashion. The country emerged from the wreckage of World War II uniquely unscathed and more powerful than ever. Among the victors, it alone was untouched and economically more powerful than at the war's outset. But it was not yet globally dominant. In the military realm and even more in the important domain of political appeal, the United States faced a formidable challenger: the likewise victorious, militarily powerful, and ideologically belligerent Soviet Union.

Relations with the Soviet Union thus became the defining issue in U.S. foreign policy. This was not initially self-evident to the

American foreign policy elite, whose illusions about an enduring post-war coalition among the major victors lingered for several years. Moreover, the decline of the British Empire was initially obscured by vivid recollections of the wartime "Big Three" communing together in Teheran and Yalta, and dividing the spoils of victory in Potsdam after Germany's defeat. But before long it became apparent that the key postwar issue was whether U.S. relations with Russia would continue to be derived from a sense of partnership or degenerate into open conflict.

By 1950, the only question was whether the political conflict with the Soviet Union would erupt into total warfare. As a result, for the next four decades, American global engagement had a clear purpose: to deter the Soviet Union from attempting armed expansion and to defeat its ideological appeal. The policy was global in scope but regional in focus, with a heavy emphasis on the Atlantic Alliance to contain the new communist empire.

The strategy was comprehensive and realistic in that it balanced the political and military dimensions. It emphasized political unity among the democracies and military deterrence of the enemy. It stressed freedom (and, for a while, even "liberation") as the key issue, and calls for human rights eventually became a powerful tool for undermining the communist rival from within. It combined American leadership with a recognition of the importance of allies. In a conflicted world of nation-states, it promoted political interdependence, recognizing the new reality of competitive transnational ideologies and of an increasingly interactive global economy. Most important, it prevailed.

Since 1990, in the course of a mere decade, the United States has articulated three major themes as the new defining principles of its engagement with the world. Under President George H.W. Bush, they were encapsulated by three words: New World Order. In some respects, the concept was reminiscent of the illusion harbored briefly after 1945 that the World War II coalition would serve as the pillar of a more peaceful and cooperative world order under the aegis of the newly established UN. The "New World Order" of the 1990s was similarly premised on a false hope: that America's Cold War victory would usher in a new global system based on legitimacy and contagious democracy. On occasion—such as on March 6, 1991, when addressing the Congress—President Bush would wax almost lyrical: "Now, we can see a new world coming into view. A world in which there is the very real prospect of a new world order....A world where the United Nations, freed from the Cold War stalemate, is poised to fulfill the historic vision of its founders. A world in which freedom and respect for human rights find a home among all nations."

Although President Bill Clinton shared that optimistic premise, he emphasized the primacy of the economic-technological revolution in shaping a world with fewer and more porous borders, with greater economic interdependence and lesser reliance on political power. To him, the issue was not so much a new world order as it was the (supposedly) benign dynamics of globalization. "It's the central reality of our time," Clinton declared to Congress on January 27, 2000. He saw in this novel phenomenon the key hope for humanity and a great opportunity for America as its standard bearer, key promoter, and major beneficiary. Globalization became Clinton's pet concept.

Both Bush Sr. and Clinton, however, underestimated the intensity of the percolating global turmoil that the protracted conflict with the Soviet Union had obscured. That turmoil—derived from national and religious conflicts and intensified by mounting social impatience with various forms of inequality or oppression—had quietly festered for a long time, only to break into the open with the Cold War's end. The hopeful visions of either a new world order or globally benign cooperation died a violent death on September 11, 2001.

Within a year, the next U.S. president, George W. Bush, articulated a more ominous vision of the future with yet a new defining concept for U.S. foreign policy: global hegemony at war with terrorism. Notions of a cooperative world order gave way to concern about "terrorism with a global reach." America-spearheaded globalization yielded to America-led "coalitions of the willing," with a Manichean "who is not with us is against us" formula serving as the global line in the sand. The administration's 2002 NSC policy statement declared both its determination to maintain America's military superiority over any other power and its claim to a special strategic right to preempt threats by military action.

Yet President Bush, even if dismissive of multilateralism and less sanguine about the global condition than his predecessors, had to recognize that American power was now being wielded in the context of an incipient global community. He placed more emphasis on the global threats facing America, but he also acknowledged the basic reality of worldwide interdependence. How to strike a balance between sovereign hegemony and an emerging global community, and how to resolve the dangerous contradiction between the values of democracy and the imperatives of global power, thus remains America's dilemma in the age of globalization.

NOTES

1   Each U.S. president also puts a personal stamp on how the more important visitors are treated. An informal protocol that emerged under President George W. Bush had the following gradations: a 30-minute meeting in the Oval Office signified serious consideration for the visitor or his country; a state dinner was reserved for special national relationships (there were only two in the first two years of the Bush administration, one for the president of Mexico and one for Poland); a meeting at Camp David (with ostentatious informality) signaled a personal closeness to the U.S. president (e.g., with Prime Minister Blair); to be hosted by Bush at his ranch in Crawford, Texas, indicated both the recognition of the importance of the visitor's country and his personal standing with the U.S. president (e.g., in addition to Blair, also Jiang of China, Abdullah of Saudi Arabia, Putin of Russia).

2   Cesare Merlini, "US Hegemony and the Roman Analogy: A European View," *The International Spectator*, no. 3 (2002), 19.

3 It has been estimated that this gathering brings together globalist business leaders who collectively control more than 70 percent of international trade. See Jenni Russell, "Where the Elite Preens Itself," *New Statesman*, January 28, 2002.

4

THE DILEMMAS OF GLOBALIZATION

For America, the buzzword "globalization" has contradictory implications. It has come to signify the onset of a novel age of worldwide accessibility, transparency, and cooperation—yet it also provides a symbol of the moral obtuseness and indifference to social injustice alleged to characterize the world's wealthiest countries, the United States in particular.

Originally, the term *globalization* emerged as a neutral description of a process that is inherent in the worldwide effects of the technological revolution. A helpful definition was offered in 2000 by Professor Charles Doran, who summed up the phenomenon as "the interaction of information technology and the global economy. It is indexed in terms of the intensity, scope, volume and value of international transactions in the informational, financial, commercial, trade and administrative spheres worldwide. A sharp increase in the rate of these transactions in the last decade, and therefore in their level, is the most measurable manifestation of the process of globalization."[1] Note the reference to "measurable" aspects of globalization, which implies that the phenomenon is at least partly objective.

By 2001, however, the seemingly neutral economic term had already become an emotionally charged political prescription. At first, globalization meant a macroeconomic restructuring that reflected, on a global scale, the central experience of the Industrial Revolution at the national level: specialization and economies of scale generate comparative advantages that prompt the relocation of manufacturing to wherever labor-intensive production is most profitable, or to where relatively cheap skilled labor is readily available, or to where opportunities for advantageous innovation are most plentiful. No wonder China became the favored showcase for the proponents of globalization.

But during the Industrial Revolution, efficiencies of scale and comparative advantages operated within internally unrestricted economies. The world, by contrast, is still politically demarcated by nation-states, which can either comply with the pressures of globalization or seek to defy them. Globalization offers these states a mix of incentives. On one hand, it presents an opportunity for economic growth, the inflow of foreign capital, and the gradual reduction of widespread poverty. On the other hand, it often threatens massive dislocation, loss of national control over basic economic assets, and social exploitation. For a select group, it provides an opening to new markets and de facto political domination. The more technologically advanced, capital-rich, and innovative a country's economy, the more enthusiastic that country's national elite tend to be about the spread of globalization.

The concept of globalization has thus acquired several meanings and serves several purposes. The term all at once provides an allegedly objective diagnosis of world conditions; encapsulates a doctrinal preference; precipitates a counter-creed (or an antithesis) that rejects that preference; and generates a pointed political-cultural critique designed to alter the existing global power hierarchy. In every one of these manifestations, the concept of globalization serves as the defining feature of either empirical or normative reality. For some, it dissects what is; for others, it defines what ought to be; for others still, what ought not to be; and for many, it does all of this at the same time.

THE NATURAL DOCTRINE OF GLOBAL HEGEMONY

With the fall of communism and the associated illusion that it brought the end of ideological conflicts, globalization has become for America a convenient catchall and an appealing interpretation of the emerging global condition. It highlights the new reality of increasing global interdependence, driven largely by the new technologies of communications, with national frontiers more relevant as demarcating lines on maps than as real barriers to the free flow of trade and of financial capital. Presented in that light, globalization has spawned a cottage industry of books hailing the onset of a glorious new age (though often forgetting that the world prior to 1914 was at least as barrier-free to trade and capital flows, and more open to migration) and purporting to find in globalization the decisive essence of the twenty-first century's global condition.

Thus, for most of the American political and economic elite, globalization is not only an observable fact, but an explicit norm. It provides an interpretative mechanism as well as a normative prescription. It is not merely a diagnostic tool but also an action program. Together, in a systematized form, these aspects of globalization amount to a doctrine, based on a morally confident assertion of its historical inevitability.

It is symptomatic that globalization, in both its diagnostic and doctrinal meanings, has been embraced most enthusiastically by the major global corporations and financial institutions, which until recently preferred to label themselves "multinational." For them, the buzzword represents a great virtue: the transcendence of the traditional restrictions on worldwide economic activity that were inherent in the national era of modern history. Some of globalization's doctrinal boosters have made exuberant claims regarding not only its economic but even its allegedly automatic political benefits.[2]

Not surprisingly, during the 1990s globalization evolved from an economic theory into a national creed. Its advantages were expounded in voluminous scholarly texts, proclaimed at international business conferences, and promoted by the global financial and trade organizations.

The diagnostic function of the concept of globalization, and its seeming objectivity, capitalized on America's anti-ideological tradition much the way that the effort to repel communism had done earlier: by elevating the rejection of doctrine itself into an alternative doctrine. Globalization thus became the informal ideology of the U.S. political and business elite, defining America's role in the world and identifying America with the benefits of the postulated new era.

President Clinton was especially relentless in preaching the historical inevitability, social desirability, and need for American political leadership of mankind's march into the era of globalization. To audiences as diverse as the Russian Duma, the Vietnamese National University, and the World Economic Forum, not to mention countless American gatherings, Clinton proclaimed that:

> Globalization is not something we can hold off or turn off. It is the economic equivalent of a force of nature—like wind and water....we cannot ignore it—and it is not going away. (Vietnam National University, November 17, 2000)
>
> Today we must embrace the inexorable logic of globalization—that everything, from the strength of our economy to the safety of our cities, to the health of our people, depends on events not only within our borders, but half a world away. (San Francisco, February 26, 1999)
>
> Those who wish to roll back the forces of globalization because they fear its disruptive consequences I believe are plainly wrong. Fifty years of experience shows that greater economic integration and political cooperation are positive forces. Those who believe globalization is only about market economies, however, are wrong, too....We must recognize first that globalization has made us all more free and more interdependent. (World Economic Forum, January 29, 2000)

Like all countries, Russia also faces a very different world. Its defining feature is globalization. (The Russian Duma, June 5, 2000)

The train of globalization cannot be reversed....If we want America to stay on the right track...we have no choice but to try to lead the train. (University of Nebraska, December 8, 2000)

Once "globalization" had been popularized as the key to understanding the meaning of change in our time and to deciphering its historical direction, and once it came to be perceived as consonant with American interests, it became easy to view globalization as at once benign and inevitable. Even if not quite as complex and dogmatic as the Marxist ideology had been in responding to the rise of industrial capitalism, globalization became the fashionable ideology of the post-ideological age. It embodied all the makings of an ideology: it was historically timely, it appealed to the key power elites that shared common interests, it offered a critique of what ought to be rejected, and it postulated a better tomorrow.

In doing so, globalization filled a major gap in America's new status as the world's only superpower. International power, in both its political and economic dimensions—even if concentrated in one nation-state—still needs social legitimacy. That legitimacy is required both by the dominant and by the dominated. The former crave it because it gives them the self-confidence, the sense of mission, and the moral conviction to pursue their goals and to assert their interests. The latter need it to justify their acquiescence, to facilitate their accommodation, and to sustain their submission. Doctrinal legitimacy reduces the costs of the exercise of power by mitigating resentment on the part of those subject to it. To this end, globalization is the natural doctrine of global hegemony.

To state this is not to slight globalization's appeal to the idealist tradition in American political behavior. Though protective of its own sovereignty as a nation-state, American society has maintained a long-standing aversion to international power politics. Globalization, through its utopian aspiration to worldwide openness and cooperation, has effectively tapped that sentiment, thereby providing a political counterweight to the strongly felt reservations of much of America's organized labor. The latter's opposition to globalization—derived from the understandable fear that domestic jobs will be transferred abroad while America is de-industrialized[3]—increasingly came to be seen as an expression of anachronistic self-interest, bound to fade as America completes its transition to the post-industrial technetronic age.

Hostility toward globalization on the part of the trade unions as well as some domestic industries thus came to seem inward-looking and myopic when compared to a vision of a world without borders, a world in which the peaceful pursuit of personal economic well-being is not obstructed by narrow nationalism and its increasingly archaic state frontiers. In that vision, the domestic American experience—with its shifting, geographically unimpeded, market-driven patterns of economic activity—was taken to be universal and was simply projected outward to the globe as a whole, with the paradoxical effect that the insistently sovereign American nation-state became the passionate propagator of the economic doctrine that would make sovereignty obsolete.

Moreover, the idealistic case for globalization was reinforced by some of its undeniably genuine benefits. By and large, the multinationals have tended to be relatively sensitive to the impropriety of exploiting child labor, a practice traditionally widespread in many of the underdeveloped and most impoverished states. While drawn to markets with available cheap labor, Western companies cannot ignore the risk of public disapproval of their practices by consumers in the more advanced countries. Thus they have largely eschewed child labor. In addition, by offering employment at somewhat higher wages than was locally customary, global companies have marginally contributed to a reduction of poverty—most notably in China, which has attracted the highest amounts of foreign direct investment. A few multinationals have gone farther and even actively embraced social responsibility. In some cases, the opening of borders to foreign companies has also arguably prompted somewhat heightened ecological sensitivity in contrast to long-established local indifference.

Of the foregoing, most significant in its social and political consequences is the contention that globalization has contributed to a noticeable diminution in worldwide poverty. Though the matter is contested among economists, it would appear that the proportion of the very poor (those living on $1/day PPP or less) lately has somewhat declined, both as a percentage of world population and in actual total numbers. Again, however, this positive trend is distorted by the special case of China, with other major parts of the Third World benefiting less.[4]

Whether the decline in the world's most acute poverty cumulatively reduces global inequality, or whether globalization instead actually furthers inequality by delivering its benefits disproportionately to the rich countries, is a hotly contested issue. In the final analysis, the claim that globalization helps to close the gap between the rich and the poor, or at least helps to make the poor better off than they otherwise could have been, represents the central moral case on its behalf. It also follows (as noted in the next section) that the case against globalization rejects this claim at its core, arguing either that globalization is a very mixed blessing or that it is purely and simply a doctrine of exploitative Western, specifically American, imperialism.

Be that as it may, for the United States in its new role as the dominant world power, globalization as a doctrine provides a useful frame of reference for defining both the contemporary world and America's relationship to it. It has the force of intellectual simplicity, offering easy comprehension of the complexities of the post-industrial and post-national age: Open access to the world economy is seen as the natural and imperative consequence of new technologies, with the World Trade Organization (WTO), the World Bank, and the International Monetary Fund (IMF) serving as institutional expressions of that fact on a global scale. The free market should be global in scale, and then let the brave and the industrious compete. Countries should be assessed not only by the degree of their internal democracy but also by how globalized they have become.

The appeal of an ideology comes not only from its vision of the future, but from its compelling myths about the present. The latter legitimate the former by providing credible reinforcement. Globalization offers several such myths. One pertains to post-Soviet Russia. Much of the U.S. policy toward Russia during the Clinton presidency was infused with mechanistic and even dogmatic notions derived from the doctrinal definition of globalization. The administration often proclaimed its assumption that the more Russia adopted the principles of the market-driven and interdependent globalized economy, the more its politics would come to partake of "universal" standards, measured by Western experience.

Therefore, almost in a deterministic Marxist fashion, the growth of democracy in Russia was expected to be largely a product of market forces rather than an outgrowth of deeper philosophical or spiritual values. The "election" of President Putin was even proclaimed by Clinton's top Russia expert as the culminating proof that democracy in Russia had become a fact. Unfortunately, Russia's subsequent retrogression from the standards of an open society and genuine democracy encapsulated some of the risks inherent in reducing the complex processes of globalization to pat formulas.

China as a showcase of globalization generates another myth. Unlike the case of Russia, American expectations of China have been confined largely to the economic domain. No official claims were made that an automatic connection between globalization and democracy was bringing China to the brink of a democratic era. Nevertheless, China has been widely cited as a globalization success story—a model of rapid economic development achieved by internal liberalization and openness to external capital. That combination did in fact generate remarkably high and sustained economic growth, and it created the preconditions for China's entry into the World Trade Organization, a major step forward in its progressive globalization. These accomplishments, however, took place under a highly authoritarian state, with an economy still heavily dominated by the state-owned sector and national frontiers that are at best only selectively porous. In essence, China's economic success falls less under the banner of globalization than of enlightened dictatorship.

Perhaps the most widespread claim among globalization's proponents in the world of business is that it promotes an open and level playing field for competitive economic activity. Just as the myth of the classless society was an important component of communist ideology (notwithstanding the highly stratified Soviet reality), so the notion that globalization promotes equitable competitive opportunity for all players is an important source of the new doctrine's historical legitimacy, irrespective of the reality.

That reality, inevitably, is more ambiguous. Some states are obviously more equal than others. It is unavoidable that the richer, stronger, and more advanced states are in a favored position to dominate the game—especially America. Whether in the WTO, the World Bank, or the IMF, the United States has by far the loudest voice.[5] There is thus a perfect fit between global hegemony and economic globalization: the United States can promote an open global system while largely defining the system's rules and choosing for itself how dependent on the system it wishes to be.

America's advantages are many. The sheer size of the American market, with the U.S. consumption of world manufactures by far outstripping that of any other country, gives its trade negotiators a potent bargaining tool. At the same time, the American economy is the globe's most innovative and most competitive (in 2002, it was again ranked first in both the Growth Competitiveness Index and the Microeconomic Competitiveness Index, formulated annually by the World Economic Forum). The United States spends more on R&D, and constitutes a considerably higher percentage of the global high-tech market, than any other state. American multinationals directly control several trillion dollars in foreign assets, while the American economy—so much larger and more diverse than any other—is the locomotive for the global economy.

No wonder, then, that the United States can formally assert that it is not bound to change its laws, lower its trade barriers, or compensate a foreign country in keeping with WTO provisions.[6] For domestic political reasons, the United States has adamantly maintained high protectionist barriers for agricultural products and imposed stiff quotas on steel and textile imports from poorer countries that desperately need access to the American market. The developing countries keep pleading that America lower its trade barriers, but lack the clout to make themselves heard.

The level playing field is a reality only between the United States and the European Union. When the two agree, together they can dictate to the entire world the rules governing global trade and finance. When they disagree, it becomes truly a heavyweight contest. At one point, for example, the EU mounted a charge that U.S. Internal Revenue codes were prejudiced in favor of American business interests. The United States at first simply disregarded the issue, but when the EU threatened to impose countermeasures and to suspend concessions in excess of $4 billion, the United States promptly requested WTO arbitration. Even when contending with the EU, however, the United States can play up its relationship with its Asian trading partners as leverage to obtain greater European accommodation of American desires.

Thus the "level" playing field is slanted whenever American interests are at stake. Moreover, America—unlike the EU, its economic peer—possesses massive military assets, and the combination of military and economic prowess generates unmatched political influence. That influence can then be engaged to advance American interests in a manner that blends a commitment to economic globalization (because it is economically convenient) with strong insistence on American state sovereignty (whenever politically expedient). Power permits America, right or wrong, to transcend the apparent inconsistency.

Not surprisingly, self-serving doctrines tend to be applied selectively, and this inconsistency also applies to the related issue of multilateralism. The Clinton administration, despite its embrace of globalization as America's key defining concept, decided for political reasons not to implement the Kyoto Protocol, which it had signed in 1998. It ultimately did not reach an agreement on containing global warming and signed the politically controversial treaty on the International Criminal Court only with reservations requiring Senate modifications. The subsequent Bush administration translated these hesitations into outright opposition. To the world at large, the message was clear: When an international arrangement collides with American hegemony and could inhibit American sovereignty, the U.S. commitment to globalization and multilateralism has strict limits.

Finally, the very scale of America's dominance means that the new phenomenon of economic globalization is almost automatically viewed worldwide as the flip side of the universal appeal of America's mass culture. In fact, globalization is more the result of modern technology's unguided breaking down of the traditional barriers of time and space than of any deliberate American doctrinal design. Still, the historical coincidence of an emerging interactive global community and a politically dominant, economically dynamic, and culturally magnetic nation is fusing the phenomena of globalization and Americanization together.

The "Made in the USA" label is thus quite visibly and unavoidably imprinted on globalization. Globalization as the natural doctrine of the world's hegemon ultimately both reflects and projects its national origin. Without a national base, globalization—even if the term would appeal to some as an analytical concept—would not be a politically powerful and internationally controversial doctrine. It becomes such only when institutionalized, just as religion became powerful when embodied in a church, or communism when identified with the Soviet system. Symbiosis with an established and powerful reality becomes, for better or worse, integral to a doctrine's identity.

THE TARGET OF COUNTER-SYMBOLIZATION

Consequently, globalization fosters an intense anti-Americanism, largely because of the widespread perception that globalization is a vehicle not only for socioeconomic change but for cultural homogenization and political domination. The doctrine of globalization thereby generates its own antithesis, with the perceived fusion of globalization with Americanization serving as a catalyst for the emergence of a counter-creed that is simultaneously anti-globalist (in effect opposed to U.S. political primacy) and anti-globalization (critical of the economic and cultural effects of globalization as such).

Victory in the Cold War left America standing astride the world. Not only was it dominant, but no globally appealing and intellectually comprehensive indictment of the American system was readily available. The "historical inevitability of mankind's march toward communism"—a Marxist claim that had stood through most of the messy twentieth century—had been dramatically refuted by the Soviet bloc's disintegration. The popular case against capitalism had collapsed: capitalism proved to be both more productive and more rewarding than socialism. Even Communist China was now seeking to preserve "communist" political rule by practicing capitalism. Democracy and the free market had no peer. Some argued that the end of history had come.

But history was not ended for long. Precisely because the moral content of globalization is at best vague and its most enthusiastic proponents' sensitivity to issues of social justice not always evident[7], it soon proved tempting for some to stigmatize globalization as the new universal doctrine of exploitation. Seen by its critics as morally neutral and spiritually empty, globalization has been charged with being the new ideology of supreme materialism, even more so than Marxism. It has been parodied as the self-serving doctrine of the corporate boardroom, lacking any concern for social justice, patriotism, morality, ethics.

That indictment reinvigorated both recidivist and disillusioned Marxists, appealed to populists and anarchists, environmentalists and ecologists, and attracted spiritually motivated cultists and chauvinistic rightists, not to mention the more serious skeptics—on the economic and even the theological levels—of globalization's allegedly automatic benefits. The outbreaks of violence in the first years of the twenty-first century at the WTO meeting in Seattle, at the World Bank meeting in

Washington, and at the IMF meeting in Prague, and elsewhere, were early warning signs that a counter-creed was emerging.

Counter-symbolization is a known phenomenon in politics. It occurs when a weaker party adopts (at least outwardly) the values and the rules of the game practiced by the stronger—and then turns them against the stronger. The classic example is the successful mobilization of the Hindu masses by Mahatma Gandhi's Congress Party, which used peaceful civil disobedience and an appeal to British liberalism to gain British political sympathy and to disarm the British rulers' opposition to India's national emancipation. The civil rights movement in America ultimately prevailed by adopting tactics that were congenial to American constitutional traditions. In Poland, Solidarity prevailed over the Soviet-imposed Communist regime by first mobilizing "the proletariat" on behalf of workers' rights before openly seeking national emancipation. One of the major failings of the Palestine Liberation Organization is that it never consistently pursued such counter-symbolization in order to gain Israeli sympathy for its efforts to win Palestinian emancipation from Israel.

The rejection of globalization similarly involves an effort to counter-symbolize issues that are central to globalization's historical appeal: the degree to which globalization is driven (or not) by moral impulses that truly seek to improve the human condition, and the factual record of its economic performance as an upward social equalizer of a world in which economic disparities increasingly coexist with heightened awareness and resentment. In brief, anti-globalization has been evolving intellectually from a vague sentiment into a counter-creed, reinforced emotionally by anti-Americanism.

As such, it is filling the void left by the collapse of communism. The new counter-creed focuses intellectual attention simultaneously on the world's central political and economic realities, namely, hegemony and globalization, and offers a critique of both. It also harnesses a variety of resentments directed especially against America, and vaguely alludes to an alternative vision of the future. Though neither as systematic as Marxism nor as comprehensively developed, it similarly appeals to both feelings and reason.

The new counter-creed also derives some of its momentum from a fundamental difference between the usually pragmatic promoters of globalization and their generally more passionate opponents. Sociopolitical militancy tends to be activated less by materialistic impulses than by vague but intense feelings of social injustice. Communism gained its first historical dynamism from such a sentiment, and it took seventy years of hypocritical Soviet experience to discredit its appeal. To the extent that globalization has come to be perceived as driven by the free market, it tends also to be perceived by its detractors as anti-humanistic and avaricious. On its more extreme fringes, the counter-creed attracts those whose dogmatic self-righteousness and intense idealism are capable of rationalizing violent political passions.[8]

To justify their professed outrage, the critics of globalization have at times sought to exploit cautious and morally motivated reservations regarding unbridled capitalism that have been voiced by the Papacy since the late nineteenth century. In more recent times, Pope John XXIII focused in his 1961 encyclical *Mater et Magistra* on "an increase in social relationships" inherent in the modern world, which in his view called for more attention to "socialization." That reference (and especially that word) was widely interpreted as conveying a fundamental critique of capitalism. Forty years later, Pope John Paul II, in his April 27 address to the Pontifical Academy of Social Sciences, stressed "that globalization, like any other system, must be at the service of the human person; it must serve solidarity and the common good." He warned that "changes in technology and work relationships are moving too quickly for cultures to respond," and he urged mankind to "respect the diversity of cultures." Although the Pope was careful to note that "globalization, *a priori*, is neither good nor bad. It will be what people make of it," his concerns underlined wide-ranging unease regarding the basic impulses motivating the case for globalization.

The emerging counter-creed, while inspired by a variety of misgivings, still lacks a central theorist and a formally stated doctrine. It is thus an ideology in the making, but as such it already partakes of some shared premises. Apart from serious scholarly critiques of globalization as an economic theory, the views of Pierre Bourdieu, the popular French sociologist who died in 2002, have been especially influential in systematizing the counter-creed's views. Bourdieu rested his indictment of globalization on a central premise—"unification profits the dominant"—and argued that the world market is a political creation, "the product of more or less consciously planned politics." He left his admirers in no doubt as to who was doing the planning.

> The model of an economy rooted in the historical particularities of a tradition of a particular society, that of American society, finds itself established simultaneously as inevitable destiny and political project of universal liberation, as the end of *a natural evolution* and as a civic and ethical ideal that, in the name of a postulated link between democracy and the market, promises political emancipation to the people of all lands.
>
> What is proposed and imposed in a universal manner as the standard of all rational economic practice is in reality the universalization of particular characteristics of one economy immersed in a particular history and social structure, that of the United States.[9]

It follows that to the subscribers of the new creed, globalization "is not an expression of evolution" produced by modern technology, but "was designed and created by human beings with a specific goal: to give primacy to economic—that is, corporate—values above all other values."[10] Globalization thus represents the universal imperialism of the economically most competitive and politically most powerful: above all, the United States.

But not exclusively the United States. Opposition to globalization on the grounds that it favors the powerful and privileged may also draw sustenance from a very specific condition peculiar to several parts of the underdeveloped world: the economic and financial dominance of rich minorities. In the words of a perceptive observer of globalization, it has not been sufficiently noted that in a number of places "Markets concentrate enormous wealth in the hands of an 'outsider' minority...fomenting ethnic envy and hatred among often chronically poor majorities."[11] These minorities, because of superior education and wider contacts, are in a much better position to attract foreign investment and to become partners for foreign businesses. Globalization thus helps them to maximize their privileged position. The result is to exacerbate ethnic inequality and spark further ethnic tensions. The painful reality is that the economic privilege of an ethnic minority is a very combustible political condition; ethnic envy can become a powerful xenophobic force, generating hostility to the perceived unfairness of globalization's effects.

Not surprisingly, the assault on globalization, and particularly on its connection to America, also has a powerful cultural motif. According to the critics, in addition to promoting globalization for selfish economic and political reasons, America is engaging in self-serving cultural imperialism. Indeed, these critics see globalization as synonymous with Americanization: the imposition on other nations of the American way of life, leading to the progressive cultural homogenization of the world on the American mode. This politically demonizing charge is reminiscent of the French communists' slogan that the United States was engaged in the "Coca-Colonization" of the world.

The cultural indictment injects a highly contentious ideological issue into the debate. It not only attracts a broad coalition of anti-globalization ideologues, but mobilizes important support from the elites of some key states, notably France and Russia.

For the French political and intellectual elite, the current American global preponderance—even if tolerated as a necessary evil for the sake of international security—represents a form of cultural hegemony. Many of them view globalization as an America-propagated design for the dissemination of a mass culture that is pervasively and perniciously undermining individual national heritages. That prospect is truly abhorrent to an elite that not only is inordinately proud of its own heritage but views it also as universally pertinent. Its cultural self-defense against the supposedly vulgarizing and homogenizing consequences of globalization, therefore, almost inevitably takes an anti-American stance.

French concerns that globalization equals homogenization are stated openly and often. In almost every walk of life, the manifestations of globalization are assessed by the degree to which they coincide with the contagious menace of American culture. That menace is said to range from the spread of the English language as the lingua franca of the globalized world—whether it be in air traffic control or as the operational language of the international bureaucracies—to the threat posed to French culinary traditions by America-fostered reliance on allegedly anti-human genetic engineering in agriculture and animal husbandry.

France and America both, to be sure, value their historic friendship based on a genuinely shared (and tested) commitment to democratic values. Nonetheless, the waning of the old Marxist challenge has been followed by new Franco-American cultural tensions that have permeated even the official dialogue. In 2000, for example, at the U.S.-sponsored meeting in Warsaw of the "Community of Democratic States" (attended by the foreign ministers of more than 100 states), the sitting French foreign minister forcefully argued that the American way of advancing global democracy did not harmonize with the need to respect international cultural diversity. He urged the assembled to avoid the temptation to "equate universalism with forced Westernization," and deplored "the dominance of the Anglo-American version of free-market politics."[12]

Such criticism by the French has given anti-globalization an elegant intellectual veneer. The Russian elite, meanwhile, has increasingly offered a more antagonistic political definition of the emerging counter-creed. Much of that elite is instinctively anti-American, but it lacks a systematic formulation that would justify and channel its hostility. It understandably regrets Moscow's fall from the top of the global hierarchy and resents America's exclusive perch on it. Communism is discredited and there is no return to it; this elementary fact most of the Russian elite realize. Reliance on nationalism, not to speak of chauvinism, can facilitate domestic political mobilization, but cannot gain Russia external allies. It would be difficult—indeed, futile—to contest America on the basis of a nationalism that inherently focuses attention on Russia's abysmal domestic conditions. To resist American "hegemony," Russia needs to mobilize international support, and that in turn requires a compelling intellectual case.

In that context, the perception that globalization is merely an extension of American global political primacy provides a heaven-sent ideological opportunity. It supplies the rationale for a comprehensive but indirect indictment of the only superpower without being overtly anti-American, and it can unite the confused and demoralized segments of the post-Communist, anti-Communist, quasi-Communist, nationalist, and chauvinistic elements in the Russian elite. It can even exploit the social residues of the old Soviet "anti-cosmopolitanism" campaigns in order to nurture a posture in which anti-globalism becomes virtual anti-Americanism. Russia cannot compete economically with America, but the contrast between Russian poverty and American plenty can be turned into the charge that America—unlike Russia—is culturally vapid, materialistically rapacious, and devoid of a spiritual vocation.

Such views have the political benefit of identifying Russia with more widely held anti-globalization sentiments elsewhere in the world. Traditionally, the Russian elite have been tempted to arrogate for Russia a uniquely universal calling, first as the Christian world's Third Rome and later as the center of the world revolution symbolized by the red flag fluttering over the Kremlin. When that flag was lowered in late December 1991, Russia was demoted—in the eyes of many Russians—to the status of a mere nation-state, no longer the embodiment of transcendental and transnational values. The temptation to embrace the counter-creed of anti-globalization is thus partly a response to the Russian yearning for renewed self-esteem and for a more effective ideological opposition to global domination by America's business interests and mass culture.[13]

There is also a self-serving domestic reason for the Moscow political elite's reservations regarding the America-led globalization. That elite has traditionally harbored a strong predilection for highly centralized government. Centralized authority serves its interests, whereas globalization threatens to dilute the power and efficacy of national policy instruments. A decentralized nation, with its regions less beholden to Moscow and more directly responsive to the world beyond Russia's borders, is not what the Russian elite instinctively favor.[14]

The official Chinese worldview also reflects strong doses of cultural hostility to American-sponsored globalization. With Marxism becoming irrelevant both domestically and globally, China's political rulers need an alternative doctrinal justification for continuing their monopoly of power at home, while internationally they need to formulate a shared intellectual perspective with like-minded opponents of America's "hegemonism." To the latter end, the proposition that globalization is inherently anti-democratic, in that it favors the strong, provides convenient reinforcement for China's advocacy of "multipolarity."[15]

One can also discern elements of the emerging counter-doctrine in the frequent Chinese suggestion that a common concept of "Asianism" (presumably with China at its forefront) be cultivated in order to guide an independent pursuit of Asia's collective interests in the face of hegemonic globalization. Chinese-sponsored "Asianism" could become an appealing alternative to globalization, exploiting the common sense of identity between the influential Chinese diaspora in Southeast Asia and the Chinese of the mainland. Two recent Chinese bestsellers, *China Can Say No* (a transparent imitation of a very popular anti-U.S. pamphlet written by a leading Japanese nationalist, entitled *The Japan That Can Say No*) and *China's Road: Under the Shadow of Globalization*, both reflect the view that globalization is an extension of American political and cultural hegemony.

Paradoxically, it is China's embrace of globalization, rather than rejection of it, that could harm America's worldwide economic dominance. As noted earlier, China is the favorite poster-child of globalization's most enthusiastic boosters. It is not only attracting American capital, which sees declining prospects for America's own home industries, it is rapidly becoming the most alluring magnet for foreign direct investment in general, drawn by the low cost and increasing productivity of China's abundant labor force. If that trend were to be coupled with a serious downturn in foreign direct investment in America, which currently offsets the negative U.S. trade balances, and with a progressive decline in the profitability of American industry, globalization's success in turning China into the world's prime industrial factory could become a major factor in America's industrial undoing.[16]

Finally, the anti-globalist argument has a more immediate and quite practical dimension. The counter-ideologues realize that the American economy is the locomotive of global development and that American power is the foundation of global stability. A significant economic downturn in America, with its resulting disruptive global impact, could reverse the trend toward increasingly free worldwide trade (strongly favored by the Washington-located global institutions). Given that American power is inseparable from a vital American economy, an economic crisis would weaken America's global influence, upend the seemingly positive connection between globalization and American security interests, and stir up more menacing nationalistic economic rivalries. Many nationally powerful economic interests, from coal miners in Germany to rice growers in Japan to the steel industry in America, would benefit—at least in the short term—from renewed protectionist sentiments.

This mélange of motivations and beliefs does not as yet add up to a comprehensive and systematic anti-globalization ideology in the manner of Marxism's linkage of quasi-rational historical determinism with idealistic fanaticism. It is more a protest against a feared future and against a resented present than an alternative design for the human condition. In short, globalization is repudiated for a variety of reasons, many of them specifically derived from hostility toward its American imprint—but the counter-creed does not yet offer a comprehensive, ideologically appealing blueprint for an alternative political and economic global order. The adherents of the counter-creed can nibble away at the dominant opponent, but they still cannot launch a decisive counteroffensive.

In time, however, a comprehensive counter-creed could emerge and provide the intellectual spark for a global political climate that is intensely hostile to the United States. At a time when it is intellectually fashionable to assume that the age of ideology is over, anti-globalization—fusing Marxist economic determinism with Christian humanitarianism with ecological anxieties, fueled by resentment of global inequality and by sheer envy—has the potential to evolve into a coherent and globally appealing anti-American doctrine.

If that were to happen, the counter-creed could become a powerful tool for worldwide mass political mobilization. At some point, it could provide the unifying ideological platform for a coalition not only of diverse cause-oriented popular movements, but also of states that coalesce to oppose American hegemony. Its more fanatically hostile ideologues and political leaders could then exploit the perception of America's unilateralism, insensitivity to the interests of the poorer and the weaker, and arbitrary use of power to target America as global enemy Number One.

The operative word in these paragraphs is "could." Public opinion polls taken around the world indicate a growing tendency toward a more critical or even hostile view of America. That trend, however, reflects more a resentment of U.S. conduct as the world's only superpower than a rejection of either the American way of life as such or the doctrine of globalization.[17] In fact, when globalization was defined as "increased trade between countries in goods and services, and investments," majorities in twenty-five countries tended to be hopeful regarding its impact on their own futures. There was far more disagreement, however, over globalization's impact on global inequality, presumably reflecting the conflicting data available in the mass media on this complex issue. But most curious—given the world's generally optimistic view of globalization—and potentially quite significant was the fact that a large proportion of the respondents also indicated vague approval for the anti-globalization movements, on the ground that "they act in my interest."[18]

That curious empathy for globalization's critics could be a warning signal. Perhaps the publics sense that globalization, by disconnecting vital economic decisions from the people most directly affected by them, creates the danger that public faith in the democratic process could collapse. The weaker or poorer countries, and especially their most socially vulnerable components, may come to feel deprived of any direct political connection to the decision making that determines their well-being. If a national economy were to falter, nobody—not remote multilateral institutions (such as the WTO or IMF), not supranational organs (such as the EU), not huge global corporations and financial institutions (located in the distant cities of the world's richer countries)—could be held to political account. For many, economic globalization could amount to political disempowerment.

A pervasive sense of social impotence would make a perfect setting for a variety of demagogues chanting nationalist slogans, mouthing Marxist rhetoric, and fulminating against the evils of a new global reality that can be blamed on rapacious exploiters from the distant America and Europe—all while counter-symbolically wrapping themselves in the flag of democracy. Globalization, instead of being understood as the consequence of a technologically shrunk world, would be transmuted into a global conspiracy against the popular will.[19]

To note that risk is neither to endorse the demagogic indictment, nor to ignore the complex connection between the phenomenon of globalization and the emergence of a novel type of global political hegemony. But it does bear saying that ambiguous popular reactions to globalization point to a potentially serious problem. Globalization is a mixed blessing, and if American policymakers do not deliberately infuse it with politically evident moral content, focused on the alleviation of the human condition, their uncritical embrace of it could backfire.

The core of this moral content must be an increasing democratization. Channels must exist for all peoples affected by globalization to voice their fundamental interests. With a greater say, the less developed world would have less ammunition—or desire—to attack the moral legitimacy of globalization writ large. The democratization of globalization will be a long, complex, and halting process that will suffer regular reversals and require enduring American leadership. Nevertheless, America can promote the needed moral infusion into its approach to globalization by toning down its doctrinaire impulses, practicing what it preaches, and focusing more on the global good.

In both its political rhetoric and its national policymaking, the United States should treat globalization less as a gospel and more as an opportunity for the betterment of the human condition. This would dilute America's currently ideological attitude toward globalization. The pursuit of open markets and lower barriers should not be an end in itself, but a means of improving economic conditions worldwide. "Free trade" and "capital mobility" would remain guiding principles, but they should not be forced indiscriminately and wholesale on all countries without regard to local political, economic, social, and institutional constraints. Eschewing ideology in favor of a nuanced and differentiated approach to globalization would demonstrate American sensitivity to the specific needs of other countries, while also gradually instilling that sensitivity in American business leaders.

America also undercuts the credibility of its moral leadership by demanding of others what it rejects for itself. When the rules prove economically disadvantageous or politically inexpedient, America often violates them. This inconsistency both reinforces suspicions of America's motivations—making its dominance all the less tolerable—and increases the incentive for others to similarly flout the system's rules. Given America's exceptional role as the main engine of globalization, some allowances may be justified. But they should be clearly circumscribed and not saturated in self-righteous dissemblance.

Since America enjoys the benefits of globalization, it should also underwrite efforts to alleviate the ills of globalization. America's welfare today depends increasingly on how the world views its own welfare. The more callous America appears toward global suffering, the more recalcitrant the world becomes to American leadership. Therefore, America must be willing to shoulder some costs of providing for the global good without expectations of immediate return.[20] At bottom, by making unreciprocated—but carefully calculated—sacrifices for the global good, America could convince the world that its global preeminence is benign, while addressing in substance the inequities that generate anti-American animus.

Ultimately, the political appeal of the counter-creed depends a great deal on how U.S. leadership is exercised and on the general state of the world economy. A faltering world economy would foster resistance to globalization, encourage new barriers to free trade, intensify social deprivation in the poor countries, and damage both American political leadership and the global appeal of democracy.

For America, the dilemmas of globalization pose the risk not only of philosophical isolation, but of the rise of a doctrine that could mobilize worldwide hostility against America. It is therefore essential for American leadership to recognize that, in this age of worldwide political awakening and shared international vulnerability to technologically advanced means of inflicting mass destruction, security depends not only on military power but also on the prevailing climate of opinion, the political definition of social passions, and the foci of fanatical hatreds.

Given the importance in world affairs of both the United States and the European Union, close cooperation between them on global matters—economic as well as political—will be a critical factor in determining the extent to which the counter-creed becomes a powerful political force. Serious conflict between these two economic giants, which happen also to be the global centers of democracy, would do more than endanger their respective economies. It would threaten efforts to promote an equitable, orderly, and increasingly democratizing globalization.

A WORLD WITHOUT BORDERS, EXCEPT FOR PEOPLE

Globalization envisages a worldwide community without borders for money or for products. When it comes to people, however, neither the proponents nor the opponents of globalization have much to say. Yet in the next several decades the combination of migratory pressures, generated by uneven demographic growth and unevenly distributed global poverty, and the social consequences of the uneven aging of national populations may very well transform the political face of the earth.

Advocates and critics of globalization alike tend to accept as their defining framework a world demarcated into nation-states, with their restrictive definitions of citizenship and residency. Some outspoken critics of globalization become almost sentimental in referring to national borders as "valued safeguards on unfettered economic activity—that is, every nation's laws that foster their economies, their citizens' health and safety, the sustainable use of their land and resources, and so on."[21] Indeed, in some of the richer states, the very same people who otherwise strongly disagree over the merits of globalization increasingly voice strident anti-immigration slogans because they wish to preserve the familiar ethnic cocoon of their nation-state.

That was not always so. Until the rise of the nation-state, and effectively until the appearance of reasonably efficient border-control systems, movement of people was impeded less by national enforcement than by indenture, prejudice against non-locals, geographical impediments to social relocation, and widespread ignorance of conditions outside one's immediate environment. Within Europe, from the early Middle Ages through the nineteenth century, the movement of tradesmen and the settlement of colonists (e.g., Germans in Eastern Europe and even Russia) were relatively free of political restraints and often even promoted by enlightened rulers. In time, moreover, trans-oceanic exploration opened up massive opportunities for relatively spontaneous relocation.

As a broad proposition, it can be said that until the twentieth century, migration was determined by socioeconomic conditions, not political decisions. The national passport, a worldwide twentieth century phenomenon, thus symbolized mankind's loss of the right—even if difficult to exercise in practice—to view the earth as its common home. A consequence of nationalism, from a humane point of view, it was a step backward.

That issue is now being painfully reopened. How tight the borders of the enlarging European Union ought to be is already a highly contested internal and external dilemma. How soon the established EU members' national restrictions on the free movement of labor from new members should be lifted was one of the most difficult matters complicating the EU's decision of late 2002 to invite ten additional countries into membership. How that latest enlargement of the EU will affect the movement of Russians (not only into the EU but through the expanded EU's territory between Russia and its Kaliningrad region), or of Ukrainians, is a challenge to the EU's external relations.

As the choice target of global migration, the United States confronts similar dilemmas. Almost one-fourth of the world's current total of over 140 million migrants are in the United States, and of its more than 30 million foreign-born residents, one-third originate from Mexico. Mexico is also the major source of illegal migration to the United States. Clearly this is a special dilemma. How to regulate the flow of immigrants so that both sides derive some benefit has been a continuing source of mutual irritation. Adaptation within America to the growing cultural and linguistic presence of the Hispanic community is part of the domestic side of that dilemma.

When viewed as an intrinsic consequence of the worldwide technological revolution and not as a doctrinal debate, globalization makes the issue of global migration urgent. The figures (in millions) on the chart below document the widening demographic imbalance between the richer Europe and America and the poorer Asia, Africa, and Latin America.

The Changing Distribution of the World Population (in millions)							
	1900		2000			2020		
	Pop.	% total	Pop.	% total	*Absolute increase (1900-2000)*	Pop.	% total	*Absolute increase (2000-2020)*
Asia	947	57%	3,672	61%	2,725	4,582	60%	910
Africa	133	8%	794	13%	661	1,231	16%	437
Latin America	74	5%	519	9%	445	664	9%	145
Europe	408	25%	727	12%	319	695	9%	-32*
North America	82	5%	314	5%	232	370	5%	56
WORLD	1,650		6,056		4,406	7,579		1,523

* As of 1999, 18 European countries had higher death rates than birth rates, with Russia and Ukraine having the highest negative ratios.
(Base data provided by the UN Population Division.)

Not only has the joint population of Europe and North America declined from 30 percent of the world total in 1900 to only 17 percent in 2000, but in the next twenty years it is likely to drop to only 14 percent of the world total. Europe's population will actually decline, while Asia's is projected to grow by as much as 910 million. At the same time, the populations of the world's wealthy countries will grow increasingly old. Immigration is therefore both an economic as well as a political necessity for the more prosperous states with aging populations, while emigration may serve as a safety valve for rising demographic pressures in the already densely populated and much poorer Third World.

Much of that Third World is becoming a massive tinderbox underpinned by anti-Western, anti-American hostility—and global demographic trends could ignite it. There is massive inequality in per capita income between the richer West, which is shrinking and aging, and the poorer East and South, which are growing and will remain relatively young. While annual income per capita in North America (calculated in terms of purchasing power parity) is well over $30,000, and in the states of the European Union it ranges from approximately $17,000 to $30,000, in the most populated states of the Third World it hovers between $875 for Nigeria, about $2,100 for Pakistan, $2,540 for India, $3,100 for Indonesia, $3,900 for Egypt, and $4,400 for China. As of 2001, fifteen African states had per capita incomes under $1,000—less than $3 per day.

In this strikingly unequal global context, some of the world's most afflicted populations will suffer the greatest demographic duress. The countries that will experience the highest population growth rates over the next half-century face some of the economically least gainful, politically least stable, socially most volatile conditions in the world, sweeping from Palestine through the Persian Gulf and including the most uncertain parts of South Asia.[22] If these countries fail to address the political aspirations and economic drives of their bloating populations—as is quite possible—locally destabilizing and internationally revisionist movements, often violent and anti-Western, could gain a vast pool of recruits.

The prospect that by 2020 the poorer regions' populations will be predominantly composed of the young, and thus of the socially and politically more restless, is likely to intensify social pressures. For Asia, the percentage of those under thirty years of age is projected to be 47 percent; for the Middle East/North Africa, 57 percent; for Sub-Saharan Africa, 70 percent; in contrast, for North America it is projected to be 42 percent and for Europe, 31 percent. The "youth bulge" will be especially acute in the Middle East and North Africa, which will pose an especial threat to the EU due to its proximity. As a 2001 CIA report noted, "The world's poorest and often most politically unstable countries—including, among others, Afghanistan, Pakistan, Colombia, Iraq, Gaza, and Yemen—will have the largest youth populations through 2020. Most will lack the economic, institutional, or political resources to effectively integrate youth into society."[23] The disenfranchised young, with little hope but ample anger, will be the most impassioned insurgents against the international order that America seeks to ensure.

These asymmetries are becoming more explosive because of the historically unprecedented awareness on the part of the poor—thanks to mass media and especially television—of better conditions elsewhere. Moreover, the world's poor are increasingly congested in chaotically growing urban mega-slums, highly vulnerable to politically radical or religiously fundamentalist appeals fueled by intense xenophobic resentments. America, Europe, a few other well-off countries, and soon perhaps Japan are thus both magnets for the socially underprivileged and increasingly focal points of their hatred.

Against this backdrop, migration is beginning to alter the socio-cultural make-up of Western Europe. In some European countries, such as Austria, Germany, and Belgium, the percentage of foreign-born is not far behind America's, with France and Sweden following suit. As a result, political and social tensions have surfaced in a number of European states, with anti-immigrant movements becoming more widespread. Yet neither Western Europe today nor Japan tomorrow can afford to halt immigration. Their economies increasingly need to import young labor—partly because prosperity has made labor-intensive employment less attractive to the native-born, but especially because of a new phenomenon that only recently has drawn public notice: progressing and accelerating global aging.[24]

The phenomenon of societal aging has far-reaching implications for economic globalization and world geopolitics. It increases the proportion of non-productive and dependent citizens in a population while also increasing these citizens' political power. It is a worldwide trend, though nationally uneven due to varying rates of mortality and fertility. According to the U.S. Census Bureau and the United Nations, in 2000 the median age in the United States was 35.5 years; in Europe (including non-EU and Russia), 37.7; in Japan, 41.2; in China, 30; and in India, 23.7—but by 2050 the median age in the United States will be 39.1; in Europe, 49.5; in Japan, 53.1; in China, 43.8; and in India, 38.

With the progressive diminution of the percentage of the population that is productively engaged and the rising percentage of those dependent on others, budgetary strains produced by increased social welfare needs, and the resulting drag on economic growth, are likely to become globally more pervasive. All countries will have more people over sixty-five, but the richer countries will also have fewer people under thirty. Making matters worse, the likelihood that the richer countries will by necessity permit increased immigration by younger migrants, and especially make a focused effort to attract better educated ones, may compound the social dilemmas of the poorer and less developed countries. They will be drained of some of the most productive, most innovative, and best educated segments of their working population. It is estimated that there are already some 1.5 million skilled migrants from the Least Developed Countries (LDCs) employed in America, the EU, Australia, and Japan. Africa alone has lost 200,000 badly needed professionals and some 30,000 PhDs in the last decade.[25]

While the longer-term effects of societal aging are likely to be global, its more immediate impact will be on the richer and more developed countries, notably Europe and Japan. Italy, Spain, and Japan are currently the "oldest" nations in the world (in terms of the ratio of elderly to total population). But societal aging is spreading, and its effects are intensified by a parallel process of depopulation, with the populations of more than thirty countries expected to shrink by mid-century. Some, like Spain's or Italy's, will shrink by perhaps 20 percent, and Japan is not far behind. Thus the problem for the richer and older countries is likely to get progressively worse. Coupled with a significant drop in the birth rate, it might shift the social old-age dependency ratio to a fiscally dangerous degree, with massive public debts and even defaults in the not-too-distant future.[26]

The American population, by contrast, will continue to grow, though at a diminishing pace and with increasing reliance on immigration and on immigrants' higher birth rates. (It is estimated that immigration and births to immigrant mothers will account for two-thirds of America's annual population growth.) As a result, America is likely to be in a more favored position than either its key allies or even some of the developing nations in terms of its old-age dependency ratio and the replenishment of its labor force.[27]

The painful reality is that neither Europe nor Japan will be able to maintain its standard of living or its social obligations toward its increasingly elderly citizens, without a very significant infusion of fresh blood—so-called "replacement migration"—and even then the remedy will only be partial. In fact, it is altogether unlikely that the most affected countries will permit immigration on the scale needed to preserve even the existing ratio of those productively employed to those dependent. The numbers of migrants these countries would have to absorb are beyond the range of practicality, literally in the multiples of millions.[28]

Initially, the European Union might be able to alleviate the demographic problem simply by expanding eastward. Assimilation of outsiders is easier if they at least come from a shared cultural legacy and have no legal barriers to cross. For France or Germany, for example, the integration of Polish immigrants is much more rapid and socially acceptable than that of North Africans or Turks, not to mention the lately growing number of South Asians. But even Eastern Europe (and especially Ukraine and Russia) will be afflicted by the combination of depopulation and aging, which will reduce the manpower available to immigrate westward.

Inevitably, people from North Africa, Turkey, the Middle East, and South Asia will be an increasing presence in Europe, with all the attendant social and cultural conflicts. The strong reaction that surfaced recently in Holland against newly resident foreigners was largely due to the social perception that the 5 percent of the country's population composed of Muslim immigrants (largely Moroccan and Turkish)—a group whose size has increased tenfold over the past thirty years—was not assimilating to Dutch mores and way of life. Similar reactions have occurred elsewhere in Europe.

This combination of migratory pressures and societal aging is likely to generate, in the richer, older, and gradually depopulating countries, a progressive redefinition of the traditional concept of the ethnically defined nation-state. That unavoidably painful process inheres in globalization. At present, almost all of the world's richer countries (the United States, Canada, and Australia being the major exceptions) are ethnically defined. Assimilation involves not only formal acceptance of citizenship and a loyal commitment to a shared future—as is the case in America—but also genuine internalization of a shared and often mythical past. Immigrants to the United States typically begin to consider themselves Americans even before they acquire citizenship. In Europe, that is much less the case, even in a country like France with its tradition of linguistic assimilation. For insular and culturally unique Japan, the very idea of absorbing millions of migrants is close to unthinkable. In these countries, national history, language, and cultural and religious identity are intricately and intimately interwoven, and identification with the national past is almost as important for full acceptance as a sense of shared national future.

There are additional consequences of the emerging conundrum, and some have significant geopolitical implications for America. The latter fall broadly into three categories: the impact of migration and aging (1) on the national ethos of the "first world" countries; (2) on the role of those countries in international security; and, most important, (3) on America's global political standing.

The contrast between the Germany of 1900 and the Germany of 2000 was aptly defined (by an unattributed source) as the difference between a country in which "more than half of the population was under 25 and poor" and a country in which "more than half of the population is over 50 and rich." Leaving aside some statistical exaggeration, this captures the essence of the change in the German national ethos: a shift from an energetic and emotive national identity to a more sedentary and "gemuetlich" existence. National ethos thus becomes more a way of life than an assertive vocation, and owning a vacation home in a neighboring country becomes more gratifying than seizing that country's territory.

Such a shift in outlook, which typifies the West European experience, suggests that the European Union will not be much inclined to translate its eventual political unity into a globally significant capability to project military power. Indeed, the financial squeeze inherent in the rising old-age dependency ratio may intensify anti-militarist sentiments and increase the difficulty of obtaining electoral approval of any major increases in European defense spending. At the same time, the looming demographic decline will further reduce the pool of available citizens of military age. These two trends are likely to make national recruitment of military volunteers more difficult.

Before too long, the EU—and eventually perhaps the United States—may have no choice but to revive recruitment policies reminiscent of the pre-national era in military affairs. With conscription-based citizen-armies (traceable to the *levée en masse* of the French Revolution) currently being replaced by technologically skilled professional militaries, the highly developed states may have to rely increasingly on mercenary migrant recruitment. With national fervor no longer the key determinant of fighting spirit, the professional armies of the more affluent countries may increasingly be composed of highly trained recruits from the Third World whose loyalty extends to their next paycheck.

For the time being, the United States will enjoy the advantage of being somewhat less vulnerable to the scissors dilemma posed by aging and a drastic decline in population growth. If current projections hold true, America will maintain a strong demographic base from which to exercise leadership on behalf of its notions of globalization. Its well-off partners will probably remain stable internally but will still be dependent on U.S. protection for global security. With their populations stagnant or shrinking, they could suffer growing ethnic tensions as they heighten their reliance on migrant manpower. Globalization may thus become less attractive to them. But much of Asia, the Middle

East, and Africa, as well as some portions of Latin America, may be subjected politically and socially to intensifying demographic pressures.

In that context, the American experience of an increasingly multicultural society with a future-oriented tradition of assimilation could be a reassuring model to others still in the grip of more integral nationalism. Moreover, because of its relative vitality, America is likely to be better positioned to promote a more cooperative global response to the varied consequences of uneven demographic dynamics. Just as the WTO became a necessity if globalization was to acquire a reasonably orderly character, so an international instrumentality for regulating (and humanizing) global migration (a WMO?) might help to introduce some common standards for the currently arbitrary and inconsistent handling of migrants. Nation-states will be reluctant, of course, to yield any control over access to their territories. Over time, however, uneven demographic dynamics will necessarily prompt searches for broader solutions than any one country can impose.

In the final analysis, a globalization that indifferently favors the rich and copes with the human misery of migration in a manner that benefits the already privileged will be a globalization that justifies its critics, mobilizes its enemies, and further divides the world. Only a world that is both increasingly imbued with a shared social conscience and more open to the movement—even if regulated—of not just goods and funds, but people as well, will fulfill the positive potential of globalization.

NOTES

1   Charles F. Doran, "Globalization and Statecraft," *SAISphere* (Winter 2000), Paul H. Nitze School of Advanced International Studies.

2   Consider for example the widely disseminated study prepared jointly in early 2001 by a leading international consulting firm, A.T. Kearny, and a respected international affairs journal, *Foreign Policy*, entitled "Globalization Index" and allegedly providing "the first comprehensive guide to globalization in fifty developed and key emerging markets." Its accompanying Kearny press release proclaimed that one of the study's "most dramatic findings" was that more globalized emerging-market countries have "greater income equality than their less globalized counterparts." As

evidence, the examples of Poland, Israel, the Czech Republic, and Hungary were cited. Nowhere was it noted that each of these countries had a strong prior history of socialist egalitarianism.

Similarly, the study claimed that "the world's most globalized countries tend to enjoy more civil liberties and political rights, as measured annually by Freedom House…." Again, the Index did not note that in each case cited (Netherlands, Sweden, Switzerland, etc.), democracy and legality had been long established, and thus the implied causal relationship was probably actually the reverse. The Index, incidentally, listed Singapore as the world's most globalized country, which presumably should have been somehow reflected in its civil rights record.

In a follow-up study, issued a year later ("Globalization Index" 2002), the claim was again made that "the world's most global countries boast greater income equality than their less global counterparts…with few exceptions, countries that scored high on the Globalization Index enjoyed greater political freedom…. And a comparison of our index rankings with Transparency International's survey of perceived corruption suggested that public officials in the most global countries are less corrupt than their counterparts in closed economies"—the implication being that globalization promotes equality, political freedom, and integrity.

3   Trade union leaders frequently cite the fact that in 1979 21 million Americans had jobs in manufacturing, accounting for about 30 percent of all employment; by 2001, manufacturing employment had shrunk to 16 million even though the labor force had increased by some 15 million.

4   The Chinese themselves contest the benign interpretation of globalization's impact. A detailed analysis in the official organ of the Chinese Communist Party ("Two Major Trends in Today's World," *People's Daily*, April 3, 2002) asserted that "globalization has led to the widening of the gap between the poor South and the rich North…in the past 30 years, the number of the least developed countries has increased to 49 from 25; the world's absolute impoverished population has increased from 1 billion five years ago to 1.2."

5   The agenda for the WTO ministerial meetings is set by the so-called "Quad" composed of the United States, Canada, Japan, and the EU, which together account for about two-thirds of world trade. Moreover, the issue of access to the U.S. market gives U.S. negotiators unparalleled leverage with which to influence the position of the other states. In the World Bank, the president has been an American as a matter of convention, and the United States has the largest percentage of the voting power. In the IMF, important decisions require an 85 percent vote in favor, and the U.S. share of the voting power is 17.11 percent, thus giving the United States an effective and sole veto power. No wonder that some have called the IMF and World Bank "wholly-owned subsidiaries of the U.S. Treasury Department."

6   According to the office of the U.S. Trade Representative, "The findings of a WTO dispute settlement panel cannot force us to change our laws....America retains full sovereignty in its decision of whether or not to implement a panel recommendation" See "America and the World Trade Organization," accessible at http://www.ustr.gov/html/wto_usa.html.

7   Illustrative of this are the results of the first annual "Commitment to Development Index" (CDI) formulated by the Center for Global Development and *Foreign Policy* magazine, which "ranks some of the world's richest nations according to how much their policies help or hinder the economic and social development of poor countries" based on a combination of aid, trade, investment, environmental sensitivity, openness to migration, and contributions to peacekeeping. The G-7 countries, which together "account for two-thirds of the world's economic output," generally fared poorly in the rankings, with the United States and Japan relegated to twentieth and twenty-first places, respectively, out of twenty-one. "Ranking the Rich," *Foreign Policy* (May/June 2003).

8   In an especially virulent celebration of 9/11 that linked that event causally to globalization, a much noted French philosopher, Jean Baudrillard, proclaimed in his pamphlet *L'Esprit du Terrorisme* (Paris 2001) that "Terrorism is immoral...and it responds to a globalization that is itself immoral," with the latter generating a collective complicity in "the vast jubilation at seeing the destruction of this world superpower, or rather, at seeing it in a sense self-destruct, a beautiful suicide." In his view, mankind is now experiencing the fourth world war, the first having been against colonialism, the second against Nazism, the third against Sovietism, and the ongoing fourth against globalization. The pamphlet was widely disseminated by *Le Monde*, November 3, 2001, which devoted two full pages to reprinting it in full.

9   Pierre Bourdieu, "Uniting to Better Dominate," contribution to "Conflicts over Civilization," *Items & Issues*, 2, no. 3–4 (Winter 2001), 1–6.

10   *Alternatives to Economic Globalization: A Better World is Possible*, ed. John Cavanagh, et al. (San Francisco: Berrett-Koehler, 2002), 18.

11   That point is made forcefully by Amy Chua in "A World on the Edge," *The Wilson Quarterly* (Autumn 2002) (in a preview of her book, *A World on Fire: How Exporting Free Market Democracy Breeds Ethnic Hatred and Global Instability*). A few examples document her basic point: In the Philippines, the Chinese 1 percent of the population controls about 60 percent of the economy (with over 60 percent of the Filipinos living on about $2 a day); in Indonesia, the Chinese 3 percent of the population dominates about 70 percent of the private economy (with anti-Chinese violence a periodic problem); and the Chinese play a similar role elsewhere in Southeast Asia

and in Burma. In West Africa, Lebanese immigrants tend to dominate some forms of trade, while in Rwanda in 1994 the Hutu majority killed some 800,000 Tutsi who traditionally had monopolized cattle-owning. Before being pushed out of East Africa, Hindu tradesmen were prevalent in commerce. A small number of white farmers until recently owned most of the agricultural land in Zimbabwe.

12   Hubert Vedrine, "Democracy has many hues," *Le Monde Diplomatique* (December 2000). *Le Monde* itself has been featuring numerous anti-globalization articles. Typical, for example, was Ignacio Ramonet's "The Other Axis of Evil," *Le Monde Diplomatique* (March 15, 2002), in which the author asserted that "There is a whole industry that aims to convince humanity that globalization will bring universal happiness....Armed with information, globalization's ideological warriors have created a dictatorship that depends on the passive complicity of those it subjugates." This theme is developed further in the same author's book *Propagandes Silencieuses* (Paris: Galilée, 2000). In fairness, it should be noted that there are also French views that are critical of the parochialism and nostalgic character of such indictments of globalization, seeing in them an overreaction to America's hegemonic tendencies and a tendency to "seek indefinite refuge behind our traditional ways of thinking that take us one step forward and two steps backward." See Jean-Claude Milleron, "La France et la mondialisation," *Commentaire*, no. 100 (Winter 2002–3), 817.

13   E.g., the linkage of globalization with U.S. global imperialism is forcefully argued by a Russian historian, Aleksandr Volkov, in a strikingly titled article, "International Totalitarianism: Never Before in History Have Conditions So Favorable for Realizing the Idea of the World Dominance of an Individual Power Ever Taken Shape," *Rossiyskaya Gazeta*, January 30, 2003. A preview of that approach was provided in early 2001 by a joint Russian-Nigerian presidential statement. It was an attempt at formulating a doctrinal platform that would link the interests of the Third World (represented by a grouping of some 135 UN-member states) with Russia in shared opposition to American globalist and globalizing manifestations.

14   See the frank discussion in "Aktual'nye voprosy globalizatsii," *Meimo*, no. 4 (1999), 39–47.

15   That case is made explicitly in "Two Major Trends in Today's World" by the organ of the CCP, *People's Daily*, April 3, 2002, which argues that globalization is politically undemocratic and economically discriminatory.

16   "China, once viewed by wide-eyed executives as the market of future riches, is instead becoming the world's factory floor....One upshot of China's emergence as a manufacturing powerhouse: It's becoming an increasingly powerful global deflationary force. China's manufacturing prowess is pushing down prices on a growing range

of industrial, consumer and even agricultural products that it sells around the world."
Moreover, unlike other recently industrialized economies, China "is holding on to
low-end industries, like toys and textiles, and garnering a growing slice of the high-
end, hi-tech sector as well." Last but not least, "China's impact on world prices and
corporate strategies is likely to increase. Its entrance into the World Trade
Organization is breeding lean and hyper-competitive private Chinese companies
turning their sights overseas to alleviate price pressure at home." See Karby Leggett,
"Burying the Competition," *Far Eastern Economic Review* (October 17, 2002). The
Chinese themselves have begun to speculate about China's potential to become "the
world's factory." For example, Fan Gang, the director of the National Economic
Research Institute, wrote in "China Must Fight to Strengthen Its Manufacturing
Industry Even As It Pursues High-Tech Industries, Services" (the PRC-owned *Ta
Kung Pao*, Hong Kong, November 15, 2002) that "If it makes good use of its strength,
namely its human resources in the form of a huge work force made up of peasants,
we believe China would become the global manufacturing base in the next one or two
decades."

17   The Pew Global Attitudes survey, conducted in forty-four countries and released
in late 2002, found that "pluralities in most of the nations surveyed complain about
American unilateralism." Moreover, in general the image of the United States has
slipped, in some cases quite significantly. The only major exceptions—Nigeria (31 percent increase), Uzbekistan (29 percent), and Russia (24 percent)—seemed to suggest
that the respondents were highly influenced by the state of *official* relations between
their governments and the United States. The survey also revealed that "the American
public is strikingly at odds with publics around the world in its views about the U.S.
role in the world and the global impact of American actions."

18   According to polls conducted in twenty-four countries for the World Economic
Forum by Environics International Ltd. between October and December 2001, the
ratio of those who felt that the anti-globalization movements were acting in their
interest versus those who disagreed was 73 percent to 8 percent, respectively, in
Turkey; 60 percent to 34 percent in India; 54 percent to 35 percent in France; 41 per-
cent to 49 percent in Italy; 39 percent to 52 percent in the United States; 35 percent
to 62 percent in South Korea; and 24 percent to 50 percent in Japan.

19   As the critics put it, "Will a small ruling elite, meeting in secret and far from
public view, be allowed to set the rules that shape the human future?
...Accountability is central to living democracy....This is not the case if the management decisions are in the hands of a foreign corporation whose directors live
thousands of miles away and, furthermore, face a legal mandate to maximize short-
term return to shareholders." See *Alternatives to Economic Globalization: A Better World is
Possible*, ed. John Cavanagh, et al. (San Francisco: Berrett-Koehler, 2002), 4, 57.

20   This might mean, for example, creating stronger incentives for U.S. pharmaceutical companies to distribute their medicines cheaply where most needed, or developing a more efficient food redistribution program to shift the surfeit of Western produce to the world's hungriest populations while investing more to help the latter develop indigenous sustainable production capabilities. Less obviously, it might entail installing more structural buffers in major international institutions, especially in financial ones like the IMF, between institutional decision-making processes and the informal access points of American pressure, thereby insulating these institutions from the overbearing influence of American domestic interests and allowing them to act more coherently toward the global benefit.

21   Ralph Nader, in preface to Lori Wallach and Michelle Sforza, *Whose Trade Organization? Corporate Globalization and the Erosion of Democracy* (Washington, DC: Public Citizen Foundation, 1999), x.

22   The regions projected to experience the most percentage growth of population both by 2025 and by 2050 are Yemen, Occupied Palestinian Territory, Oman, Afghanistan, Saudi Arabia, Bhutan, Pakistan, Jordan, Iraq, and Cambodia. See United Nations, Population Division, Department of Economic and Social Affairs, *World Population Prospects: The 2000 Revision*, February 2001.

23   Central Intelligence Agency, *Long-Term Global Demographic Trends: Reshaping the Geopolitical Landscape*, July 2001, 36.

24   Truly pioneering work on the emerging reality and implications of global aging has been conducted by a team of researchers at the Center for Strategic and International Studies (CSIS), which was headed by Dr. Paul Hewitt. For a summary, see the CSIS Report, "Meeting the Challenge of Global Aging," March 2002, on which the above discussion draws.

25   "Growing Global Migration and Its Implications for the United States," Central Intelligence Agency, March 2001, 23. A countervailing partial compensation is that remittances to lands of origin do help their economies.

26   The OECD estimates that the ratio of working age population to those over sixty-five will decline in the EU and Japan from 5-to-1 in 2000 to 3-to-1 already by 2015.

27   In 1950, the United States was fourth among the world's twelve most populated countries, along with four other advanced societies; in 2000, it was third among the twelve, with three other advanced societies; by 2050, it may still be third but none of the other twelve will be from among the advanced societies.

28   Estimates of what might be needed vary widely. The aforementioned March 2001 CIA report estimates that Japan would have to admit *3.2 million immigrants a year and for years to come* to preserve its current old-age dependency ratio, and *The Economist* (October 31, 2002) estimates that just maintaining the working-age population at its current size would require 5 million migrants per annum for Japan, 6 million per annum for Germany, and 6.5 million per annum for Italy—all obviously not practicable. But even the more cautious analysis by Kenneth Prewitt, in "Demography, Diversity, and Democracy," *The Brookings Review* (Winter 2002), 6, concludes that "to maintain Italy's working-age population...would require 370,000 new migrants each year; Germany's, just short of half a million."

5

THE DILEMMAS OF
HEGEMONIC DEMOCRACY

America today is simultaneously an internationally hegemonic power and a democracy. This unique combination justifies asking whether the outward projection of America's mass democracy is compatible with a quasi-imperial responsibility, whether the democratic American polity can provide direction for a changing world that is now much more complex than during the earlier bipolar competition, and whether American democracy at home is congenial to the prolonged exercise of hegemonic power abroad, however carefully that hegemony is camouflaged by democratic rhetoric.

Hegemonic power can defend and even promote democracy, but it can also threaten democracy. American power was central to the defeat of the Soviet Union and remains central to both the national security of the United States and the preservation of basic global stability. Hegemonic power can promote democracy abroad if it is applied in a manner that is sensitive to the aspirations and rights of others and if it is not discredited by overblown and evidently hypocritical democratic sloganeering. Nevertheless, hegemonic power can also threaten domestic democracy if its assertion, in the face of new vulnerabilities, fails to discriminate between the imperatives of prudent national security and the phantasms of self-induced social panic.

Ultimately, it is the balanced combination of American democracy and American hegemony that presently offers mankind its best hope for avoiding debilitating global strife. Given that the social appeal of democracy is a key component of the prevailing U.S. global power, several questions follow: What is the political significance of the undeniably massive global attraction to America's mass culture? How does the ongoing transformation of America into a multicultural society affect the cohesion of America's strategic vision? What risks for America's internal democracy inhere in the exercise of its external hegemonic role?

AMERICA AS THE GLOBAL CULTURAL SEDUCTION

The term "cultural revolution" originated in a massive human tragedy produced by a monstrous political crime: Mao Zedong's brutal attempt to upend Communist China's power structure in order to revive what he felt was the waning vitality of the original communist revolution. By stirring up the young and by turning them against the ruling elite and its lifestyles, as well as against China's own historic and cultural traditions, the aging dictator hoped to ignite a permanent revolutionary flame.

The social impact of America on the world also entails a phenomenon akin to a cultural revolution, but a seductive and non-violent one that is farther-reaching, more enduring, and thus ultimately more truly transforming. Neither based on political direction nor derived from demagogic propaganda, the American-inspired global cultural revolution is redefining the social mores, cultural values, sexual conduct, personal tastes, and individual material expectations of almost the entire world's younger generation. That generation, especially its urban portion, is increasingly characterized by common aspirations, amusements, and acquisitive instincts. Although the material means available to the world's 2.7 billion individuals in the age bracket of 10–34 differ enormously from country to country—reflecting the general disparities in standards of living—there is a remarkable degree of similarity worldwide in the subjective desire for the latest CDs, in the fascination with American films and television serials, in the magnetic attraction of rock music, in the spread of digital games, in the ubiquity of jeans, and in the absorption even into local traditions of the American popular culture. The result may be a mishmash of the locally distinctive with the universal, but the latter is clearly traceable to America.

The extraordinary seductiveness of American mass culture flows from the underpinnings of American democracy, which places special value on social egalitarianism combined with the opportunity for unlimited individual self-fulfillment and enrichment. The quest for individual wealth is the strongest social impulse in American life and the basis of the American myth. But it is accompanied by a truly egalitarian ethic that exalts the individual as the central unit of society, rewards individual creativity and constructive competitiveness, and entitles each individual to an equal opportunity to become a personal success or (though largely left unsaid) a failure. The failures unavoidably outnumber the successes, but it is the latter that the myth popularizes, thereby focusing the individual dreams of many millions on an alluring America.

Propelled by this appeal, America has become the unplanned and politically unguided vehicle for a cultural seduction that seeps in, pervades, absorbs, and reshapes the external behavior and eventually the inner life of a growing portion of mankind. Quite literally, not a single continent, perhaps not even a single country (with the probable exception of North Korea), is immune to the irresistible penetration of this diffuse but cumulatively redefining lifestyle.

Even in the heyday of the Cold War, with the Soviet system still in the grip of Stalinist controls, it was evident to a casual foreign visitor that the Iron Curtain simply could not isolate Soviet youth from "pernicious" and "decadent" Western (and specifically American) influences. It was somehow easier for the KGB to isolate Soviet intellectuals from foreign doctrinal contagion than to prevent the otherwise disciplined members of the Komsomol (Communist Youth League) from donning jeans and privately savoring jazz while eagerly quizzing visitors about the latest American fads. And once the Soviet controls slackened, imitation and internalization of what was previously forbidden became a massive wave.

With ideological controls today more difficult to assert, given the spread of global communications and the absence of any ideologically self-confident alternative, the only countries that can resist the new global mass culture are those with highly traditional and still primarily rural societies. In effect, passive resistance derived from a delayed historical timeline and rooted in the strength of self-isolation provides the only effective impediment to the new cultural seduction. Otherwise, even culturally proud and highly self-conscious nations like France[1] or Japan are unable to seal themselves off or distract their younger generation from the allure of the latest fads and newest attractions, which ultimately—even if not always overtly—bear the "Made in USA" label. That allure then becomes part of a virtual reality vaguely associated with America, at once both distant and immediate.

This historically novel situation is not the product of a political stratagem. It is a dynamic reality produced in large measure by the open-ended, creatively enterprising, and highly competitive American democratic system. In that system, innovation is the determinant of success in almost every walk of life, including in areas that together produce a mass culture. The result is a globally dominant position in films, in popular music, on the Internet, in brand recognition, in mass culinary habits, and in language, as well as in graduate education and management skills—in short, what scholars have described as the "soft power" of America's hegemony.

The sheer scale of American cultural predominance has neither a peer nor any historical precedent. Nor is there any rival on the horizon. If anything, America's cultural domination is intensifying as the world increasingly urbanizes, as mankind becomes more interwoven and interactive, and as the more traditional and largely rural segments of the world shrink and become more permeable. That is as true of Lagos as of Shanghai.

Perhaps the most visible and dramatic global impact of America's mass culture comes through films and television serials. Not only has Hollywood been the global symbol of an industry that over the twentieth century became the world's most important source of entertainment (as well as cultural influence), but American-made films have been the world's most widely disseminated and financially rewarding. U.S. movies account for nearly 80 percent of the film industry's worldwide income. Even in France, U.S. movies account for about 60 percent of box office revenues and constitute somewhere between 30 percent and 40 percent of films nationally distributed. In China, the initial importation of just a limited number of Hollywood films—which became instant box-office successes—forced the government to abandon its efforts to produce its own "politically correct," essentially propagandistic films. Much the same can be said of the appeal of American television serials, some of which (e.g., "Dallas" and "Baywatch") have already given hundreds of millions around the world their (idealized and distorted) conceptions of American life.

For the young, new popular music is a captivating source of absorption and self-expression. Much of it originates from the United States. According to the music industry's weekly tracking, even in India, nine of the top twenty albums in January 2003 were by American acts—and the statistic is similar or higher elsewhere. In addition, MTV, with its thirty-three channels worldwide, VH1 (music programming oriented toward the slightly older), and Nickelodeon (general children's programming) combined reach some 1 billion people in 164 countries. As with films and television, the attraction of the new music carries with it worship of specific superstars, including an intense interest in their "private" lives as deliberately sensationalized by pulp magazines often sponsored by the industry itself.

The Internet also contributes to the world's virtual and instant identification with America. With some 70 percent of all web sites originating from the United States and with English the most widely used language of communication for both play and work (96 percent of all e-commerce web sites are in English), the rapidly expanding global chatter is heavily influenced by its American component. Though itself culturally "neutral," the Internet facilitates a rapid, direct, and informal style of communication, accelerates commercial processes, frustrates political controls over the flow of information, and thus cumulatively makes for a more intimate globe, in which the deliberate exclusion of American mass culture becomes more difficult.

American cultural influence extends even to eating habits, with its emphasis on culinary convenience. The notion that rapid ingestion of needed food can be economically productive, relatively esthetic, and affordable for the many is at the heart of the fast-food industry, which originated in America but is making increasing inroads worldwide and even prompting imitation by local entrepreneurs. Quick meals make more time available for work, neatly packaged mass food-products gain devotees, and relatively low costs attract mass consumers—mainly urban workers and the younger generation. In the 1950s, "Coca-Colonization" was the anti-American slogan of the European left; half a century later, the McDonald's logo, present in almost every major foreign city, is often associated—for better or worse—with the Stars and Stripes.

More generally, through its dynamism and innovation, American business has made a distinctive impression on the world's growing number of consumers. In a typical international poll conducted by *BusinessWeek* in the fall of 2002, respondents were asked to identify various brands. Eight of the ten brands most widely recognized worldwide were American, including the top five. It is noteworthy that four of the eight most familiar American brands were directly associated with lifestyle products (Coca-Cola, which occupied first place, Disney, McDonald's, and Marlboro), while the remaining most widely recognized American brands were in the area of technological innovation (Microsoft, IBM, GE, and Intel).

Even the world's political styles are changing under American influence. In some respects, the spreading imitation of the American political style reflects the generally increased standing of democracy following its victory over totalitarianism. It is also, however, very much a matter of the contagion of American mass marketing, the export abroad of American techniques of mass-media advertising (including the political attack ad), and the manipulative packaging of the profiles of political leaders. The growing popularity among politicians of using personal nicknames (Jimmy instead of James, Bill instead of William) reflects the studied informality of the American mass culture.

The worldwide cultural seduction is facilitated by the rapid spread of the English language as the international lingua franca. Among those who educate the younger generation, English is increasingly being viewed not so much as a foreign language but as a basic skill on a par with arithmetic. It is the operational language of international air traffic, as well as of travel more generally, and it is also becoming the official internal language of the most important internationally active (but not necessarily U.S.-based) corporations. It should be noted, however, that the version actually spoken is not English as such, but increasingly its American variant. The American idiom is spreading globally, with purely American words and expressions often penetrating into (and, some purists would argue, corrupting) national languages.

It is thus not surprising that socially privileged and individually ambitious people around the world seek enrollment at an American university. The top U.S. graduate schools represent a global academic Mecca whose degrees provide instant status, but attendance at even an average American college is considered a ticket to greater personal opportunity. Many of the foreign students who come to America with the intention of returning home are subsequently seduced by better professional opportunities and higher material compensation, to America's special benefit.

The growth of foreign student enrollment in the United States has been enormous. In the 1954–55 academic year, the total number of foreign students in American colleges was 34,232 (or 1.4 percent of total U.S. enrollment).[2] In 1964–65, it was 82,045 (1.5 percent); in 1974–75, 154,580 (1.5 percent); in 1984–85, 343,113 (2.7 percent); in 1994–95, 452,653 (3.3 percent); and by 2001–02 it had climbed to

582,996 (4.3 percent). The largest numbers came from India and China, with over 60,000 originating from each in the year 2001–02. With Europe and Japan collectively accounting for under 130,000 of the grand total, it is evident that America is a major training ground for the future leaders of Asia, the Middle East, Africa, and Latin America.

The impact abroad of this varied, occasionally personal but more often virtual exposure to American mass culture is revolutionary. It liberates the individual personality, upends prevailing custom, generates largely unattainable social aspirations, and undermines the traditional order. It also homogenizes human cultural diversity, but this is a matter of choice: It spreads by imitation, not by imposition—which suggests that for the masses, it is an appealing and benign cultural revolution. If its political effect is to destabilize the existing social order, it does so because what disseminates from America is more appealing than what exists locally. Esthetes can fault mass culture, but their tastes are not socially contagious. America as the source of cultural seduction cannot be stopped by political fiat.

In short, in the words of a perceptive European observer, "history's first global civilization is 'Made in USA,' and it needs no gun to travel." But what are its political implications? Does it facilitate the exercise of American power? Is mankind's increasingly intimate familiarity with America breeding affection or antagonism? The European commentator just cited has no doubts: "Seduction is worse than imposition. It makes you feel weak, and so you hate the soft-pawed corrupter as well as yourself."[3] But reality is more ambiguous.

The world's virtual familiarity with America involves the complex interaction of America's global cultural effluence and its globally pervasive power. Just as the call of American culture seduces foreign societies, so American policy has a profound impact on foreign polities. The world's virtual experience of America and its reaction to that experience depend on the dynamic intermingling of the two.

Polls of worldwide public opinion suggest that virtual familiarity breeds affection for much of the American way of life even as it intensifies resentment of U.S. policies. Although such polls, because they reflect instant personal reactions to changing circumstances, are inherently volatile, certain patterns seem evident. A review of several polls[4] indicates that an overwhelming number of countries worldwide, including even France, China, and Japan (the major exceptions being Russia and the Middle East, followed to a lesser extent by Pakistan, India, and Bangladesh), view American popular culture favorably. At the same time, however, the spread of American "customs" is viewed predominantly as "bad" in a majority of countries (with even 50 percent of Britons reacting critically), the only major exception being Japan. Unlike American culture, American foreign policy is largely viewed negatively. Its perceived bias in favor of Israel against the Palestinians is frequently cited as the specific reason, as is America's perceived indifference to other countries' interests. Majorities in most countries believe that the United States is actually intensifying the gap between rich nations and poor ones.

Thus the cultural impact of virtual familiarity with America collides with the political. The major political consequence of America's cultural seduction is that more is expected of America than of other states. To act selfishly in the name of "the national interest" is generally viewed as normal international behavior—yet America tends to be held to a higher standard. In the aforementioned polls, those who were most dissatisfied with the state of their own countries tended to entertain a more jaundiced view of America, reinforcing the hypothesis that they expect more of America and hold it somehow accountable for the deplorable state of the world. This may partly be due to the highly self-righteous rhetoric of American political leaders, with its heavy reliance on idealistic and religious invocations. But the global public opinion polls suggest that it is also a double-edged compliment by those who truly expect more from America and resent its failure to meet such elevated expectations when it comes to actual policy. Anti-Americanism bears the trappings of betrayed affection.

America is thus admired and resented at the same time. Envy contributes to but is not the sole cause of the resentment. It stems from the sense that America's global reach affects almost everyone, especially those who have vicariously become an extension of America through virtual experience. They are captives of, and even more frequently willing participants in, the American mass-cultural sphere, but they feel that they are not heard in the American process of decision-making. The historic (American) slogan "No taxation without representation" finds its contemporary global equivalent in "No Americanization without representation."

Global Americanization also elicits an antithesis, but largely as an elite phenomenon and not a mass one. The deliberate repudiation of the American way is common largely among intellectuals who deplore the cultural homogenization and debasement that they associate with the spread of American mass culture. Given the absence of an appealing mass cultural alternative, however, these elites' largely futile attempts at cultural counter-identification have to rely either on local traditions or on the more generalized rejection of globalization. When U.S. policies are especially offensive, it is the advocates of cultural counter-identification who tend to provide the political leadership in galvanizing populist resentment against America's failure to live up to popular expectations.

The dilemma for U.S. foreign policy is that the cultural transformation unleashed by America is inimical to traditional stability. It contains a strong democratic and egalitarian content, while its emphasis on innovation as the key to personal and collective success is also revolutionary in its dynamics. In many parts of the world, the cumulative impact of American mass culture is politically destabilizing, even as U.S. foreign policy places a premium on international stability. Admittedly, the proclaimed U.S. goal is peaceful (and thus "stable") change, but in many parts of the world, real change necessarily involves upheaval. The consequences can be inimical to America's more immediate strategic interests.

Moreover, the world's fascination with America leaves no room for neutrality or indifference toward it. Unlike the British Empire—which was vaguely envied but incurred hostility only from its immediate rivals—America is experienced worldwide, both immediately and virtually, by elites and publics alike. It is globally admired or resented or both simultaneously, with a force and intensity commensurate to its pervasiveness.

By sparking political instability while drawing to America an unavoidably intense concentration of global sentiment, America's global cultural seduction limits the leeway of U.S. policymakers to derive U.S. foreign policy from a narrow view of the American national interest. America sits at the epicenter of a cultural maelstrom of its own creation; its security depends on whether it can calm the surrounding storm. Only if it places a higher premium on the emerging awareness of a shared global interest will America derive any political benefit from its globally radiant cultural appeal.

MULTICULTURALISM AND STRATEGIC COHESION

Societal strategic cohesion is the necessary precondition for the effective conduct of a democracy's foreign policy. A dictatorship can conduct foreign policy on the basis of elite consensus and firm personal leadership at the top. A democracy, however, must mobilize its consensus not only from the top down, but also from a shared, basic, almost instinctive notion of the national interest on the part of an electorate that is not especially inclined to follow the intricacies and complexities of world affairs. The electorate's sensibility reflects ingrained instincts, common likes and dislikes, and in the case of America, a remarkable record of future-oriented assimilation. Most of the time, this underlying strategic cohesion is latent—but it can be activated, mobilized, and even manipulated in a time of crisis.

It is uncertain whether such strategic cohesion will be sustained as the globally assertive and seductive America evolves into a multicultural society in which its citizens' primary self-identification becomes more directly linked to their own ethnic origins, and foreign issues germane to that particular self-identification become more paramount. In these circumstances, the definition of the national interest and the exercise of global leadership could become vastly more difficult. The looming paradox is that as America increasingly becomes everyone's (real or virtual) alternative home, the making of American foreign policy could become more disjointed, reflecting the conflicting pulls of this or that special ethnic interest. Should that come to pass, despite America's worldwide popularity, American foreign policy would be unable to coherently address the larger global good.

The transformation of America's national essence over the last two centuries has followed a distinctive and pointed trajectory: from unity, to diversity in unity, to diversity. When the first American census was taken in 1790, the dominant white population accounted for 80 percent of the grand total (the rest being African slaves and Native Americans, all disenfranchised), and of those, 87 percent were Anglo-Saxon and 13 percent Germanic. America was thus ethnically a traditional nation-state, socially united by historic and linguistic bonds in addition to its pioneering and self-proclaimed identification with tomorrow's vast opportunities.

But even then its leaders were concerned—with some justification—that "every citizen would take pride in the name of an American, and act as if he felt the importance of the character by considering that we ourselves are now a distinct nation the dignity of which will be absorbed, if not annihilated, if we enlist ourselves...under the banners of any other nation whatsoever....we should guard against the Intrigues of any and every foreign Nation who shall endeavor to intermingle (however covertly and indiscreetly) in the internal concerns of our country."[5] That George Washington considered using these words in his Farewell Address (in the end he did not) suggests a painful awareness that even some of the fathers of the Constitution had not only foreign affinities but even some receptivity to foreign inducements.

For much of the subsequent century, the fledgling America was largely a homogenous WASP (White Anglo-Saxon Protestant) nation, acquisitive and expanding territorially while protected by two oceans from major external intrusion. Both politically and culturally, the tone was set by an elite with an arrogant and distinctive sense of its identity. It should be noted that the internal composition of the nation was changing substantially, even if not yet very visibly. By 1850, Roman Catholics (largely from Ireland) were already the single largest Christian denomination, and by the end of the century their ranks were infused with a significant number of Italian immigrants and early in the next also with a growing number of Poles. The simultaneous wave of German, Jewish, Scandinavian, and Christian Orthodox immigrants was cumulatively diluting the ethnic and religious homogeneity of the earlier America, transforming it into a trans-European amalgam—but still with a WASP veneer and social elite. In keeping with the concept of the melting pot, to be an American it was best to change your name and to become a WASP by self-adoption.

It was not until the twentieth century that the veneer faded, the composition of the elite became a reflection of the new ethnic diversity, and long-lasting taboos were broken. The first attempt to elect a Catholic president, in 1928, failed because of manifest prejudice, but the second one, in 1960, was successful. Jews became members of the president's cabinet by the third decade but, aware of social prejudice, they were initially inclined to deliberately de-emphasize their Jewish identity.[6] But by the second half of the twentieth century, the de facto social legitimacy of the new diversity of America was reflected in the appointment in the late 1960s of a Jewish refugee of German origin as National Security Advisor to the President and then as Secretary of State, followed in the mid-1970s by a Polish American (with a difficult to pronounce, non-WASP-sounding name) as National Security Advisor. Two decades later, the ending of the shameful exclusion of African Americans from genuine participation in American life—initiated belatedly by the civil rights revolution of the 1960s—was symbolized even more dramatically by the simultaneous appointment of two African Americans as Secretary of State and National Security Advisor to the President, respectively.

That new diversity in unity was still predominantly trans-European in origin. From roughly the middle of the nineteenth century to the middle of the twentieth, the vast majority of immigrants into America came from Europe. Their proportion declined only gradually, from about nine-out-of-ten during the earlier period to about three-out-of-four by 1950 or so. The two world wars had a varied impact on the different European components of the increasingly diversified American mosaic. The conflict with imperial Germany during World War I prompted the increasingly numerous German Americans to become ostentatious WASPs, while the Poles and other Slavs developed an overt interest (especially after Wilson's famous Fourteen Points) in the political independence of their original homelands. The contest with the Axis powers during World War II (and the emergence of a Jewish state in its aftermath) stimulated in Jewish Americans a similarly heightened identification with Israel's interests, while Italian and Japanese immigrants sought to emphasize their lack of any political connection with their former homelands.

Since the middle of the twentieth century, however, the American mosaic—replacing the melting pot as the essence of the American experience—has been evolving beyond its European character. The new American mosaic is a multicultural mélange of ethnicities that are at once more distinct, more assertive, and more globally varied than ever before. The civil rights revolution pierced the invisibility and exclusion of African Americans, while immigration from abroad ceased to be a predominantly European phenomenon. The 2000 census figures show that three-out-of-four foreign-born residents of America now originate from Latin America and Asia, and that proportion is growing. America is becoming the world in microcosm.

This change in the make-up of America indicates more than the unprecedented variety among the so-called minorities; at some point, the question arises as to whether any distinct ethnic or racial majority prevails in America at all. The U.S. population currently totals 285 million people, with Hispanic Americans accounting for 37 million, African Americans for just under 37 million, Asian Americans for 11 million, and Native Americans, Hawaiians, and Alaskans for over 3 million. The European-by-origin component of the total population is dropping drastically while the Hispanic and Asian components—with much higher fertility rates and immigration—are rising. California will soon become the first state without a racial majority.

More important from a political perspective is the rise of distinctive awareness and consequent political activism among ethnic groups with a special interest in particular foreign policy issues. Interest groups are a reality of democratic pluralism, and business, labor, and professional groups have special interests as well. Nonetheless, the rise of ethnic priorities as a major influence on foreign policy could at some point become a serious complication, especially if it is accompanied by a more general dilution of the common American identity and redefines how the emerging multicultural American mosaic is being politicized.

Over the last century or so, ethnic lobbies have made themselves felt in a variety of ways. Most typically, they have exploited their voting strength in the country at large (for example, Central Europeans located from the Northeast through much of the Midwest), their concentration in some key states (Jews in New York and Cubans in Florida), or their willingness to put their money behind their political causes (Armenians, Greeks, and Jews). Polish Americans during World War II were able to project such a degree of political concern over their ancestral homeland's fate that President Roosevelt felt compelled to explain to Stalin that the United States could not approve Soviet designs on Poland until after the 1944 presidential elections. President Clinton similarly and quite deliberately chose Detroit, a city with a major Polish community, as the site for his announcement in 1996 that the United States would support the expansion of NATO to Central Europe.

Broadly speaking, today's most active, influential, and best-financed ethnic lobbies with foreign policy priorities are the Jewish, Cuban, Greek, and Armenian. Each has made its weight felt on foreign policy matters, be it the Arab-Israeli conflict, the embargo on Castro's

Cuba, the status of Cyprus, or the prohibition of aid to Azerbaijan. Among other ethnic groups, the Central Europeans have significant voting strength but lack organizational cohesion and serious financial resources. In the future, these lobbies may be joined by the potentially influential Hispanic (largely Mexican) one in the making, by black Americans who share a growing concern for Africa, and perhaps even by emerging Iranian, Chinese, and Indian (Hindu) lobbies, as well as the religiously based Muslim one.

Before too long, these ethnic groups and others may be playing an increasing role in shaping U.S. foreign policy on issues of intense significance to them. Though the Asian Americans have a record of remarkable social advancement, they are still politically relatively passive. For the time being, they are more inclined—like the Germans, the Japanese, and the Italians before them—to stress their Americanism as a way of overcoming the occasionally lingering social misgivings regarding the depth of their assimilation. A survey by *Newsweek* in April 2002 showed that about one-third of respondents suspected Chinese Americans of being more loyal to China than America, and 23 percent admitted they would feel uncomfortable voting for an Asian American for president (a higher level of prejudice than against a Jewish candidate for president). But with the passage of time, it is likely that Asian Americans will increasingly make their voices heard on issues pertaining to America's role in Asia.

A very significant ethnic community that is likely before long to make its presence felt in the shaping of a multicultural America's foreign policy is the Hispanic one, specifically its Mexican component. The 10 million people born in Mexico constitute the single largest immigrant group in the United States, and they have a strong geographic base and a rising sense of their political clout. The predominantly Mexican Hispanic Congressional Caucus and its California equivalent have already proclaimed that "Latino issues are American issues." They have been supportive of multiculturalism, even of bilingualism. If U.S.-Mexican relations were to become strained, the

Mexican Americans could become a major and highly motivated player in the domestic American foreign policy dialogue.

Similarly, the African American community is bound to become more assertive regarding U.S. policy toward Africa. The first black American secretary of state openly embraced a number of causes connected with the humanitarian threat that millions of Africans have been facing, and his influence has had a compelling impact on U.S. priorities abroad. It is quite likely, however, that the concerns of African Americans will be focused on the African continent as a whole, and will not have the specific and intense focus on particular African nations that is more typical of the ethnic lobbies.[7]

This growing role of distinctive cultural and political identities coincides with the breakup of the once exclusive WASP elite and the surfacing of greater acceptance of diversity in an America once intensely devoted to assimilation. The waning of WASP dominance has been followed by the rise in the social standing and political influence of the Jewish community. Its story is a remarkable transition—almost within one generation—from being the object of widespread, even if not always overt, prejudice to securing a position of prominence in the influential sectors of American life: within academia, in the mass media, in the entertainment industry, and in political fundraising. Its 5–6 million people are also far better educated and have higher incomes than the American median.

More importantly, in keeping with the new diversity, Jews no longer feel pressed to de-emphasize their Jewish identity—a pressure still felt by many as recently as fifty years ago—or to downplay their natural commitment to the well-being of Israel. The role of the Jewish community in the shaping of U.S. Middle Eastern policy has moved in the last several decades from largely passive to increasingly influential to perhaps even decisive.[8] The natural opponents of the Jewish American community in regard to that issue—the oil industry and the Muslim community—were outmatched. The oil industry, with its focus on profits, could not compete on the moral-sentimental level, while the Muslim American community (though numerically comparable to the Jewish) is still under-organized and financially much poorer, and has a very limited presence in the institutions that shape American public opinion.

During the nineteenth century, American goals abroad were defined first as splendid isolation (non-entanglement) and then as a mission to expand, occasionally reinforced by strong doses of jingoism. During the twentieth century, U.S. foreign policy became transoceanic and focused largely on Europe, with increased emphasis on shared democratic aspirations. In both world wars, America's ethnic cohesion, even if somewhat diluted by the increasingly trans-European inflow of immigrants, enabled its still largely WASP leadership to shape a popularly mandated national strategy. During the Cold War, the predominant focus on Europe was sustained by the especially strong backing of ethnically conscious and strongly anti-Communist Central Europeans.

In the post-Cold War era, the scale and complexity of global turbulence would make the definition of clear foreign policy priorities inherently more difficult even if there were a dominant national consensus. But with what are essentially ethnic veto groups potentially exercising a decisive influence on major regional policies—all legitimated by the hallowed notions of pluralism and lately by the supremacy of multiculturalism over traditional future-oriented assimilation—shaping national policy could become increasingly unmanageable. In the age of American hegemony and globalization, no particular group is endowed with a uniquely insightful understanding of the overall American national interest.

Moreover, many of the worst problems that America must confront as the global hegemon tend to pit the interests of one American ethnic constituency against those of another. Which ethnic group has the right to decide American policy toward Israel and the Arab world? Toward China and Taiwan? Toward India and Pakistan? In the absence of an underlying cohesion centered on the shared sense of a common American future, the American mosaic could become a contest among groups, each of which will claim (and try to assert) its special expertise, as well as its right, to define policy in a universe of conflicting foreign interests.

This tendency is already evident in the U.S. Congress. Special ethnic interests have become adept at introducing congressional resolutions and promoting legislative amendments that restrict American global policies. The use of campaign funds to obtain congressional support for ethnic causes is now an overt reality, be it in denying financial aid to Azerbaijan for the sake of the Armenians or in financially favoring Israel. Congressional caucuses specifically identified with ethnic interests have become more common. Congressmen and senators who have become spokesmen for, and even tools of, specific ethnic lobbies are not a rarity, and they are likely to proliferate as the country moves toward more assertive, socially acceptable, and politically defined multiculturalism.

As it is, Congress—as a collective and very diverse body—finds it difficult, except in times of acute national challenge, to articulate the essential strategic direction of a U.S. policy that is coherently global in scope. The executive branch is more inclined to do so, especially if the president has a reasonably defined worldview. But if the president lacks such a view of his own, he could himself become a prisoner of the perspectives of a particularly influential group. In any case, the president's ability to exercise leadership is constrained by the separation of powers and the decisive role of Congress in controlling the purse. In exercising that control, Congress is especially susceptible to the influence of particular lobbies, with the result that the flow of U.S. funds to specific foreign countries has come to reflect the clout of particular groups more than the national interest.

Creating institutional constraints on the divisive consequences of multicultural political assertion will be difficult. What may be required instead is a more deliberate public articulation—both by the president using his bully pulpit and by the private sector, including educational foundations—of a unifying, non-ethnically-hyphenated, forward-looking conception of American citizenship. Any such effort would face formidable challenges, not the least of which is how to encourage a consistent civics curriculum among federal, state, and local jurisdictions. Moreover, this common conception of citizenship would have to respect America's mounting multicultural impulses while nonetheless promoting the strategic cohesion of American society.

It is sometimes argued that Canada's policy of multiculturalism may be America's future. But Canada does not have to sustain a global foreign policy. For America, the competitive interplay of multicultural interests, with its resulting reduction in the scope of instinctively shared consensus regarding the common national interest, is likely to produce conflicting pressures that could eventually prove inimical to America's global leadership. Without an underlying and spontaneously felt strategic cohesion, a globally involved America may find it difficult to chart a steady historical direction.

HEGEMONY AND DEMOCRACY

American global hegemony is wielded by American democracy; never before has a global hegemony been exercised by a truly democratic and pluralistic state. The imperatives of hegemony, however, could clash fundamentally with the virtues of democracy, pitting national security against civil rights, decisiveness against deliberation. It is timely, therefore, to ask whether global hegemony could endanger American democracy itself.

Democracy is deeply ingrained in the very fabric of American society. The freedom to choose one's political leaders, the rights to vote and to speak freely, equality before the law and the subordination of everyone to the rule of law (including the president, as both Nixon and Clinton painfully learned) are sacred principles, central to the definition of American democracy. National policy is formulated in keeping with constitutional provisions and, as such, reflects the will of the American people. It follows that the exercise of hegemonic power abroad should also be subject to democratic public oversight.

Public opinion polls indicate that the fundamental attitude of the American people toward the exercise of that power continues to be sober, sensible, and imbued with cautious idealism. The American people have erroneously assumed that the United States gives more foreign aid than other rich states (81 percent thought so, according to the Program on International Policy Attitudes (PIPA), January 1995), but a majority still broadly approves of such (exaggerated) generosity. In general, Americans support the UN, and even as of 2002, only 30 percent felt that "the U.S. should mind its own business internationally" (in contrast to 41 percent in 1995, according to the Pew poll of December 2002).

It is fair to assert that following the end of the Cold War, Americans have been predominantly espousing a multilateralist view of the world. They have favored procedural legitimacy as a matter of principle, acknowledged the growing reality of globalization, and believed in the necessity of working through international organizations. In polls taken at the turn of the century, some 67 percent favored strengthening the UN; 60 percent the WTO; 56 percent the World Court; and 44 percent the IMF. Sixty-six percent supported the idea of an International Criminal Court.[9] Clearly, the mindset of the American people regarding its hegemonic world role has been basically benign. Unilateralism has no widespread appeal.

Then came September 11, 2001. The resulting shift from a relatively benign definition of America's world role to a preoccupation with America's vulnerability has been reflected most dramatically not on the popular level but rather at the top political strata. Indeed, despite months of sustained official propagation of an allegedly imminent threat from Iraq, as late as February 2003, a month before the outset of the war, the majority of the American people believed that war should not be undertaken outside the UN framework. Late in 2002, some 85 percent felt more generally that America "should take into account the views of its major allies."[10] That, however, was not the attitude of the White House, and it was the White House—notably the president himself—that set the tone.

That tone was simultaneously alarmist and highly assertive. In a natural reaction to the scale of the brutal crime committed, the administration stressed the hostility of the post-9/11 global environment, with evil and largely elusive forces posing a mortal danger to national security. The president himself promulgated a dichotomous view of the world, neatly divided into forces of good and evil. Failure to support America was tantamount to hostility toward America.

A computer check of presidential comments following 9/11 showed that by mid-February 2003—a period of about fifteen months—the president used publicly some variant of the Manichean phrase "who is not with us is against us" (actually popularized by Lenin!) no less than ninety-nine times. The people of America were now called upon to defend nothing less than civilization itself from the apocalyptic threat posed by global terrorism. That new mission inescapably increased the pressures on American democracy that were already inherent in America's global hegemonic role.

Even in the best of circumstances, tension between the traditions of domestic democracy and the imperatives of global hegemony would be unavoidable. In the past, an imperial motivation was inherently elitist and an imperial leadership role required an elite endowed with its own special sense of mission, destiny, and even privilege. That was certainly true of the British Empire as well as its equally grand Roman and Chinese predecessors, not to mention a variety of less illustrious imperial legacies. The responsibilities of the Cold War and of the subsequent U.S. hegemony have generated some American equivalents of such an elite, best symbolized by the power and status of the several regional U.S. CINCs (Commanders-in-Chief of Unified and Specified Commands) deployed in effect as viceroys in key external security zones, and by the enormous U.S. professional bureaucracy serving abroad. The U.S. occupation of Iraq, with an American proconsul in Baghdad, provides the most recent example.

The emergence of an American hegemonic elite is a corollary of the growth of American power over the past fifty years. As the United States discharged its far-flung global duties during the Cold War and after, a politico-military web—directed by the executive branch—arose strand by strand to cope with America's increasingly complex role in the world. Over time, a colossal apparatus of diplomatic relationships, military deployments, intelligence-gathering systems, and bureaucratic interests coalesced to manage America's comprehensive global engagement. Animated by a forceful concentration of knowledge, interests, power, and responsibility, the imperial bureaucrats view themselves as singularly equipped to determine America's conduct in a complicated and dangerous world.

The influence of America's new hegemonic elite on national policy, however, is tempered by continued oversight—notably through the power of the purse—by a Congress that is highly sensitive to the moods of the American public. The congressional committees that supervise the conduct of U.S. diplomacy, the organization and priorities of the military establishment, and the operations of the intelligence community have provided powerful obstacles to the formation of a quasi-autonomous imperial establishment in the executive branch. Without such legislative checks, reinforced by a probing free press, a hegemonic mindset reflecting the special hegemonic interests of a relatively homogenous bureaucratic elite might have become pervasive in the vast bureaucracies of the Defense Department, the State Department, the CIA, and the various dependent government agencies and semi-private organizations that they fund.

Nonetheless, a vast web of expertise, access to information, and interests abroad is inherent in the exercise of political-military power. Its very scope creates a multifaceted community capable at any one point of marshaling a powerful combination of experience, facts, and persuasion on behalf of a preferred policy. In the delicately balanced separation of powers, the equilibrium in foreign policy tends to tip in favor of the executive branch. That imbalance becomes even more marked if the issue at hand is an emotionally charged one and the presidential bully pulpit becomes fully engaged in stirring up public opinion.

In part, that is as it should be. The president is the necessary focal point for the definition of the national interest in a threatening world. It would be futile for the Congress to try to shape the fundaments of U.S. foreign policy, especially given the crosscutting interests of various ethnic and business groups. Only the executive branch, organized hierarchically and subject ultimately to the president, can do so—and, for the sake of national security, it must do so.

Nevertheless, for U.S. foreign policy to continue to enjoy public support and for it to be defined in a manner that is in keeping with the nation's underlying democratic values, the sustained participation of the Congress is a necessity. Otherwise, American priorities could acquire a crude imperial cast. The increasingly urgent question, therefore, is how such early congressional participation in the shaping of policy—and not just the reviewing of policy—can best be enhanced, lest the Congress become increasingly reduced to a rubber stamp for strategic decisions with which it is suddenly confronted.

This is largely what happened when the U.S. Congress decided in 2002 to give the president a free hand to undertake military action against Iraq, with or without a UN mandate and without any requirement for subsequent congressional approval. The congressional leadership was unable to resist a case that arose with sudden intensity and for which the president mounted a highly charged public campaign, conflating the issue of terrorism with the failure of the Iraqi regime to abide by a host of earlier UN resolutions while claiming that Iraq was armed with weapons of mass destruction. Whatever the merits of that case, its outcome—a congressional abdication of the right to declare war—demonstrated the extent to which the imperatives as well as the dynamics of hegemonic power have been skewing the finely crafted constitutional balance between the two primary policy-defining branches of government.

That trend is the inevitable consequence of the scale of America's global involvement, and thus difficult to mitigate—but the difficulty is compounded by the absence anywhere in the U.S. government of a central strategic planning organ that engages in a sustained dialogue with the pertinent congressional leadership. The Policy Planning Council in the Department of State is quite naturally concerned mainly with diplomacy, which it tends to view as the main content of foreign policy. The Department of Defense has its own large policy planning mechanism, but it unavoidably infuses its output with a heavily militaristic content. The NSC in the White House attempts to integrate military and diplomatic concerns, but its main responsibility is operational coordination of policy. It has few resources and little time for systematic strategic planning, and its orientation is also necessarily influenced by the president's political interests. The result of this rather ad hoc process eventually surfaces as the president's policy, for Congress to either support or oppose.

This state of affairs could be ameliorated by a more formal consultative relationship between the senior leaders of the congressional committees that deal with foreign affairs and a more formally structured global-strategy planning organ in the NSC. A visible and central strategic planning group in the White House, headed by a senior official to whom the pertinent senior planners in the State and Defense departments would report, could serve as a forum for periodic consultations with appropriate congressional leaders regarding longer-range plans, emerging new problems, and needed initiatives. That might somewhat mitigate the current risk that the exercise of quasi-imperial global power will gradually slip away from democratic public oversight.

The risk has intensified since 9/11. The peremptory manner in which the administration decided, in mid-2002, to go to war against Iraq reflected the degree to which the rise of a threat with global reach—transnational terrorism—created among American officials a disposition to make far-reaching strategic decisions in a narrow circle of insiders whose true motivations are obscure to the public. Personal impulses, specific group interests, and political calculations produced in stealth a sudden policy lurch with major international implications, justified publicly with very dramatic and occasionally demagogic rhetoric as well as questionable evidence. The sudden and almost simultaneous surfacing of the new strategic doctrine of preemptive war, reversing long-established international convention, further underscored the proposition that a beleaguered hegemony suffused with heightened domestic insecurity may not be congenial to a democratically open and deliberate formulation of foreign policy.[11]

The interaction after 9/11 between global hegemony and domestic democracy raises especially troubling questions. At the very core of American democracy are the civil rights of Americans. The events of 9/11 set in motion a chain of reactions in which the executive and legislative branches had to adopt emergency responses to counter an elusive threat as well as tangible mass anxiety. But their actions against the former intensified the latter. Because the dangers were so difficult to define precisely and yet so very grave, the balance between prudence and panic was hard to maintain. Even if unintentionally, civil rights were being put at risk.

Matters were not helped by the charged rhetoric employed by very senior officials, who spoke of the threat in sweeping terms[12], or by bureaucrats' fears that a repeat of the surprise of 9/11 could bring accusations of bureaucratic incompetence. The sporadic national alerts over completely unspecified threats contributed to a mood in which concern over personal security tended to overshadow traditional attachment to civil rights. That has happened before in American history. The adoption in 1798 of the Alien and Sedition Acts during the conflict with France, the suspension of the writ of habeas corpus during the Civil War, the Espionage Act of 1918 and the crackdown on pacifists and radicals in connection with America's participation in World War I, and the World War II internment of about 120,000 Japanese Americans as well as other aliens—these were not proud moments in American history. Though popularly supported as emergency measures, they have come to be viewed as overreactions.

The current reactions to 9/11 may prove more permanent because the challenges intrinsic to America's new global role are more enduring. Even if American power had been exercised after 9/11 with greater respect for international consensus, the very fact of American hegemony was bound to breed resentment and then resistance, with consequent dangers to America's sense of security. With the need for intensified security thus a new but enduring reality, the resulting risks to American civil rights are not merely a passing phenomenon.

The impact of the principal piece of post-9/11 legislation, the Patriot Act of 2001 (passed by Congress under strong presidential pressure) has been to limit the courts' jurisdiction over such sensitive activities as government eavesdropping, to infringe the attorney-client relationship, and to widen governmental access to personal medical and credit and travel records—all in the name of national security. It also expanded the government's powers of surveillance by lowering the standards needed for authorization. Hopefully, some of the initial legal measures affecting civil rights, adopted after 9/11 to facilitate the campaign against terrorism, will prove temporary, like some of the earlier overreactions in American history. The Patriot Act has sunset provisions for some of its rules, requiring a new vote after four years lest they automatically lapse.

Nonetheless, the trend has been toward restriction of civil rights, especially when it comes to non-citizen residents of the United States. It now suffices, for example, for the attorney general to conclude that he has "reasonable grounds to believe" that a suspect is "engaged in any activity that endangers the national security of the United States" for that person to be detained indefinitely. Moreover, the executive branch issued rules permitting the continued detention of non-citizens even if an immigration judge has ordered them released, and it established military tribunals for trying foreigners without any appeal to a civilian court. Additional steps have involved initiatives to increase unilateral and arbitrary access by governmental agencies to private e-mail and commercial databases, cumulatively narrowing the area of privacy for citizens and especially for aliens.[13]

Given the aroused political atmosphere after 9/11, some excesses and even miscarriages of justice were unavoidable. The main brunt was borne by foreign residents, some of whom were arbitrarily arrested and detained without charges for long periods, while many others were summarily deported (in some cases after prolonged residence in America) without much regard for their rights, their families, or their well-being. Targeted and humiliating immigration procedures were imposed on specified nationals attempting to visit the United States.

These overreactions may not be comparable to some of the earlier phases of American social hysteria. Nonetheless, they contribute to a declining image of America and provide ideological fodder for foreign critics only too eager to cast aspersions on the country's democratic credentials. If that perception were to spread widely, it would add to the growing hostility toward America. Even America's friends are asking whether, especially after 9/11, the hegemonic dimension of America's world role might not be overshadowing its democratic vocation.

The longer-range issue is whether the understandably intense American reactions to the 9/11 attacks will prompt a redefinition of the delicate traditional balance in America between individual liberty and national security. Such a fundamental redefinition, especially when coupled with America's unique technological capabilities in the area of security, could progressively transform America into an isolated, intensely security-conscious, somewhat xenophobic hybrid of democracy and autocracy, perhaps even with overtones of a vigilant garrison state.[14]

Two states already exist that may foreshadow this future: Israel and Singapore. Both are basically democratic, but both feature strong autocratic elements, introduced because of security concerns and made feasible by the intellectual and technological skills available to them. Each has adopted sophisticated methods to safeguard the population from hostile external intrusion and provide the state with the capacity for prompt emergency responses. And the civil rights of citizens have been somewhat constrained—especially those of the 1.2 million Israeli citizens of Palestinian nationality, and even more so the Palestinians under Israeli occupation.

Given its vulnerability to terrorist attacks, Israel has had no choice but to acquire the characteristics of a garrison state. The very latest techniques have been harnessed to monitor suspicious movements, access to public (including non-governmental) facilities is carefully controlled, vehicles and individuals are subject to searches, and many citizens carry arms openly for self-protection. Video surveillance, radiological and biochemical monitoring, infrared and electronic systems to detect even rubber rafts along the shores, extensive and technologically sophisticated perimeter zones for vital industries and public services, personal data-loaded I.D. cards, proactive penetration of potentially hostile groups, and forceful interrogation techniques have helped to anticipate and thus to thwart a majority of would-be terrorist attacks.

Israel's geographical setting is incomparably more vulnerable than America's, but the American people may have a lower threshold of tolerance for terrorist attack. Moreover, America's quest for domestic security is likely to be complicated by its simultaneous engagement in a variety of national, ethnic, and religious conflicts around the world, each of which may generate separate hostile responses. They are more likely to do this if America's global power is applied unilaterally, without a collective umbrella and hence without global legitimacy. Worldwide hostility could thus be as threatening to America, despite its global power, as regional hostility has proven to be for Israel.

Looking much further ahead, beyond more immediate security concerns, an altogether new dilemma must be anticipated. It pertains to the potential emergence of a truly widespread differentiation in the human condition. In the course of this century, scientific advances such as genomic profiling, biomedical engineering, and genetic modification might not only significantly prolong the human lifespan, but also dramatically improve the quality of personal life and even individual intelligence. The richer countries, and the richer people within them, will be the first beneficiaries of this new capability. The poorer countries and people will come later, if ever. America, as the richest and socially most innovative society, would most likely be among those in which the advantages of enhanced human engineering are first exploited on a socially significant scale. For those who can afford them, the promise of extraordinary improvements in personal health, in the prolongation of life, in the expansion of intelligence, and (on a more trivial level) in personal appearance will be very hard to resist.

The result will be a new human inequality. Existing global inequalities based on wealth and ethnicity would be sharpened and given a very visible and potentially nasty political dimension. Such a development could challenge America's role as the world's leading democracy and even the meaning of democracy itself.

The global reaction against any such new human inequality would doubtless capitalize on as well as mobilize existing resentments against more familiar inequalities. As gaps in the human condition widen, the governments of the poorer nations would come under growing pressure to fashion policies that redress the new inequality and point to some alternative global conception. The anti-globalist counter-creed would thus be infused with an additional and exceedingly powerful appeal. As the experience of Marxism during the twentieth century has shown, mass resentment of inequality is particularly susceptible to political mobilization in the cause of hateful ideas. With the American state already being portrayed by counter-ideologues as engaged in the ruthless promotion of globalization as its universal doctrine, anti-Americanism would in turn gain additional legitimacy.

The potential new inequality in the human condition has significant implications not only for American hegemony but for American democracy as well. When President Bush declared in August 2001 that the U.S. government would not support an outright ban on stem cell research—a ban his more conservative supporters had strongly advocated—he made a statement of historic import. He was acknowledging, in effect, the inevitability of a new era in human evolution. The decision signaled mankind's reluctant acquiescence to an unfolding revolution in human affairs propelled by a growing scientific capability that one day might even redefine the meaning and essence of human life. Where it will ultimately take humanity, no one knows, but we do know that doors are being unlocked that, decades from now, could lead to far-reaching human self-alteration.

There is, therefore, a serious risk that as the century unfolds, the revolution in biotechnology will spawn a whole host of unexpected psychological, intellectual, and religious/philosophical dilemmas. The traditional responses offered by the great religions, as well as traditional democratic principles, could be severely challenged.

In terms of democracy, new questions could arise regarding the political definition of the human being itself. The traditional linkage of political liberty and political equality—a legal concept that is central to the functioning of a democracy—was derived from the idea that "all men are created equal," a conviction that the process of human creation is inherently egalitarian. But preferential human enhancement, by selectively manipulating the elemental code that defines the parameters of human possibility, could imperil that idea and all the political and legal constructs based on it. What becomes of the axiom of equality when some individuals' intellectual and even moral capacities are artificially magnified far beyond those of others?

The danger is that some states may be tempted to pursue preferential human enhancement as a national policy. In the past, a self-centered sense of innate superiority on the part of certain peoples provided the justification for colonial exploitation, slavery, and in the extreme case, the monstrous racial doctrines of the Nazis. What if such superiority, rather than being merely a self-serving illusion, should become real? Perceptible differences in intelligence, health, and longevity between peoples could challenge the very unity of humanity that globalization is said to be advancing and the very democracy that America seeks to promote.

It must be reiterated that the emergence of such a new human inequality is likely to be slow, uncertain, and subject to many checks and restraints. Greater social awareness of the implications might by itself induce more deliberation about the future of mankind and less demagogy about the present danger. Americans still have time to reflect, more deliberately than they have yet done, on the elusive and complex tradeoffs between the values of traditional democracy and the imperatives of national security, on the implications of the scientific revolution, and on the manner in which America wields its novel global hegemony. But they no longer have the luxury of not doing so.

NOTES

1   The fate of the French business mogul Jean-Marie Messier, who headed the entertainment conglomerate *Vivendi Universal*, is quite telling. His efforts to acquire a Hollywood studio and expand his American assets, and eventually his decision to move his headquarters from Paris to New York, produced massive controversy and culminated in his dismissal. His public explanation to the effect that "The Franco-French cultural exception is dead" precipitated, in turn, public denunciations by no less than President Jacques Chirac himself, who deplored Messier's "mental aberration," France's minister of culture confessed to having been "scandalized," and a leading French magazine headlined its cover with the question "Has Messier Gone Crazy?"

2   According to data collected by the Institute for International Education, *Open Doors 2002*, accessible online at http://opendoors.iienetwork.org/.

3   Josef Joffe, "Who's Afraid of Mr. Big?" *The National Interest* (Summer 2001).

4   Notably, "What the World Thinks in 2002," released December 4, 2002, by the Pew Research Center for the People and the Press, as well as the "Worldviews 2002" polls released in September 2002 jointly by the Chicago Council on Foreign Relations and the German Marshall Fund of the United States. See especially pp. 63–69 of the Pew polling data.

5   From a May 1796 draft of George Washington's Farewell Address, as cited by Tony Smith, *Foreign Attachments: The Power of Ethnic Groups in the Making of American Foreign Policy* (Cambridge, MA: Harvard University Press, 2000), 32.

6   Particularly gripping and revealing in this regard is the account of Henry Morgenthau's service as the first Jewish Secretary of the Treasury in FDR's cabinet, including the frequent and quite overt use of anti-Semitic language among contending members of that cabinet. See Michael Beschloss, *The Conquerors* (New York: Simon & Schuster, 2002).

7   This in part is a legacy of slavery—many black Americans have no familial connections with African relatives, and very often do not know from where in Africa their ancestors originated.

8   It has been a source of frequent complaint by Arab Americans that whereas Jewish Americans in recent years have occupied the top policy slots pertaining to the Middle East in the NSC, the State Department, and the DoD, Arab Americans in effect have been locked out.

9   According to PIPA polls of October 1999 and March 2000.

10 Pew, December 2002.

11 Whither such rhetoric, and the atmosphere it generates, could even take U.S. foreign policy is illustrated by an article published in a scholarly journal by a former assistant general counsel at the CIA and an adjunct professor at Georgetown University. It states that "As an instrument of foreign policy to combat WMD and act in self-defense, killing regime leaders not only might be fair game, but also might be the best alternative under certain circumstances....In the absence of an effective collective security system, and in a world with increasingly dangerous weapons in the hands of actors willing to use them, killing regime leaders, however regrettable, may be an appropriate policy option." See Catherine Lotrionte, "When to Target Leaders," *The Washington Quarterly* (Summer 2003), 73, 84. The decision to undertake such assassinations, the author implies, would be made by U.S. "policy-makers." That it might have far-reaching international consequences, and also spawn foreign imitation, is not considered.

12 Regrettably, the lead was taken by the president himself, who frequently resorted to highly demagogic language in order to rouse public opinion against Saddam Hussein personally and the Iraqi regime in general, exploiting to that end the threat posed by terrorism. In the fifteen months since 9/11, the president referred publicly to otherwise unidentified "killers" 224 times, "murderers" 53 times, etc., declaring also that "They hate things; we love things" (August 29, 2002). He was forcefully echoed by his attorney general: e.g., "A calculated, malignant, devastating evil has arisen in our world" (Robert F. Worth, "Truth, Right and the American Way," *The New York Times*, February 24, 2002), again without much effort to narrow down the practical sources of the threat.

13 It is too early to tell what might prove to be the longer-range consequences for civil rights of the Homeland Security Act of 2002. The Department of Homeland Security is to have a division that will gather information from other intelligence and law-enforcement agencies regarding the terrorist threat. A proposed Cyber Security Enhancement Act was to give the Department the capability to promptly obtain needed information from Internet service providers regarding their clients, while a DoD initiative, originally designated as the Total Information Awareness project (later changed to "Terrorism Information Awareness" after loud public outcry), was being designed to "enable a team of intelligence analysts to gather and view information from databases, pursue links between individuals and groups, respond to automatic alerts, and share information, all from their individual computers. It could link such different electronic sources as video feeds from airport surveillance cameras, credit card transactions, airline reservations and records of telephone calls." Adam Clymer, "Congress Agrees to Bar Pentagon From Terror Watch of Americans," *The New York Times*, February 12, 2003.

14   A disturbing preview of that is provided by the electronic billboards across the Washington, D.C. beltways that flash the following vague admonition: "Report Suspicious Activity."

CONCLUSION AND SUMMARY: DOMINATION OR LEADERSHIP

American global hegemony is now a fact of life. No one, including America, has any choice in the matter. Indeed, America would imperil its own existence were it somehow to decide—like China more than half a millennium ago—to withdraw suddenly from the world. Unlike China, America would not be able to isolate itself from the global chaos that would quickly ensue. But as in life, so in political affairs: someday, everything must wane. A hegemony is a transient historical phase. Eventually, even if not soon, America's global dominance will fade. It is therefore not too early for Americans to seek to determine the shape of their hegemony's eventual legacy.

The real choices pertain to how America should exercise its hegemony, how and with whom that hegemony might be shared, and to what ultimate goals it should be dedicated. What is the central purpose of America's unprecedented global power? The answer will ultimately determine whether international consensus legitimates and reinforces American leadership, or whether American primacy relies largely on assertive domination based on might. Consensual leadership would increase America's supremacy in world affairs, with legitimacy enhancing America's status as the world's sole superpower; domination would require a greater expenditure of U.S. power, even if still leaving

213

America in a uniquely preponderant position. In other words, as the former, America would be a Superpower Plus; as the latter, a Superpower Minus.

It almost goes without saying that America's own security has to be the first and foremost purpose of the exercise of national power. In the increasingly elusive global security environment, especially given the growing ability not only of states but of covert organizations to unleash massive lethality, the security of the American people must be the primary goal of America's global policy. But in our age, solitary national security is a chimera. The quest for security must include efforts to garner greater global support. Otherwise, international resentment and envy of America's primacy could turn into a rising security threat.

In some measure, that ominous trend has already begun. America emerged triumphant from the end of the Cold War, truly a Superpower Plus. A decade later, it risks becoming a Superpower Minus. In the two years since 9/11, the initial global solidarity with America has increasingly been transmuted into American solitude, while global sympathy has given way to widespread suspicion of the true motivations of the exercise of American power.

In particular, the militarily successful but internationally controversial invasion of Iraq produced a perplexing paradox: America's global military credibility has never been higher, yet its global political credibility has never been lower. It is universally recognized that the United States is the only power capable of mounting and winning a military operation anywhere in the world. But the justification for the war against Iraq—that Iraq was armed with weapons of mass destruction, a charge stated categorically as a fact by the president and his top officials—has turned out not to have been true. That has damaged America's global standing, not only among the frequently anti-American left but also among the right. Since international legitimacy in significant degree is derived from trust, the costs to America's global standing should not be viewed as negligible.

It is therefore all the more important how America defines for itself—and for the world as well—the central purposes of its hegemony. That definition has to capture and articulate the essential strategic challenge that America confronts and against which America seeks to mobilize the world. How it does so—with how much clarity and moral force, with what degree of comprehension of the needs and aspirations of others—will largely determine the effective scope and burdens of the exercise of America's power. In brief, it will determine whether America will be a Superpower Plus or a Superpower Minus.

Since 9/11, to much of the world it appears that the predominant emphasis of U.S. security policy, both domestically and internationally, is on "the war against terrorism with a global reach." Efforts to rivet public attention on that phenomenon have been the major public concern of the Bush administration. Terrorism—defined vaguely, reviled in largely theological or moralistic terms, castigated as unrelated to any regional conundrum though generally linked to Islam—is to be combated through ad hoc coalitions with like-minded partners who share (or expediently profess to share) a similar preoccupation with terrorism as the central security challenge of our time. The eradication of that scourge is thus presented as America's most urgent task, the success of which is expected to facilitate the more general promotion of global security.

The primary focus on terrorism is politically captivating in the short run. It has the advantage of simplicity. By demonizing an unknown enemy and exploiting vague fears, it can rally popular support. But as a longer-range strategy, it lacks staying power, can be internationally divisive, can breed intolerance of others ("he who is not with us is against us") and unleash jingoist emotions, and can serve as the point of departure for America's arbitrary designation of other states as "outlaws."[1] Consequently, it poses the risk that America will be perceived abroad as self-absorbed and that anti-American ideologues will gain international credence by labeling the United States a self-appointed vigilante.

215

The three main strategic conclusions drawn from the definition of terrorism as the central threat to American security—that "he who is not with us is against us," that military preemption and prevention are equally justifiable and can be conflated into a single interchangeable proposition, and that enduring alliances may be supplanted by ad hoc coalitions—have prompted widespread concerns abroad. The first is viewed as dangerously polarizing, the second as inviting strategic unpredictability, and the third as politically unsettling. Cumulatively, they have contributed to the image of America as an increasingly arbitrary superpower.

An experienced European observer, comparing contemporary America to ancient Rome, noted perceptively that "World powers without rivals are a class unto themselves. They do not accept anyone as equal, and are quick to call loyal followers friends, or *amicus populi Romani*. They no longer know any foes, just rebels, terrorists, and rogue states. They no longer fight, merely punish. They no longer wage wars but merely create peace. They are honestly outraged when vassals fail to act like vassals."[2] (One is tempted to add, they do not invade other countries, they only liberate.) The author wrote before 9/11, but his comment strikingly captured the attitude some U.S. policymakers displayed during the UN debates surrounding the 2003 decision to go to war against Iraq.

The alternative approach to defining America's central strategic challenge is to focus more broadly on global turmoil in its several regional and social manifestations—of which terrorism is a genuinely menacing symptom—in order to lead an enduring and enlarging alliance of like-minded democracies in a comprehensive campaign against the conditions that precipitate that turmoil. To this end, the magnetic success of America's democracy and its outward projection through a humane definition of globalization would reinforce the effectiveness and legitimacy of America's power and enhance U.S. ability to overcome—together with others—both the consequences and the causes of global turmoil.

Global turmoil manifests itself in a variety of ways. It is intensified, though not entirely caused, by persistent mass poverty and social injustice. In some regions, it involves ethnic oppression; in others, tribal conflicts; elsewhere, religious fundamentalism. It is expressed through bursts of violence as well as pervasive disorder throughout the southern rim of Eurasia, the Middle East, much of Africa, and some portions of Latin America. It generates hate and envy of the dominant and prosperous and is likely to become more sophisticated in its lethality, especially with the proliferation of WMD. Some of that violence is much more indiscriminate than terrorism in its victims, with tens of thousands killed every year, hundreds of thousands maimed, and millions afflicted by primitive combat.

Recognition of global turmoil as the basic challenge of our time requires confronting complexity. That is the weakness of the issue insofar as the American political scene is concerned. It does not lend itself to sloganeering or rouse the American people as viscerally as terrorism. It is more difficult to personalize without a demonic figure like Osama bin Laden. Nor is it congenial to self-gratifying proclamations of an epic confrontation between good and evil on the model of the titanic struggles with Nazism and Communism. Yet not to focus on global turmoil is to ignore a central reality of our times: the massive worldwide political awakening of mankind and its intensifying awareness of intolerable disparities in the human condition.

The key issue for the future is whether that awakening will be seized and exploited by hate-mongering anti-American demagogues, or whether a compelling vision of a global community of shared interest will come to be identified with America's global role. To be sure, as with the narrower focus on terrorism, an effective response to global turmoil requires major reliance on American power as the essential prerequisite to global stability. But it also calls for a long-haul commitment, derived from a sense of moral justice as well as from America's own national interest, to progressively transform America's prevailing power into a co-optive hegemony—one in which leadership is exercised more through shared conviction with enduring allies than by assertive domination.

A global community of shared interest should not be confused with world government. A world government is not a practical goal at this stage of history. America certainly would not yield its sovereignty—nor should it—to a supranational authority in a world that lacks even the minimum of consensus needed for a common government. The only "world government" currently even remotely possible would be an American global dictatorship—and that would be an unstable and ultimately self-defeating enterprise. World government is either a pipe dream or a nightmare, but not a serious prospect for some generations to come.

A global community of shared interest, on the other hand, is not only possible and desirable but actually emerging. It is partially the outgrowth of a spontaneous process inherent in the dynamics of globalization and partially the consequence of more deliberate efforts, especially by the United States and the European Union, to weave together a broader fabric of binding and institutionalized international cooperation.[3] Bilateral and multilateral free trade agreements, regional policy forums, and formal alliances all contribute to a web of interdependent relations, at this stage more on the regional level but increasingly also on the global. Cumulatively, they represent the natural evolution of interstate relations into an informal international governance structure.

That process needs to be encouraged, expanded, and institutionalized, so as to promote a growing awareness of the common destiny of mankind. Shared interest entails a balance of benefits and responsibilities, empowerment and not dictation. America is in a unique position to lead this process because it is both secure in its power and democratic in its governance. Since a selfish hegemony will inevitably breed its own antithesis but democracy breeds its own contagion, it is the common-sense dictate of hard-nosed realism that America should rise to this calling.

The practical issue of preserving its position thus pertains to the character of America's global leadership. Leadership entails a sense of direction that mobilizes others. Power for the sake of power, domination dedicated to the perpetuation of domination—these are not a formula for enduring success. Domination as an end in itself is a dead-end street. It eventually mobilizes countervailing opposition while its very arrogance produces self-deluding historical blindness. The ultimate destination of the globe, as argued in the preceding chapters, will be either steady movement over the next two decades or so toward a community of shared interest, or an accelerating plunge into global chaos. The acceptance of American leadership by others is the sine qua non for avoiding chaos.

In practice, wise leadership in world affairs calls, first of all, for a rational and balanced policy of self-protection in order to mitigate the most likely and most threatening risks to American society without stimulating a paranoiac sense of national insecurity. Second, it calls for a patient and protracted effort to pacify the more volatile regions of the globe, which generate much of the emotional hostility that fuels violence. Third, it requires a sustained effort to engage the most vital and friendly parts of the world in a joint framework to contain and, if possible, eliminate the likely sources of the greatest dangers. Fourth, it requires recognizing globalization as more than just an opportunity for enhanced trade and profit, but a phenomenon having a deeper moral dimension. And fifth, it requires fostering a domestic political culture that is actively aware of the complex responsibilities inherent in global interdependence.

The required co-optive global leadership calls for a conscious, strategically coherent, and intellectually demanding effort by whomever the American people choose to be their president. The president must do more than stir the American people; he must also educate them. The political education of a large democracy cannot be pursued by patriotic slogans, fear-mongering, or self-righteous arrogance. Every politician faces that temptation, and it is politically rewarding to yield to it. But harping on terrorism distorts the public's vision of the world. It breeds the risk of defensive self-isolation, fails to give the public a realistic understanding of the world's complexities, and furthers the fragmentation of the nation's strategic cohesion. America will be able to exercise global leadership over the long haul only if there is greater public understanding of the interdependence between U.S. national security and global security, of the burdens of global primacy, and of the resulting need for enduring democratic alliances to overcome the challenge of global turmoil.

The grand strategic choice facing America points to several specific implications. The foremost is the critical importance of a complementary and increasingly binding American-European global partnership. A mutually complementary if still asymmetrical Atlantic alliance with a global reach is clearly in the interest of both. With such an alliance, America becomes a Superpower Plus, and Europe can steadily unite. Without Europe, America is still preponderant but not globally omnipotent, while without America, Europe is rich but impotent. Some European leaders and nations may be tempted to pursue unity through an anti-American (or, rather, an anti-Atlanticist) self-definition, but both America and Europe itself would be the ultimate losers in the effort. As a Superpower Minus, America would find the costs of exercising its global leadership considerably higher, while Europe would then be even less likely to unite, because an anti-Atlanticist platform would not attract a majority of the EU members and prospective members.

Only the two sides of the Atlantic working together can chart a truly global course that may significantly improve the worldwide state of affairs. To do so, Europe must wake up from its current coma, realize that its security is even more inseparable from global security than is America's, and draw the inevitable practical conclusions. It cannot be secure without America, it cannot unite against America, and it cannot significantly influence America without being willing to act jointly with America. For some time to come, the much-discussed "autonomous" European political-military role outside of Europe will remain quite limited, largely because the European slogans about it outrun any determination to pay for it.

At the same time, America must resist the temptation to divide its most important strategic partner. There is no "old" or "new" Europe. That too is a slogan with no geographical or historical content. Moreover, the gradual unification of Europe does not threaten America; on the contrary, it can only benefit America by increasing the overall weight of the Atlantic community. A policy of *divide et impera*, even if tactically tempting for settling scores, would be shortsighted and counterproductive.

An important reality that also needs to be faced is that the Atlantic Alliance cannot be a perfectly balanced 50-50 partnership. The very idea of such a finely tuned and symmetrical equality is a political myth. Even in business, where shares can be precisely counted, a 50-50 arrangement is not workable. A demographically younger, more vigorous, and politically united America cannot be matched politically and militarily by a Europe of diverse and aging nation-states that are unifying but far from united. Nevertheless, each side of the Atlantic has assets the other needs. America will remain for some time to come the ultimate guarantor of global security even if. Europe progressively enhances its still rather meager military capabilities. Europe can reinforce U.S. military power, while the combined economic resources of the United States and the EU would make the Atlantic community globally omnipotent.

The only real option, therefore, is not a European partner of equal weight, and even less a counterweight, but a European partner with weighty influence in the shaping and implementation of a shared global policy. The exercise of critically important influence, even if it does not involve exactly an equal share of decision-making, requires a willingness on both sides to act together when action is needed. It also means, when action is necessary, that the party with the greater means for action or greater interest in the outcome ultimately has the greater say. American primacy need not imply the automatic subordination of Europe, and partnership need not imply general paralysis in cases of initial disagreement. Both sides must foster the spirit of accommodation, nurture shared strategic perspectives, and promote additional Atlantic mechanisms for sustained global political planning.[4]

Though Europe's economic unification will move more rapidly than political unification, it is not too early to consider some restructuring of NATO's decision-making in order to take into account the EU's slowly emerging political profile. As the EU's constitution becomes embedded in the fabric of European society, a common European political orientation will take shape. Given that the vast majority of NATO's members are also members of the EU, alliance procedures will have to reflect the fact that the alliance is becoming less a composite of twenty-six nation-states (one of them much more powerful than all the others) and more a two-pillar North American-European structure. To fail to take that reality into account would only encourage advocates of a separate and potentially duplicative European defense effort.

A transatlantic convention to discuss the implications of this emerging reality would be timely. It should consider not only the long-term strategic agenda for a redefined and perhaps restructured alliance but also the wider global implications of the fact that America and Europe together are genuinely omnipotent. Implicit in that fact is Europe's obligation to become more engaged in promoting global security. Europe's security perspective can no longer be limited to the continent and its periphery. With NATO already present in Afghanistan, indirectly also in Iraq, and soon perhaps along the Palestinian-Israeli frontier, the Atlantic Alliance's strategic scope eventually will have to include all of Eurasia.

A genuine U.S.-EU transatlantic alliance, based on a shared global perspective, must be derived from a similarly shared strategic understanding of the nature of our era, of the central threat that the world faces, and of the role and mission of the West as a whole. That calls for a serious and searching joint dialogue, and not mutual recriminations (often based on contrived argumentation that America and Europe are drifting in fundamentally divergent directions). The truth remains that the West as a whole has much to offer to the world, but it will be able to do so only if it articulates a common vision. The West's current deficit is neither in military power (America has a surfeit of it) nor in financial resources (Europe's match those of America). Rather, it is in the ability to transcend parochial concerns and narrow interests. At a time of unprecedented challenges to mankind's security and well-being, the leadership of the West often seems intellectually barren. A conscious strategic debate might inspire the needed global political innovation.

In any case, short of such an ambitious grand review, the transatlantic alliance needs to address a more specific agenda. In Europe, it involves the steady and complementary expansion of both the EU itself and NATO. That expansion is now entering its third phase. The first, the Warsaw round, involved coping with the immediate geostrategic legacy of the Cold War era by promptly admitting Poland, the Czech Republic, and Hungary into NATO; the second, the Vilnius round, pertained to the almost simultaneous and geographically largely overlapping decision to enlarge both NATO and the EU by seven and ten new states, respectively; the third and next (the Kyiv round?) looks further east, to Ukraine and maybe the Caucasus, and may even consider the eventual admission of Russia.

Outside of Europe itself, the Middle East is an area of strong American interest and of immediate concern to Europe. A roadmap for the Israeli-Palestinian peace—dependent in large part on joint and persistent efforts by America and Europe—is inseparable from a roadmap for Iraq's rehabilitation as a stable, independent, and democratizing state. Without both, peace in the region is not possible. Working together, the United States and the EU can also be more effective in avoiding a head-on collision between the West and Islam and in promoting the more positive tendencies within the world of Islam that favor its eventual incorporation into the modern and democratic world.

But joint pursuit of that goal requires also a subtle understanding of the contending forces within Islam, and Europe has the advantage over America in that regard. In addition, American sympathy for the security of the Israelis is balanced by European sympathy for the plight of the Palestinians. No peaceful outcome for the Israeli-Palestinian conflict is possible without both concerns being taken fully into account.[5] A peaceful outcome will facilitate, in turn, the needed and much delayed internal transformation of the adjoining Arab societies and will reduce anti-American hostility. The unwillingness of several U.S. administrations to bite the bullet on this issue has been a major contributing factor in the rise of extremism in the region.

America also has a unique role to play in the promotion of democracy in the Arab world. For more than two centuries, America has been the cradle of liberty, the destination point for those who seek to live in freedom, and the source of inspiration for those who want to make their own countries as free as America itself. During the Cold War, it was America alone that clearly proclaimed—through Radio Free Europe—that it would not accept as permanent the subjugation of Central Europe to Moscow's control. It was America under President Carter that promoted the cause of human rights, thereby placing the Soviet Union on the ideological defensive. America thus propagated a shared aspiration; it did not seek to impose its own political culture.

It is important to recall this at a time when the now globally dominant America is publicly asserting its determination to democratize the Muslim countries. That goal is a noble one, and also practical in that the spread of democracy is generally congenial to global peace. But it is important not to lose sight of a basic lesson of history: any just cause, in the hands of fanatics, will degenerate into its antithesis. That is what happened when religious fervor in medieval Europe translated a uniquely compassionate and meek faith into the horror of the Inquisition. In more recent times, that is also what happened when the French Revolution, on behalf of "liberté–fraternité–égalité," came to be symbolized by the guillotine. The century that just ended experienced unprecedented human suffering because of the degeneration of the idealism of socialism into the inhuman totalitarianism of Leninism-Stalinism.

The promotion of democracy, if pursued with a fanatical zeal that ignores the historical and cultural traditions of Islam, could similarly produce democracy's very negation. The argument that America after World War II successfully imposed democracy upon both Germany and Japan ignores historically relevant facts. To cite but two: In 2003, Berlin celebrated the one hundredth anniversary of the victory of the German Socialist Party in its municipal elections—in the capital of imperial Germany, no less. Japanese compliance with U.S. postwar reforms gained social legitimacy because the Japanese emperor publicly endorsed them. In both cases, there were social foundations on which the United States after World War II was able to construct democratic constitutions.

There are some grounds, though more limited ones, for seeking the same outcome in the Middle East; but doing so will require historical patience and cultural sensitivity. The experience of several Muslim countries located on the periphery of the West—especially Turkey but also Morocco and (despite its fundamentalist veneer) Iran—suggests that, when democratization takes place through organic growth and not through dogmatic imposition by an alien force, Islamic societies also gradually absorb and assimilate a democratic political culture.

Given America's new prominence in the political life of the Arab Middle East in the aftermath of its occupation of Iraq, it is essential that U.S. policymakers not be seduced by doctrinaire advocates of an externally imposed and impatient democratization—a democratization "from above," so to speak. Sloganeering to that effect in some cases may reflect contempt for Islamic traditions. For others it may be tactical, rooted in the hope that the focus on democratization will provide a diversion from efforts to press both the Israelis and the Arabs to accept the compromises necessary for peace. Whatever the motivation, the fact is that genuine and enduring democracy is nurtured best in conditions that gradually foster spontaneous change and do not combine compulsion with haste. The former approach can indeed transform a political culture; the latter can only coerce a political correctness that is inherently unlikely to endure.

The strategic scope of the Atlantic agenda extends further east than the Middle East itself. The new Global Balkans—the arc of crisis ranging from the Persian Gulf to Xinjiang—will become less explosive if the resources of the three most successful regions of the world—the politically energetic America, the economically unifying Europe, and the commercially dynamic East Asia—are harnessed in a joint response to the security threat posed by turmoil in that large region. That threat is exacerbated by the acquisition of nuclear weaponry by two neighboring but hostile powers, India and Pakistan, each beset also by domestic tensions. Both America and Europe will need to keep pressing Japan and China, in particular, to become more engaged in joint efforts to contain disintegrative trends. Given that both of these states are already highly dependent on energy flows from the Persian Gulf and Central Asia—and becoming more so—they cannot remain bystanders in the face of a common challenge in this volatile area, which could become quicksand for America alone.

America has already greatly expanded its military involvement in Eurasia. It now has a continuing military presence in Afghanistan and in some of the newly independent Central Asian states. Given the growing Chinese commercial and political outreach to Central Asia, a zone until recently exclusively dominated by Russia, the need for wider international cooperation to cope with local instability has gained urgency. Both Japan and China should be pressed to become material participants in promoting the region's political and social stabilization.

How the power dynamics in the Far East are shaped by the interrelationship among America, Japan, and China will also affect global stability. The United States should seek to translate the emerging equilibrium among itself, Japan, and China into a more structured security relationship. Geopolitically, Asia roughly resembles Europe prior to World War I. America has stabilized Europe but it still faces a potential structural crisis in Asia, where several major powers still contend, though checked by America's peripheral strategic presence. That presence is anchored by the American-Japanese connection, but the rise of a regionally dominant China and the unpredictability of North Korea signal the need for a more active U.S. policy to promote, at a minimum, a triangular security relationship. As argued earlier, such a triangular equilibrium, to be enduring, will require a more internationally engaged Japan that will have gradually assumed a wider range of military responsibilities.

Creating this equilibrium might entail, in turn, fostering a trans-Eurasian multilateral security structure for coping with the novel dimensions of global security. Failure to engage China and Japan in at least a de facto security structure could eventually trigger a dangerous tectonic shift, perhaps involving the unilateral remilitarization of Japan, which already has the potential to very quickly become a nuclear power, in addition to the already grave challenge posed by North Korea's quest for a nuclear arsenal of its own. The need for a collective regional response to North Korea reinforces the more general point that only a co-optive American hegemony can cope effectively with the increasingly pervasive spread of weaponry of mass destruction, whether among states or extremist organizations.

America will have to cope with these dilemmas in the context of a historical marriage between U.S. global power and global interdependence in the age of instant communications. Striking a balance between an existential sovereign hegemony and an emerging global community, and between the values of democracy and the imperatives of global power, will continue to be America's major dilemma. Globalization, which America both favors and promotes, can help to dampen global turmoil—provided it does not disfranchise but empowers the poorer countries, and provided it is infused with humane concerns and not defined by economic self-interest alone. The U.S. attitude toward multilateral obligations, especially those that do not conveniently coincide with America's narrower and more immediate objectives, is thus a litmus test of its readiness to promote a globalization that genuinely advances equitable interdependence and not uneven dependence.[6] The U.S. record in recent years regarding multilateral obligations has created a widespread perception that a level worldwide playing field is not its primary goal.

America must be more sensitive to the risk that its identification with an unjust version of globalization could prompt a worldwide reaction leading to the emergence of a new anti-American creed. Given that security depends not only on military power but also, in this age of global political awakening, on the foci of social passions and fanatical hatreds, how America defines and pursues globalization will bear directly on its long-term security.

Similarly, it behooves America to be sensitive to the unexpected political consequences of its unique worldwide cultural impact. America's globally seductive power has had the unanticipated effect of engendering singularly lofty expectations in the world's people. They hold America to a higher standard than they do other states, often including their own. Indeed, anti-Americanism has many trappings of betrayed affection. As a consequence, the dissatisfied of the world, because they expect more from America, tend to be especially outraged when they feel it is not doing enough to help them rectify their own deplorable circumstances. In effect, America's cultural seduction is politically destabilizing even as America seeks to promote global stability for its larger strategic interests. Thus only if America places a higher premium on a truly shared global cause will it derive any political benefit from the cultural revolution it is unleashing worldwide.

Since a critically important source of America's global appeal, and thus of its power, is the magnetic attraction of its democratic system, it is likewise essential for Americans to carefully preserve the delicate balance between their civil rights and the requirements of their national security. That is easier to do when wars are distant and their costs socially acceptable. But the intense public reactions to the crime of 9/11—reactions perhaps deliberately fanned for political reasons—could be leading to a more basic redefinition of that balance. A garrison-state mentality can poison any democracy. What regional hostility has been doing to Israel, fear fomented by world-wide hostility can do to America.

It follows that domestic security must be pursued in a manner that enhances both sovereign American power and the global legitimacy of that power. To repeat what was said earlier, America is now engaged in the third grand debate since its inception as an independent state regarding the requirements of its national defense. That debate is understandably focused on societal survivability in the novel setting of diffusion and diversification of weapons of mass destruction, percolating global turbulence, and widespread fear of terrorism.

That is a new historical condition for America. It creates an intimate interdependence between the security of the American homeland and the overall state of the world. Given its global security role and its extraordinary global ubiquity, America thus has the right to seek more security than other countries. It needs forces with a decisive worldwide deployment capability. It must enhance its intelligence (rather than waste resources on a huge homeland security bureaucracy) so that threats to America can be forestalled. It must maintain a comprehensive technological edge over all potential rivals in both its strategic and conventional forces. But it should also define its security in ways that help mobilize the self-interest of others. That comprehensive task can be pursued more effectively if the world understands that the trajectory of America's grand strategy is toward a global community of shared interest.

A fortress on a hill can only stand alone, casting a menacing shadow over all beneath. As such, America would become the focus of global hatred. A city on a hill, by contrast, could illuminate the world with the hope of human progress—but only in an environment in which that progress is both the focus of a vision and an attainable reality for all. "A city that is set on a hill cannot be hid....Let your light so shine before men, that they may see your good works."[7] So let America shine.

NOTES

1 A special complication is caused by the way the United States officially defines terrorism. By stressing that terrorism is violence perpetrated against innocent civilians by outlaw private groups in order to attain their political objectives, it exonerates state-inflicted terrorism, as in the case of the massive Russian bombing of Grozny and of the "zachistki" designed to intimidate the Chechen population, as well as in the cases of other states when they use indiscriminate force against civilians to repress terrorism.

2 Peter Bender, "America: The New Roman Empire?" *Orbis* (Winter 2003), 155.

3 The scale of America's commitment in this regard is not that well known to the U.S. public. During the first 150 years of the nation's existence, between 1789 and 1939, the United States concluded 799 formal treaties and 1,182 executive agreements. Between 1939 and 1999—thus during just the last sixty years—the United States concluded 951 treaties and 14,555 executive agreements. See "Treaties and Other International Agreements: The Role of the United States Senate," Congressional Research Service, Library of Congress, January 2001, S.Prt.106-71.

4 Many Europeans are quite realistic about this: e.g., the strong case for a renewed Atlantic Alliance made by Laurent Cohen-Tanugi, *Les Sentinelles de la Liberté: l'Europe et l'Amerique au seuil du XXI siècle* (Paris: Jacob), 2003.

5 As this book was going to print, the lack of global support for the increasingly one-sided U.S. policy of favoring Israel was dramatically highlighted by the lopsided vote of the UN General Assembly of September 19, 2003, on a resolution "On Illegal Israeli Activities in Occupied Palestinian Territory." The vote was 133 in favor, 4 against, and 15 abstentions. The four were the United States, Israel, Micronesia, and Marshall Islands. All of America's closest allies in Europe (including Great Britain) and in Asia voted for the resolution. So did India, Russia, and Brazil, among many others.

6 Though the specific U.S. objections to particular international conventions may have merit, the list of those rejected by the United States in recent years conveys a troubling symbolic message: the Kyoto Protocol on climate control, the International Criminal Court, the Convention on the Rights of the Child (U.S. opposition was supported only by Somalia), the draft protocol for an enforcement mechanism to implement the ban on biological weapons, the ABM Treaty, the treaty on banning landmines, etc.

7 Matthew 5:14–16.

ACKNOWLEDGMENTS

I want to acknowledge my gratitude to two institutions and to several close collaborators for helping to make this book possible.

For more than twenty years, the Center for Strategic and International Studies (CSIS) has provided me with a global policy-oriented setting in which debates about U.S. grand strategy are a daily routine among unusually well-informed and uniquely experienced colleagues. CSIS is truly Washington's Strategic Center.

I have also benefited from my association with the School of Advanced International Studies (SAIS) of the Johns Hopkins University. Its gifted faculty as well as resident and foreign visiting scholars joined me in regular bimonthly reviews of current foreign policy issues, during which I tested some of the arguments developed in this book.

My executive assistant, Trudy Werner, runs my CSIS office. She was with me in the White House, earlier at the Trilateral Commission, and also at CSIS since 1981. I depend on her for matters serious or trivial, knowing that I can rely on her. She is the source of order and continuity in my often hectic schedule. Without her I would have fallen victim to the chaos that—at a much higher level of magnitude—I portray in the book as the principal threat to global stability.

Two research assistants played a significant role in helping me to master the several strands of argumentation developed in this personal statement of mine about America's role in the world. Scott Lindsay was present at the conception and Nikhil Patel at the creation. Scott's initial research memoranda filled major gaps in my knowledge, while Nikhil provided very constructive criticisms and important inserts while meticulously reviewing the entire draft. Both also briefed me systematically on current developments around the world, prepared background papers on topics pertinent to the book, and helped me to broaden my own horizons. Their dedication was of the highest order and their help was invaluable.

My editor at Basic Books, William Frucht, guided the book in its final stages. He was an ideal editor, for he refined its argument, smoothed its flow, and polished its presentation without seeking to alter its contents. He was also instrumental in the final "choice" of the title...

As always, my wife was relentless in her criticisms but also truly encouraging. Her central role is difficult to define but is perhaps best captured by the subtitle of this book!

INDEX

ABM Treaty, 9
Aging, of population, 167–168, 177n26
Algeria, 50
Alien and Sedition Acts, 204
Alliances
  with China, 115, 128n7, 226–227
  with Europe, 66–67, 88, 220–223
  with India, 64–65
  with Israel, 63–64
  with Japan, 67, 114–115, 117–118, 226–227
  with Russia, 66, 73, 87, 88, 100–103
  with South Korea, 121–122
  with Turkey, 61–63
Anthrax, 22
"Arab Human Development Report 2002," 80n6
Arab-Israeli conflict, 68–71. *See also* Middle East.
Armageddon, 12–13
Armenia, 98–99
Assimilation, 170
Asymmetrical wars, 44
Atatürk, 62
Atlantic Alliance, 34
Atomic weapons, 14

Axis of Evil, 27
Azerbaijan, 98–99, 100

Baudrillard, Jean, 174n8
Bin Laden, Osama, 45, 48
Biotechnology, 207–209
Blair, Tony, 1
Bourdieu, Pierre, 153
Bush, George H.W., 136–137
Bush, George W., 21, 26, 27, 35–36, 137–138, 138n1

Canada, multiculturalism in, 198
Caucasus, stabilization of, 98–100
Caucasus Stability Pact, 75, 82n14
Chechnya, 31, 66, 78n1, 82n14, 99
Chen, Shui-bian, 114
Child labor, 144
China, 2
  Asian leadership role of, 118–119, 125–126, 130n21
  cultural revolution of, 180
  domestic unrest in, 119–120, 129n17
  in G-8 summit, 123
  globalization and, 146–147, 157–158, 173n4, 175–176n16
  historical resentments of, 108–109

China (*continued*)
historical world ranking of, 3,
5n3
Hollywood films in, 183
Internet use in, 119
Japanese threat to, 110–114, 116
on Japan-U.S. alliance, 114–115
military capabilities of, 38n3,
118, 121
missile defense and, 19
naval arms development in, 110
Pakistan's ties to, 65
security perspective of, 111–112,
129n14
Taiwan issue and, 115–116, 123
as U.S. ally, 115, 128n7, 226–227
Chua, Amy, 174–175n10
Civil rights, 204–206, 228–229
Civil Rights movement, 151
Clinton, William J., 20–21, 137
on globalization, 142–143
on Kyoto Protocol, 148–149
Coalition of the willing, 34–35
Coca-Colonization, 184
Cold War, 8–9, 33–34, 41–42,
59–60
U.S. cultural export during,
181–182
Commitment to Development
Index, 174n7
Community of Democratic States,
Warsaw meeting of, 155

Computer systems, terrorist
attacks on, 22
Conscription, 171
Consumer culture, 180–181,
184–185
Corruption, 51
Counter-symbolization, 57,
149–163
Cuban Missile Crisis, 9
Cultural seduction, 180–189, 228
consumer culture and, 180–181,
184–185
destabilizing effect of, 188, 189
vs. foreign policy, 186–189
intellectual repudiation of, 188
resistance to, 182
Cyber-attacks, 22

Demirel, Suleyman, 82n14
Democracy, 135, 198–209
civil rights under, 204–206,
228–229
human evolution and, 208–209
imperialist policy and, 200
Islam and, 58, 225
permeability and, 45
Doran, Charles, 139

East Asia, 107–123
historical resentments in,
108–109
naval arms development in,
109–110
stability of, 107–108

Messier, Jean-Marie, 210n1
Mexico, U.S. policy toward,
194–195
Middle East, 223–224
democracy in, 225–226
European perspective on, 91, 96,
106
nuclear weapons in, 32,
38–39n5, 82–83n16
political history of, 30–31
Migration, 45, 163–165, 169–170,
178n28
illegal, 15
international standards for, 172
Military affairs, technology-driven
revolution in. *See* Revolution
in Military Affairs (RMA).
Missile defense system, 21
Mobility, 45
Modernity, 52
Morgenthau, Henry, 210n6
Morocco, democracy in, 225
Multiculturalism, 189–198
policy effects of, 193–197
Multilateralism, 199, 218
Music industry, 183
Muslim Brotherhood, 50
Muslims, 48–50. *See also* Islam.

Nagasaki, 14
New World Order, 136–137
Nigeria, 51
North Atlantic Treaty, 24

North Atlantic Treaty
Organization, 222, 223
expansion of, 96–98, 100
global security role of, 104–106
Russian membership in,
101–102, 122
North Korea, 20–21, 27, 32, 33
nuclear weapons of, 121, 122
Nuclear deterrence, 18–19
Nuclear weapons
Japanese capability for, 113
in Middle East, 32, 38–39n5,
82–83n16
in North Korea, 121, 122
proliferation of, 31–32, 33,
75–78

Oil and gas reserves, 60, 71–72
Oil reserves, 60
Oklahoma City bombing, 48
Organization for Security and
Cooperation in Europe, 122
Oversimplification, tactical, 46–47

Pakistan, 15, 19, 51, 53, 65, 75–77
Palestinian issue, 30, 64, 68–71
Pan-Asianism, 124–125, 127,
130n22
Chinese role in, 125–126,
157–158
Pan-Europeanism, 124–125, 127,
130n19
Patriot Act, 205

War on terrorism, 27–28, 32, 42, 215–216

Wars

asymmetrical, 44

local, 12, 19–20, 38n4, 216–218

world, 12, 14–15, 18–19, 24

Washington, D.C., as global capital, 132–133, 138n1

Washington, George, 190

Weakness, 43–47

Weapons of mass destruction, 21. *See also* Nuclear weapons.

covert use of, 22

proliferation of, 75–78

surreptitious acquisition of, 34

West Point Speech, 35–36

World Bank, 145, 173n5

World Economic Forum, 134

World government, 218

World Trade Organization, 145, 173n5, 174n6

China's entry into, 146–147

World War I, 24

World War II, 14–15

World wars, 12, 14–15, 18–19, 24

Yourcenar, Marguerite, 133